The PR Agency Handbook

Gina:
For Todd, Emma, and Avery

Luke:
For Mom, Dad, Sarah, and Joel

The PR Agency Handbook

Regina M. Luttrell

Syracuse University

Luke W. Capizzo

University of Maryland, College Park

Los Angeles | London | New Delhi
Singapore | Washington DC | Melbourne

FOR INFORMATION:

SAGE Publications, Inc.
2455 Teller Road
Thousand Oaks, California 91320
E-mail: order@sagepub.com

SAGE Publications Ltd.
1 Oliver's Yard
55 City Road
London, EC1Y 1SP
United Kingdom

SAGE Publications India Pvt. Ltd.
B 1/I 1 Mohan Cooperative Industrial Area
Mathura Road, New Delhi 110 044
India

SAGE Publications Asia-Pacific Pte. Ltd.
3 Church Street
#10-04 Samsung Hub
Singapore 049483

Acquisitions Editor: Terri Accomazzo
Editorial Assistant: Sarah Wilson
Production Editor: Karen Wiley
Copy Editor: Erin Livingston
Typesetter: Hurix Digital
Proofreader: Jeff Bryant
Indexer: Jean Casalegno
Cover Designer: Janet Kiesel
Marketing Manager: Allison Henry

Copyright © 2019 by SAGE Publications, Inc.

Printed in the United States of America

Library of Congress Cataloging-in-Publication Data

Names: Luttrell, Regina, author. | Capizzo, Luke W., author.

Title: The PR agency handbook / Regina Luttrell, Luke Capizzo.

Description: First Edition. | Thousand Oaks : SAGE Publications, [2018] | Includes bibliographical references and index.

Identifiers: LCCN 2017049106 | ISBN 9781506329055 (pbk. : alk. paper)

Subjects: LCSH: Public relations—Handbooks, manuals, etc.

Classification: LCC HD59 .L88 2018 | DDC 659.2—dc23
LC record available at https://lccn.loc.gov/2017049106

This book is printed on acid-free paper.

SFI label applies to text stock

18 19 20 21 22 10 9 8 7 6 5 4 3 2 1

Brief Contents

Detailed Contents

Foreword

In a perfect world, the discipline of public relations would not need to exist. Organizations and individuals would communicate clearly and consistently, and there would be no competition for attention from the audiences they intend to reach. Customers, investors, policy makers, and employees would feel that their voices were heard and understood, and there would be ample opportunities to exchange information. Products and services would never fail. Customer service would be seamless and effective. Employees would create value in their work, feel fulfilled, and grow into new roles or find new jobs easily. And Regina Luttrell and Luke Capizzo would not have to write this book.

Of course, we don't live in that perfect world.

Every day, companies, brands, institutions, politicians, and celebrities plan their messaging to build visibility and credibility, engage audiences, and stimulate action. How do they do it? Very often, they turn to communications practitioners either in their own organizations or in public relations (PR) firms.

An experienced in-house communications team can be sufficient in many instances, possessing intimate knowledge about the business needs. However, as an organization grows, it needs to manage shifting relationships and demands for rapidly changing information. This is especially true when the need to communicate reflects a new or unfamiliar challenge, a major initiative or campaign, the response to a threat, the need to generate attention, or the building of new relationships. An outside agency may be appropriate when ongoing communications needs stretch the capacity or abilities of an inside team.

Why Clients Use an Outside PR Agency

As an expandable resource or a source of fresh ideas, a capable PR agency adds value in numerous areas, including objectivity, frequency, and reach. Ideally, an outside agency provides each element quickly and in an efficient and cost-effective way.

Not surprisingly, the most common reason for hiring an outside agency is to extend the communications team. A PR agency can provide the human resources necessary to expand or accelerate communications outreach. This relationship allows for additional people to research, connect a client with an audience, create content, or engage influencers and policy makers. In a crisis situation, it may allow for a specialized team to address inquiries and comments that shape the future reputation of an organization. In the best circumstances, the outside PR professionals and in-house team create a seamless cooperative to get more done.

The value of an agency is not necessarily defined by size or cost; rather, there are other qualities that clients tend to look for in an appropriate partner. One of the most important is objectivity.

Is the Client Always Right?

While it is useful to start with the approach that "the client is always right" in any service business, it is also necessary to push back when dealing with a client who wants the impossible or asks for communications activities that may backfire. Communications risk management—the ability to weigh risk versus reward—is a shared responsibility. Ultimately, clients expect agencies to anticipate and adjust strategies and tactics based on their ability to ask the right questions.

However, in the event that the client's original request simply isn't feasible, a good agency will find a way to shape the strategy and content to reflect the closest intersection of the client's business needs and the audiences' interests. Calibration of these intersections requires experience and skill in research and analytics to shape the successful approach. A client is right to assume that the best agency partner will be one that knows, or can quickly figure out, how to gather information, navigate competing content, and analyze results to refine a desired communications approach.

Clients also hope to leverage the frequency with which an agency carries out communications tasks. For example, new product introductions, changes in leadership, initial public offerings, response to a crisis, opening new facilities, and a range of other events all require specific experience, tactics, and evaluation. Some agencies may even repeat these processes multiple times a year, and most will have more experience than their clients do. In these cases, the benefit of using an agency provides a better chance of comprehensive anticipation, smooth execution, and accurate evaluation.

Another client expectation from an agency is improved access to media and influencers. This presents both an opportunity and a challenge for agencies and their employees. While clients may prefer to use an agency's contacts, agencies and their account teams are sensitive to the quality of the content that flows through their network.

This is an important concept to understand as an agency employee because the relationships you build over time with journalists, bloggers, influencers, and experts become part of your value to current and future employers. Plus, there is a natural quality control that takes place when agencies work with clients, since agencies and their employees naturally want to improve and focus the client's content before they take it to their own networks.

Efficiency and Responsiveness

In addition to objectivity, frequency, and reach, a successful agency will also deliver speed and efficiency to its clients. This can be challenging. Organizations, especially large ones, often evolve their structures and approval processes to limit risk rather than to encourage swift decisions and immediate responses. This can mean many steps, multiple conversations, and a lot of documentation.

Very often, clients hire agencies for access to best practices, including communications planning and tracking processes that make it easier to justify the costs involved in a successful program. Early in your career, you may ask yourself, what does this meeting have to do with getting more likes on the client's social media post or getting the product launched? But the fact is, processes grow to keep people and relationships safe in the context of organizational priorities and approval cycles. Agency professionals soon learn that showcasing the value of their services doesn't stop once a relationship is won. Avoiding mistakes and waste from the point of view of the client's organization requires a lot of people to understand what, why, and how communications will happen.

Who Is Best Suited for Agency Life?

For many communications professionals, the career path of agency versus in-house is not a binary choice. Most of us complete elements of each in the course of a career. Whichever route you pursue, know that there are a number of characteristics that predict whether a person will like agency life and be successful. Most consistently, agency professionals seek variety; possess a natural curiosity, a built-in sense of urgency, and some natural entrepreneurism; and have a tendency to be business minded.

The opportunity to work on three or more projects at a time may be appealing to some, but not always for others. The trade-off for agency professionals is that they often don't get to see the long-term results of a communications program. It can certainly take that long to make a big impact on a company, brand, or institution, but agency assignments tend to change from year to year, if not more frequently.

Another marker of a successful agency employee is an appreciation for teamwork. This does not necessarily mean being a "people person." If you find yourself energized by brainstorming and sharing work with a team, you'll be comfortable in most PR agencies. This isn't to say that teamwork isn't important for in-house PR teams, but roles can be increasingly defined for individual contributors.

Perhaps it is obvious, but when an organization is paying for your time, as is the case in most client/agency relationships, working quickly and staying on task is very important. In an agency, deadlines are a fact of life, and those who are most successful require less supervision and are more self-motivated than others. If you are a person who needs a lot of reassurance to feel confident about your work, have patience within an agency career and trust the judgment of those who have the responsibility to bring your career along at a pace that serves your future appropriately.

In a good agency, the management team spends a lot of time thinking about all three priorities and considers employees' needs individually. This makes sense when you realize that the people and their experience are most valued to a client. At the same time, agency professionals need to consistently identify ways to create value, generate opportunities, and help the business grow. There is a constant two-track conversation in any agency, one about finding and satisfying clients, the other about finding talent and paying salaries and expenses associated with the business.

The need for a business-minded approach doesn't stop at the agency's doors. For agency people, getting to "yes" with a client requires far more than communications creativity. Anyone who creates value for a client ultimately has to understand the client's business and what makes it successful. An ability to think ahead will make your advice on communications strategy and tactics much more effective and make it easier and more likely that the client will see the logic of what you want them to do.

How to Succeed

Possessing a fundamental understanding of communications and having the ability to write, research, and develop communications tactics will set you up well for success in an agency. Agency life is a constant stream of learning about new topics, companies or products, issues, and trends. With time, you will be able to apply learnings from one situation or industry to another and make creative leaps by identifying a communications opportunity that your client's competitors haven't yet discovered.

You'll also need flexibility and dedication. PR agency life means serving the interests and the schedule of your clients. Your plans will change, but it's never the same day twice, and that's a reward in itself.

The lessons and insights offered by Regina and Luke allow readers to peek behind the curtain of agency life. Enjoy what you learn. If you do choose to pursue a career working in PR agencies, I wish you luck and success. By placing your clients and your colleagues first and learning from every assignment, you will become a valuable and very welcome member of our industry.

Peter J. Verrengia
President and Sr. Partner |
Communications Consulting Worldwide | FleishmanHillard

Preface

Agency public relations will introduce you to some of the most brilliant, hardest working, and genuinely inspiring people in the industry. These individuals are not afraid of tackling immense challenges and do not hesitate to challenge clients when ethical dilemmas arise. Agency professionals also take deep pride in the quality of the product as well as the value of their words.

Why a Book About Agency Life?

Many undergraduate PR students possess only a vague notion of what life at an agency entails. A lucky few secure internships that expose them to the possibilities and realities of top agencies, but the majority of students are unable to experience this side of public relations prior to graduation.

The agency world is diverse and cannot be painted in overly broad strokes. From individual practitioners and small local firms to global agencies with thousands of employees and offices around the world, there is not a stereotypical agency environment. The overarching goal of this book is to highlight the many different functional components found within an agency as well as reinforce the positive impact that excellent agency work can have on organizations. The authors have included numerous interviews with industry professionals from across the country and around the world at the end of each chapter to provide readers with snapshots of the agency experience.

Arising from a need for a practical, honest guide outlining the inner workings of agency life, this text can be utilized as a reference by both students and professionals. The topics discussed in the book may even convince a few readers that the consulting approach is the right avenue for them. Chapters cover many of the subfields of integrated communication practice, including traditional public relations and corporate communication, marketing, social media, creative production (print, digital, video, audio), web and user experience design, and search engine optimization (SEO). Of course, each topic should be considered as a brief introduction, providing context and language useful when working with, for example, professional designers, developers, and videographers. It is important to understand that an agency practitioner who can do everything simply does not exist, but we can each benefit from expanding our vocabularies and adding knowledge that makes it easier to collaborate with those who bring complementary skills.

We envision this book as a useful core text for student-run agency classes as well as a valuable supplement for courses in PR campaigns, cases, or other capstones. Topics are introduced, contextualized among PR on principles, and explained through best practices. Several real-world examples are highlighted throughout the book to ensure that the practical concepts presented become concrete for readers. The text leverages the PESO (paid, earned, shared, and owned) model of integrated media outreach and the ROSTIR model (research/diagnosis, objectives, strategies, tactics, implementation, reporting/evaluation) of campaign planning. We see these approaches as the most appropriate models for the needs of today's integrated agency environment, where there are few walls separating public relations, social media, and marketing.

Acknowledgments

The authors would like to thank the many individuals who have helped make this book possible. First, we share our gratitude to the team at SAGE (particularly Terri Accomazzo and Anna Villarruel) for their patience, encouragement, and expert guidance throughout this process. We would also like to thank Erin Livingston for her keen editorial eye and Erik Helton for his quick responses and attention to detail. Additionally, this book would be far narrower in perspective without the many practitioners who shared their time and varied expertise for the professional interviews that add so much to each chapter: Nadine Ahfat, Emily Bader, Stephanie Baumer, Michael DiFrisco, Mike Driehorst, Susan Emerick, Kelly Fletcher, Melinda Machado, Michael Meath, Nicole Moreo, Heather Sliwinski, Joe Sloan, Valerie Stachurski, Peter J. Verrengia, Darryl Villacorta, and Mark Winter. To our reviewers, a hearty "thank you" for your insights and comments, which have made a positive impact on the quality of this book and the value it will have for readers.

Regina would like to take moment to thank her husband, Todd, and daughters, Emma and Avery, for championing her writing endeavors (even when they creep into the weekend). I am ever humbled by the sacrifices you make. No illustration of appreciation is enough.

Luke would like to thank his family, particularly his parents and Sarah and Joel, for their constant support and encouragement through all of changes and adventures over the three years of this project. This writing process would have been much less enjoyable without exceptional mentors and colleagues at the University of Maryland: You've all helped me to ask better questions, to understand the immense value of PR research, and to know precisely what excellent teaching looks like. And, finally, to his agency teammates: This book would not have been possible without the camaraderie and learning opportunities of my years at Identity, made possible by the leadership, brilliance, and compassion of Andrea Trapani and Mark Winter. Thank you all!

Finally, we would like to share our admiration for the countless agency professionals who work every day to counsel organizations toward more effective, efficient, ethical, and inclusive communication. Better communication strengthens organizations, and stronger organizations create better communities.

Agency Life

CHAPTER 1

Working in an Agency

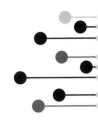

"Welcome. We're thrilled to have you here. I hope you like coffee."

These words, or something to their effect, have been shared with generations of practitioners beginning their careers at a **public relations** (PR) agency. While these individuals, the clients, and even the core skills needed to perform this work can be dynamic in nature, much of the agency experience is universal. Agencies can be a great place to build a career on the leading edge of the PR industry.

Agencies attract whip-smart, motivated individuals. They are often people who are not satisfied with punching a clock and performing work that is considered "good enough." The archetypal agency individual is a driven multitasker, someone who wants to be involved in every part of a process. Smart leaders hire the grown-up version of the kid who did everyone else's work on group projects in elementary school—and stayed up late to ensure that every last magazine cutout was glued correctly to the poster board.

PR agencies offer a path to responsibility for young practitioners. They provide both the opportunity for and responsibility of counseling clients. The bar for success may be high, but so are the possibilities—both personally and professionally.

Working with a team of these Type-A personalities can be challenging and stressful, but it can also be incredibly productive and rewarding. It has provided a nurturing, motivating, and positive place for many young PR professionals to learn and grow in their careers. Yet, without the right support structures or the necessary personal motivation, agency life can also leave many budding practitioners tired and burned out after only a short time. In order to increase the probability of success, individuals should approach agency life with an open mind in order to understand and appreciate the unique demands and rewards of the environment—and with the understanding that it isn't for everyone.

Objectives

- Clarify the characteristics of agency public relations work as opposed to in-house work.

- Understand the difference between niche and full-service agencies.

- Define the practitioner roles within a public relations agency.

- Introduce the benefits and challenges of agency careers.

It's also critical to remember that not all agencies are created equal. There are big and small companies and well-established and brand-new firms as well as those that are well-run and those that are less so. Even within these categories, some agencies are the right fit for the right person at a certain time in their careers but not at others. The difference between the right firm and the wrong firm for you can be night and day, so it's critical to be aware of the characteristics that define them.

If these traits, environments, and opportunities speak to you, this text can provide a window into the world of balancing the agency- and client-focused work needed to succeed. Working with leading agency professionals and serving a variety of clients is engaging, invigorating, challenging and rewarding work . . . that is, if you enjoy working hard and learn to appreciate the value of strong coffee.

Work Environment

You wake up. You make yourself look presentable and check your calendar to see if you have any meetings with more buttoned-down clients that day. You check email. You check your media alerts. You scan your client's **social media** channels and notifications. If nothing caught fire overnight, you make your way in to the office. You email two clients about stories that went live that morning—thankfully both positive. If you have a moment to breathe, you make a list of eight tasks you should accomplish that day and star five of them that need to be done. You get started on one of the items but are quickly distracted when a partner at your firm lets you know that he needs your help for an urgent client proposal. This puts you behind in preparing for a client call that afternoon, but you're still able to distribute a press release and provide the competitor research results needed for the proposal. By the time you wrap up the client call, make some reporter follow-up calls, and take care of an unexpected—but positive—media inquiry requiring client outreach and compiling talking points as well as the draft of an internal agency report, you realize that you've accomplished an incredible amount of work, but only one-third of it was on your original to-do list!

They may not have federal government-level benefits, a Google-style cafeteria, or Wall Street bonuses, but PR agencies tend to be some of the more fun, engaging, and rewarding places to work in the marketing and communication field.

In-House Public Relations or Agency Life?

One key distinction to keep in mind between an in-house PR position and that of an agency job is the size, skill, and makeup of your department. At many small companies, the communication/marketing/PR department may only be one or two people. Even recent graduates can quickly find themselves as the top communicator within this type of organization. While this responsibility can also have its rewards, it may not offer the opportunities to learn from and work alongside top industry professionals. Additionally, in very large companies, the responsibility of communication is often so segmented that junior practitioners end up with a very narrow exposure and skill set. While the opportunities for advancement may be exceptional over the long term, seniority often plays a larger role in the advancement process.

Many PR agencies have earned a reputation for supporting a youthful office environment with many junior professionals, providing numerous opportunities for recent college graduates. In part, agencies attract young professionals because they are fast-paced, vibrant places to learn. They can also offer rapid advancement opportunities and the potential for increased responsibility early in a practitioner's career.

Of course, there is another side to those same opportunities: PR firms are inherently high-pressure, no-excuse environments. Agencies ask a lot from all members of a team. They tend to hire a significant number of recent graduates due to a heightened level of attrition. Many young professionals in this industry have very high expectations placed upon them by senior staff, and the training, credit, and compensation do not always match these expectations. That said, these high expectations are precisely why well-run agencies attract top talent.

©iStockphoto.com/XiXinXing

PR agencies provide a multitude of experiences and opportunities for young professionals.

Whatever the circumstances, the formula for success is usually straightforward: Work hard, show results for your clients, and support the agency team. At most firms, those who do this well are rewarded, and those who do not eventually look to move on. In an era of gold stars and participation trophies, this can be a rude awakening. Either way, working at a PR agency can be an intensely rewarding experience, especially knowing that the work one does is impactful, valued, and rewarded.

Long-term career success requires exposure to a variety of experiences and skills and the subsequent refinement of them. PR agencies can facilitate this process as well as, if not better than, any other type of organization due to the dynamic nature of the business.

Expectations

While every PR agency environment is unique due to the leadership, geography, client base, and a multitude of other factors, the following list highlights a few of the key expectations that all incoming practitioners would be well served to work toward. Think of these as adjectives that describe the ideal agency professional.

Effective

One of the most rewarding parts of agency life is working with a group of people who are singularly focused on execution by collectively working diligently toward their personal, agency, and client goals. It's not simply the volume of work and the amount of time it takes to complete that work; prioritization, focus, and delivering on expectations are all essential for company success. The most successful agency team members are equally effective at executing both internal and external projects and are conscientious in their work with both fellow agency peers and client partners.

Efficient

Agency professionals are expected to work hard and be efficient. The structure of an agency, built on the professional services model, means that clients are generally not paying *a la carte* for specific deliverables but for professional time to complete the desired services. To oversimplify, it means that the faster a junior team member can write a strong press release, the more valuable he or she to the agency. That said, success is also determined by the results or outcomes of a specific project, rather than only the outputs,[1] as explained in the leading measurement guidelines described in the Barcelona Principles. Therefore, writing a press release that takes twice as long but gets picked up by three times as many media outlets is more valuable in the long run. Ultimately, it's about doing impactful work that fulfills a client's business **objectives**.

Empowered

Life in an agency world is all about finding solutions. Top agency leaders cultivate strong teams by giving them important responsibilities and empowering them to make decisions and work toward a goal. They allow their teams to make

---

[1] Grupp, R. W. (2010, June 18). The Barcelona declaration of research principles. *Institute for public relations.* Retrieved August 2, 2015, from http://www.instituteforpr.org/the-barcelona-declaration-of-research-principles/

choices—and, occasionally, mistakes—as part of the learning process. By providing their team members with the responsibility to plan and execute increasingly larger swaths of client work, agency practitioners build skills and confidence while increasing the sense of personal ownership and investment. This means that individuals must be willing to take on the responsibility and burden of driving client campaigns forward to success.

Energized

Effective public relations does not happen by accident. While there is a significant amount of skill necessary in order to be successful in the field, drive, willpower, and energy are also essential to get the job done. In walking through the office door each morning, it's critical to carry with you the desire to do your best work and a positivity undaunted by the obstacles placed in your way. Confidence and energy are critical for any PR practitioner, but the agency professional requires more of both—whether it's to help convince a hesitating client that a thoughtful strategic approach is right for them or to get through a to-do list made extra-long by multiple client projects.

One of the more rewarding aspects of a well-run agency is that each of these traits is developed and cultivated during the life cycle and proper execution of **integrated marketing communication (IMC)** campaigns.

PR agencies value professionalism and personality, since the percentage of public, external-facing, or client-facing team members is generally higher than at most organizations. This means that one's ability to look, sound, and perform in a professional manner is critical from the first day of hire. To be an active and valuable participant in meetings, one needs to be prepared, flexible, confident, and able to think on one's feet.

None of these skills are developed overnight, but they are cultivated through observation of senior professionals in action; development of depth related to a client's businesses, objectives, and industries; and understanding the process of producing news and content.

Agency Structure

As noted previously, PR agencies come in all shapes and sizes—from boutique firms with 3 to 5 practitioners to massive organizations with multiple offices and hundreds of employees. Nearly all agencies are structured with a top-down (pyramid) hierarchy, with fewer senior executives at the top, vying for new business and setting strategy, and a larger number of junior practitioners executing much of the day-to-day work. Depending on the **scope** of the agency's efforts, there may be multiple departments for different practice areas. Except for the smallest firms, there is also a support team that handles much of the behind-the-scenes work of running the business.

Work environments can also be strikingly different from firm to firm. A local boutique firm in a small media market may have a relatively targeted and stable client base, a reasonable pace of work, and experience success through strong

Media relations involves working with a variety of media outlets on behalf of clients, including print, broadcast, and digital channels for consumer and industry audiences.

relationships with local reporters and editors. They offer organizations in their market an opportunity to better leverage local media channels and engage with the community for local events, political issues, and causes. These firms often handle a mix of business-to-consumer (B2C) and business-to-business (B2B) clients. **Media relations** account team members work on multiple accounts, and firm partners are heavily involved in the day-to-day execution of deliverables. Such firms can be great opportunities for practitioners to develop skill sets on how to build strong relationships with clients and interact with the media.

One potential downside of a smaller boutique firm is that the scope of work is often limited in comparison to a larger agency. There may not be as many significant opportunities for professional growth or to gain experience in different client industries. There is often less exposure to larger clients or diverse groups of reporters and editors. Smaller firms may be located in smaller markets; be younger, less mature companies; or be run by practitioners who restrict their clients based on size or geography. That said, by working on smaller accounts, team members may be exposed to more clients simultaneously. Entry-level professionals are more likely to be working with, and learning from, agency principals.

Larger firms, on the other hand, are generally located in major metropolitan areas and tend to have larger accounts, bigger client teams, and more senior practitioners. They are much more likely to have multiple offices in multiple markets and to have more layers separating the top and bottom of the firm's hierarchy. Partners are often not as involved in the day-to-day media and client outreach. A group relatively separate from account management may handle business development. With larger accounts, the team members and scope of work are often more specialized. The responsibilities for social media and media relations may be split not only between different individuals, but also even into different departments or different offices. These firms can offer greater opportunities for advancement to the highest levels of the industry; to work with the largest accounts; and to engage in major public relations, social media **community relations**, **crisis communication**, or media outreach campaigns.

At the same time, larger firms often expect significant commitment from their team members, requiring long hours and applying substantial pressure to succeed. For the right person, it can be a challenging and invigorating environment. For the wrong person, it can become a burden. The long hours and client demands can mean extended workdays, late-night events, and even missed personal/family functions.

Whether your preference is to experience life at a large agency or a small one, geography has become less of a determining factor in success with clients. More and more, technology is allowing PR firms to perform outreach and build media relationships far beyond traditional media market boundaries. Geography is simply less of a determining factor in agency/client relationships today than it has been historically. Positively for the industry as a whole, expertise and effectiveness are the most critical drivers.

Agency Roles and Job Titles

PR agencies can vary greatly in their use of job titles and the responsibilities that each title carries. That said, they usually maintain a hierarchy with more seasoned professionals defining direction through goals, objectives, and **strategies** for client accounts, while junior practitioners are often tasked with the execution of the **tactics** and tasks built into these plans.

The division of labor within the agency structure is also important in establishing a balance and organization for each function, including media relations, **marketing**, **advertising**, media monitoring and reporting, events management, digital/**search engine optimization (SEO)**, social media channel/community management, content creation/editorial, and client management. Often, members from different discipline-based teams are pulled together to create an effective, comprehensive client team based on the account requirements.

While even the largest firms tend to combine at least some of these tasks within a single role, others may be wholly organized by client rather than by discipline. In this model, each member of an account team may engage in media relations, marketing, social media, and website oversight for an individual client. The workload is based more on the knowledge of the industry, geographic market, or unique client needs rather than the skill set of each task in an integrated marketing communication approach.

Understanding that these differing approaches to organization within an agency environment can promote distinct workloads and work environments is an important point. What may seem like the right fit for certain individuals may not be for others. Researching the operational structure of a PR agency can be one of the most critical insights prior to applying for jobs at specific firms.

From entry level to management, here is a relatively standard sample hierarchy of job descriptions and the main differentiators for each position: interns, account assistants, account executives,[2] account directors, vice presidents, and partners.

---

[2]One potential point of confusion for those entering the industry and job searching is that many media companies, including newspapers, magazine, radio stations, and television stations, use similar *account executive* job titles on their ad sales teams. In this context—and unlike the majority of PR firms—these are pure sales jobs soliciting print, radio, or TV advertising, usually paid in large part on commission.

Intern

Many PR agencies rely heavily on interns for tasks such as **social media monitoring**, **media clipping**, and client reporting as well as key outreach efforts, including media list building and **research**, media pitching and follow up, drafting press releases, and other external-facing documents. While the experience, job tasks, and overall educational value can range dramatically from one firm to another, the nature of agencies today means that the work of interns, particularly in the content-hungry world of social media, is as critical as ever. While largely unpaid, PR firms often lean on interns to increase their efficiency in meeting the demands of simultaneously working with multiple clients.

The opportunities for interns can be seen as either a positive or a negative for those looking to enter the industry. The chance to do real, practical work has meant that PR interns, more than many other professions, reap great value from their early work experiences. After completing an agency internship, most students or recent graduates will have a clear sense of whether agency life is for them. The potential downsides may include, but are certainly not limited to, unreasonable expectations of the position, questionable legality[3] of working without compensation, long hours, and not always having the full support and direction needed to succeed.[4] Agencies must take the necessary steps to build a viable program with clear objectives and thorough preparation and training for interns.

Today, students often complete multiple internships, giving themselves valuable perspectives of agency and in-house PR opportunities as well as a variety of contacts and connections in the field upon graduation. For those seeking internships, ensure that you ask questions about the work environment, the expectations, the job duties, the clients, the industry, the pace, and the responsibilities of the position. Identifying an internship opportunity that truly fits your appetite and your career goals is the best first step to having a positive PR agency experience.

Account Assistant

Recent graduates are often hired to be account assistants, focusing on client, issue, and media research; drafting and coordinating distribution of basic account and agency news; and ensuring that all media coverage on a specific client is fully captured, catalogued, and reported.

These positions may or may not be client facing but they do command a significant amount of responsibility. While the tasks that they perform may not be glamorous, they are vital to the agency's function and success. Through constant monitoring of a variety of news channels, account assistants are presented with an opportunity for firsthand involvement in understanding and decoding media trends to understand the most appropriate timing for connecting client experts with reporters.

---

[3]Appelbaum, L. (2010, April 16). Making internships work (without breaking the law). *PRSA news*. Retrieved July 20, 2015, from http://prsay.prsa.org/index.php/2010/04/16/making-internships-work-without-breaking-the-law/

[4]Barber, M.D. (n.d.). Solo PR Pro. Retrieved March 5, 2018, from http://soloprpro.com/pr-interns-or-assistants/

Agencies that make good use of their account assistants start them researching and writing early and often, allowing them to develop a deeper understanding of individual accounts and relevant industries. In executing this work effectively, account assistants gain exposure to the objectives and strategies—not simply the tactics—involved in planning and executing client campaigns.

Diligent account assistants do their best to soak up all of the information around them, to manage their time efficiently, and to ask for more whenever they can. This could include tagging along to client meetings or events, being a part of proposal development teams for new business, or taking advantage of educational opportunities with their local Public Relations Society of America (PRSA) chapter. Most importantly, this role is about learning the approaches, the pace, and the effort that goes into developing valuable integrated campaigns and programs for clients.

Account Executive

Professionals leading the day-to-day account work are considered the heart of any agency. The account executive role demands that team members are self-sufficient and can manage the majority of account tasks and tactics. These individuals know when the best times are to contact reporters and how to prioritize work over the balance of a day for maximum efficiency and are developing the key client management skills that allow them to build trust. At this level within an agency, practitioners are finding their groove, focusing on perfecting specific skills (based on industry or discipline), and understanding the style and size of an agency that is best suited for them.

Key facets of their work on the media relations side include direct media outreach, collaborating to create strategic plans, and implementing campaigns. They are often tasked with training and overseeing the work of interns and account assistants as well as ensuring that client teams are prepared for internal and client-facing meetings. In this respect, account executives play a critical role in the definition and execution of the firm's values and client experience on a daily basis.

Account Director

The glue of a strong PR firm is the management at the account director level. This position involves the critical training of increasingly larger internal teams that are managing the more visible critical client accounts. They often oversee the creation, training, and execution of internal and client communication processes.

Account directors are the most visible day-to-day client contacts, ensuring that work is delivered to meet goals, objectives, and strategies within required timelines and quality standards. As such, they are able to build very strong relationships with their clients and the media, translating these relationships into more effective and efficient work over the long term.

In directing client teams and ensuring that deadlines are met, this critical position manages the enforcement of firm policies and procedures, which may include hiring, **onboarding**, and training processes as well as best practices for media outreach or social media strategy. Account directors often meet with junior team members to mentor, answer questions, check progress, and provide feedback on their performance.

Vice President

The vice president–level roles in PR firms are often organized by function (media relations, social media, digital, **creativity**, etc.) or by practice area, often broken down by industry. In larger, multi-office firms, vice presidents often oversee specific geographic territories, large clients, or industry practice groups.

Their day-to-day work consists of a significant number of meetings (both internal and client facing) to define strategies for accounts and to ensure that each individual client team is executing them appropriately. This governance may come through a weekly meeting pulse, a series of reporting documents, or more informal methods. It often means that a vice president will step in to help during difficult circumstances or when a crisis emerges—making the work both challenging and rewarding.

At this level, their strategic contributions often extend to the agency itself, helping to define the direction of the firm. A vice president supports the partners in identifying new opportunities, networking to expand their exposure to potential clients, and building proposals and presentations for new business meetings. Vice presidents may be tasked with watching for and responding to requests for proposal (RFPs), formal documents that many organizations use to provide organizational background information for potential agency partners when soliciting proposals for their marketing and PR work.

The ability of these individuals to develop and maintain good relationships with the media and with current and potential clients takes on an even greater level of importance. As executives, they are often expected to hold leadership positions within local organizations—from their PRSA chapter to nonprofit organizations in the community. In this way, they demonstrate their leadership and organizational management skills both within the agency and beyond it.

Partner/Principal/Owner

Many boutique and regional PR firms are named for their founders and partners. These individuals are generally the owners and main stakeholders in the business and thus serve the dual role of overseeing the PR activities of the firm along with running the company. Many great practitioners have risen to the challenge and expanded their entrepreneurial skill set, while others have struggled; however, all have been forced to delegate and give up some degree of day-to-day responsibility in order to succeed.

The best PR agency leaders find ways to act as visionaries and teachers while simultaneously empowering their teams to tackle the vast majority of client work. These individuals must leverage and integrate their own strengths and skill sets, hard-earned media and client relationships, and exceptional media relations or social media skills as well as business acumen and insights. They also must nurture these skills within the rest of the organization in order to support up-and-coming talent.

Individuals in these roles often lead the business development and strategy initiatives, helping to win new clients and set the tone for the work to be completed. In the best circumstances, this setup leverages their vision and experience while allowing others to hone their skills in executing the work under their tutelage. However, successful execution does involve a distinct balancing act. When this approach misfires, clients are left feeling that their initial outreach was a bait-and-switch or that they've been left in the hands of less-skilled professionals. The best leaders create a strong team, involve them deeply in all processes, and set expectations from the outset as to the role that a firm partner will play long-term in a client relationship.

The size and scope of any individual firm is largely determined by the owners' skill, drive, and ambition. This may include consistent growth in order to challenge the top firms in their city, state, or region or may simply focus on the development of stable relationships with a core set of clients, employees, and industries.

Of course, *stable* is always a relative term in an agency environment. The pace of change, evolution of news and journalism, and the cycles of outreach tools and team members at any firm create an environment that challenges the best leaders and practitioners. PR firm leaders are among the most talented business professionals— they are doers, they are builders, and they are entrepreneurs, representing the highest echelon of media relations and communication practitioners.

Additional and Alternative Job Titles

Agencies may also have further organization within specific disciplines, for example, their social media practice. This approach could produce job titles such as *media relations account executive* and *social media account executive*. Those firms that have a significant design or creative department often follow advertising agency naming conventions, including *creative director*, *graphic designer*, *developer*, *production coordinator*, and *copywriter*. Other agencies have adopted a movement toward unconventional titles, which can range in quality and value and from inspiring to nauseating. A 2014 *Forbes* article listed some of the best creative job titles, from *project meanie* (a project manager at InsightShare LLC) to *crayon evangelist* (the graphic design lead at InteQ Corp).[5]

There is also a move by many agencies to remove these layers of hierarchy and adopt a less stratified structure. This can mean more direct contact with agency partners and executives—a benefit for younger team members—but also more responsibility and less room for advancement. Whatever the result, smart agencies develop their structure based on their strengths and the best ways to serve their client base.

---

[5]Linkner, J. (2014, December 4). The 21 most creative job titles. *Forbes*. Retrieved September 14, 2015, from https://www.forbes.com/sites/joshlinkner/2014/12/04/the-21-most-creative-job-titles/#448c0a322933

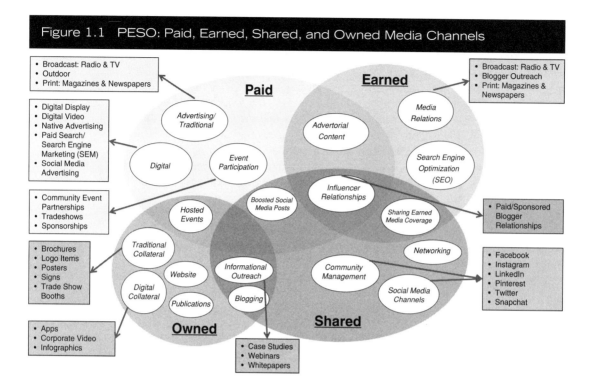

Figure 1.1   PESO: Paid, Earned, Shared, and Owned Media Channels

That said, the same job title can entail drastically different responsibilities from firm to firm. Before accepting any agency job, it's critical to fully understand the expectations for a certain role and where it fits into a firm's overall hierarchy.

The Impact of an Integrated Marketing Communication (IMC) Approach

The flattening of many agency's job structures and the growing convergence of the public relations, advertising, social media, and digital marketing disciplines has made it increasingly difficult to separate out the functions of a traditional PR firm. This is reflected in the success of older firms with PR and marketing/advertising backgrounds that are now crossing over and doing fully integrated work as well as newer digital firms that are taking on increasingly larger slices of overall marketing **budgets**—and seeking opportunities to integrate **earned** and **paid media** into their own mix.

In addition to traditional media relations, many PR firms today incorporate tactics from marketing and advertising, creative design and production, web design, and SEO as well as social media from both a **content creation** and community management perspective.

In most cases, and for our industry as a whole, this is a vital and positive progression. The historical, and somewhat arbitrary, barriers between practitioners in different areas of marketing communication are not relevant to a consumer, to a community, or to most business and organizational leaders. What should be most important is that the agency professional is making an impact toward a goal, not necessarily the tactic or tool that they have used to achieve it.

This approach does create challenges for PR agencies across the country and around the world. Very few agencies, and certainly no individual PR professional, is skilled in every facet of our increasingly complex communication networks.

Today's practitioners must have a firm grasp of broad strategies across disciplines and the self-awareness to understand their own limitations in terms of execution. With this approach, agency leaders can act as true counselors and put their client's needs ahead of their own skills. This means analyzing and diagnosing communication challenges based on the research and insights available, not necessarily based on the strengths of the individual practitioner or the firm. Practitioners may find themselves turning clients away or recommending supplementary services beyond their own reach. That said, by maintaining the role of strategist, public relations can remain at the center of the **messaging**, marketing, and outreach approaches that move an organization's business goals forward.

Agency Types: Niche Versus Full Service

Running any successful organization entails defining and understanding your limits. PR agencies are no exception. Understandably, there is significant variation as to how individual firms define these boundaries for themselves. Some agencies have a focus defined by geography or media market that leverages local media relationships, while other agencies offer a focus or core strength based on client industry expertise, such as health care, manufacturing, or tourism. They may also build a practice around types of PR outreach, such as product launches, crisis communication, **investor relations,** or community relations.

What separates a true niche agency from the others is how clearly they define these boundaries. When agencies build solid walls around a specific discipline or industry, they make themselves stand out from their competitors and appeal more strongly to a certain type of client.

Attributes of Niche Agencies

Many smaller, and sometimes even larger agencies, are very successful because they take the time to develop a specific area of expertise. Oftentimes, they will pursue only a single type of client and subsequently only hire PR practitioners that bring experience from within a specific industry or area of practice.

In order to provide the services desired by their clients, niche agencies often engage in more partnerships with outside experts or other firms to bolster their efforts. This may entail relationships with graphic designers, web developers, advertising and marketing agencies, media buyers, social media practitioners, and media relations professionals with complementary geographic or industry expertise.

In general, a smaller agency tends to service smaller clients and run with a flatter organizational hierarchy. An organization such as this may employ a higher percentage of senior practitioners possessing specific expertise. For example, these firms may specialize in a discipline such as media relations, social media, crisis communication, investor relations, **government relations**, product launches, or **branding**. They may also serve specific types of clients, industries, or groups of industries (technology, real estate, sports, manufacturing, or nonprofit, for example). As noted previously, these organizations generally have a clearly defined set of operational boundaries that support their service offerings to the majority of their clients.

For the right clients, these firms execute their work extremely well and can be valuable training grounds for younger practitioners. For the wrong clients, these organizations can lead to problems of misdiagnosis and attempting to solve a given challenge with the wrong tool. For the wrong practitioner, or even the right practitioner at the wrong time in their career, the daily tasks can be overwhelming or overly limiting and repetitive.

Attributes of Full-Service Agencies

Many agencies self-identify as full-service or integrated. These firms support their clients with a much broader range of services than a boutique firm and often have much less clearly defined walls around the types of clients or industries they work with. Today, nearly all large firms are built around the full-service model. The main group of potential clients that they exclude by subscribing to this business model are small businesses or nonprofits that cannot afford their lowest retainers or clients that potentially pose a conflict of interest with current clients.

While most full-service agencies do take the time to set boundaries in terms of the facets of integrated marketing communication that they cover, these organizations face the challenge of clearly presenting themselves in order to attract a wide range of clients without overreaching their capabilities.

Even the largest PR agencies must address the question of when to outsource and when to bring certain skills in house. At minimum, agency staff will nearly always handle the work of strategic planning and media relations. Social media is generally offered in-house. Creative design, advertising, web development, and SEO are more likely to be outsourced. With increased convergence of these varied communication disciplines, PR firms have ever-increasing capabilities but also realize a growing burden of balancing what's right for the firm and best for the client base.

Emily Bader

Emily Bader, an agency founder, leads planning at Zócalo Group. Emily guides client teams to develop social media programs founded in result-motivating insight. Her work includes guiding teams to uncover information to motivate audiences; crystallizing the role of social media to achieve companies' goals; unlocking social voice, persona, and sharable stories; and creating engaging content strategies. Her experience spans industries and category challenges for consumer and corporate brands, including Johnson & Johnson, The Home Depot, Subway, Frito-Lay, and Unilever.

Prior to the birth of Zócalo Group, Emily spent ten years at Ketchum and finished her tenure there as the Midwest Director of the Food and Nutrition Practice. Prior to Ketchum, Emily grew through the ranks at Shandwick in Minneapolis (pre-Weber). And she started her career at Kendrick Communications, a specialized consultancy focused on the automotive aftermarket. Emily serves on the board of the Word of Mouth Marketing Association and is a member of its ethics committee. We sat down with Emily to ask her what it is like to work at the Zócalo Group, and here's what she had to say.

How is your agency structured?

Our agency is set up more like an advertising agency than a PR agency; we have different groups.

- We have the account team; there are people who manage the business relationship, who oversee programming and try to identify new opportunities where we can help our clients. Within our account teams are community management; there are people dedicated to managing social media communities and ensuring that we are looking at engaging content and also

(Continued)

(Continued)

managing engagement with consumers as well as identifying and flagging issues that come up. The account team is really the nucleus of client management.

- Our creative team is almost as big as our account team, and within the creative team, we have art directors and copywriters and a lot of people who are creating digital and social experiences to drive word of mouth. The account managers make sure the creative team has what they need and are well briefed to deliver upon the work we get.

- Strategy team is all about account planning and guides teams toward what the social insight is in order to develop compelling campaigns, social media posts, and content theories.

- There is also a research and analytics team, which conducts consumer research, studies, mining resources for consumer trends, etc.

- The digital media and technology team plans media buying and the tools we use to make the ideas stronger.

How many people are on the account teams?

It depends on the size of the client. We have some clients that are very lean and some that are very big. There can be as many as ten on an account team or as few as three. It depends on how much of a budget we have.

What job roles do you hire for?

We hire on all levels. We have two recent graduates: one who works in the research and analytics team, and another who joined our media team. We have people supporting creative and account teams in community management on the account side. As our new generation becomes ever more social, it becomes incredibly valuable for us to hire young talent because it helps us make sure we're being true to what's social. Our creative team is always hiring young, fresh-out-of-college folks to help them on the creative side. There really is a full gamut of opportunity in an agency environment.

How would you describe your office environment?

It's very fun! We have scooters; even our CEO scoots around from office to office. We have the foosball table when we have beer Friday. Our creative teams do pranks with one another. For example, our product manager came in one day and his whole cube was wrapped in aluminum foil. Another guy walked in one morning and his entire office was filled with plastic volleyballs. There are tons of antics, but we do have a formal side and we have a formal conference room. We're in a high-rise building so our office right now is pretty standard. Most agencies are in an open plan where there are open desks and people sit looking at one another—we're going to be moving to that shortly.

What kind of a person should work in an agency setting like that?

If you're expecting to do the same thing every day, you shouldn't go into agency. There's always something that comes up, there's always a last-minute need to be met, there's always a client emergency, a client opportunity, or a new business pitch. You can never expect every day to be the same, so that kind of flexibility is important. I like to hire people who have been servers in restaurants. While there is a lot of creativity and thinking and puzzles to be solved, we are in the service business and that means the customer is right. There's finessing to making sure that clients' expectations are exceeded and that we are able to respond to their different types of personalities. That takes having a service mind-set and a level of patience and understanding and really strong listening skills.

How would you suggest someone just starting out deal with that best?

Make sure that from the beginning that you understand it isn't personal and that it's business. As much as creative work becomes personal and you become invested in ideas and way of thinking, at the end of the day, an agency is a business. When clients are challenging, that's part of the business, and it's something you learn to overcome. It's important for someone starting out to not get deflated by crazy clients but to learn from and listen when they are challenging things.

How does someone highlight service experience on his or her resume? How do they illustrate that it is important?

Teamwork is important; there is a very strong element of teamwork that is very important in this world. There's often too much work for the time that you have and when teams get together and deal with that, that's what makes the work rewarding as a team. Highlight what skills have come up from that restaurant work in terms of client service: being recognized as being a strong customer service person but also the elements of team. What you're hiring is the person and the raw material that the person has and if you can get through a busy Saturday night shift, to me, that's a life skill that is very important.

Do you think our industry is moving toward an integrated environment?

Yes, and PR agencies that don't are going to fail. News media is very important and one piece of the puzzle. A PR agency needs to know how to interact with consumers as marketers, and work within digital environments, appreciate the power, and understand how paid media works, including the nuances of **native advertising** and engagements. There's a lot more blurring of lines in the industry, which makes things challenging for agencies. If you don't understand how the lines are blurring and you can't speak the language of cross disciplines, then it becomes even harder.

What does today's agency look like to you?

What companies are hiring for is having a defined expertise, but creativity has never been more important. The ability to have a specialty and to really define that specialty but to be fluent in all the disciplines around your focus is important. Everything is working together, particularly with social and digital.

Do you consider your agency a niche or full-service agency?

We do a lot of things. Our specialty really is social and digital work that drives word of mouth.

You have a very relaxed environment. When someone is coming in for an interview, how do you expect him or her to dress?

Dressy business casual. Long gone are the days where you have to wear a suit every day, so I think it's almost weird when someone comes in with a full suit.

(Continued)

(Continued)

Tell us about your mentorship program.

We have a mentorship program that extends the length of the time at the agency. Mentorship should be something one asks for and people should seek that out. The employee needs to understand that part of their job is to learn the business.

Top 5 Characteristics Every PR Professional Should Have

1. Pride and pleasure in making clients happy: In an agency, the clients pay the bills. An agency's success is based on attaining clients and growing them. There is an art form to client service: truly understanding what they need, what their business meta-story is, and frankly, making them look good. Great agency people get jazzed by making clients happy.

2. Love working in teams: The best work comes from teamwork and so does the fastest work. Tight agency deadlines can be daunting—especially when clients seek big creative ideas and heavy strategies. It's important for teams to work together to ensure great work and service—breakthrough ideas, quality work, and consideration of all the details.

3. Flexibility: Every day is different in Agency Land and completely unpredictable. The happiest agency people go with the flow and can adjust nimbly.

4. Insatiable curiosity: There are so many businesses and clients and opportunities and disciplines and technologies to explore and discover in the world of agency. The more you embrace these learning opportunities, the easier it is to soar in your agency career.

5. Thick skin: As often as there are good, exciting days in this kind of environment, there are days where the clients don't like the work, when you don't win a new business pitch, or when someone else gets a new opportunity that you wanted—and more. The key is to never take any of this personally, to learn from every not-so-fun experience, and to apply those learnings to the next experience.

Top Must-Knows

- The smaller the agency, the quicker you learn. When starting out, choose an agency that has a small but nimble team. You will get way more experience from a small agency than a big one. They will need you more and throw you into juicier assignments from the get-go versus supporting bigger teams.

- Don't ask? Don't get. Be proactive about experiences you want, positions to try, people to meet. Sometimes people in senior management posts aren't as proactive about giving junior professionals opportunities. So *you* need to be. The answer may be "no," but you will get credit for asking.

- The agency business is a business. Agencies make money by ensuring their teams are *billable*. This means that every hour you spend is worth cold hard cash to the agency. Take that seriously, and appreciate that your time is valuable. Spend it as productively as you can. Always ask for more work if you don't feel like you have enough.

Top Must-Haves

- **Must-download app:** any of the many news-sharing apps. I like the good old-fashioned *New York Times*. It's critical in public relations and marketing that you stay current on the news and not just what interests you—the whole of what's going on around you in your city, the nation, in the world, and in the business world.

- **Must-read book/blog/news outlet:** Adweek or Ad Age. This is where the best marketers are featured, which provides incredible inspiration and competitive intelligence.

- **Must-use tool:** Newsmap. This helps you stay in real-time with what's happening in the world around you (http://newsmap.jp/#/b, e, m, n, t, w/us/view/).

Working With Clients

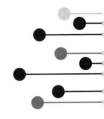

A re all clients the right client? Simply put, no. The largest agencies could service the needs of a nearly infinite variety of clients, but even they choose not to. Why is this? Even the most flexible public relations (PR) agency model is not the appropriate or efficient fit for all clients, and some clients are not a good fit for using agency partners at all.

From the sole practitioner, commonly referred to as a *solo practice PR professional*,[1] to the largest international firms, each has a specific type or number of client types that they best serve. Industry knowledge, tactical skill set, and geographic location can all point toward closer alignment and potential for success. Agencies and client partners may choose to *not* work together based on cost (retainer or project cost), industry (such as political or entertainment), personality (including overly demanding, overly rigid, or unresponsive), or conflicting interests (such as similar industries to current clients).

The challenge that each firm faces is to clearly define what types of clients that they intend to represent, with some even identifying a "perfect client" model that allows the organization and choose how far they are willing to stray from their ideal client base. Smart agency leaders learn how to best evaluate potential clients for both personal and structural factors in order to allow their account

Objectives

- Understand the distinct public relations needs of various sizes and types of organizations.

- Connect an organization's publics and goals to its public relations expectations.

- Organize, segment, and recognize client types.

- Consider the problems that may arise in agency–client relationships and how to approach solving them.

---

[1] While both can mean *an individual practicing public relations* or, in essence, *an agency of one*, technically, a sole practitioner is an unincorporated business. It's an individual taking on (in this case) media relations, marketing, or social media clients for his or her own profit. While a sole practitioner is the simplest way to practice public relations as an individual, it does mean that the individual is personally taking on all of the risks and liabilities of the business. A *solo practice* or *solo practitioner* refers to an individual functioning as an incorporated or unincorporated business (LLC or corporation). A *sole proprietor* is a specific type of *sole practitioner*. See http://info.legalzoom.com/difference-between-solo-practice-sole-proprietorship-24908.html for more info.

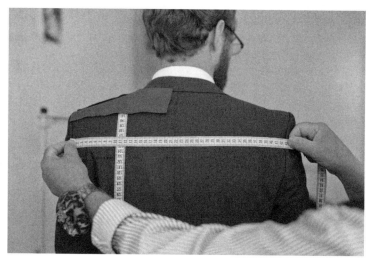

teams the greatest chance of success. Ultimately, since agencies are for-profit companies, their leaders must look to provide service to the clients that will be the best customers over the length of the relationship. This means that clients who have their own financial difficulties or who are unable to provide the internal support required for the partnership should be evaluated appropriately.

Choosing a Client: The Right Fit

The chances of contracting with the truly great, perfect-fit clients are few and far between. PR agencies could not survive on these clients alone. Yet, an Achilles heel for many of the most successful agencies and agency leaders is the amount of time and energy that their teams spend managing current clients that fall into the category of *poor fit*. Since every firm can and should set their boundaries differently, the value of planning for a desired clientele is especially important. The following guidelines can help in identifying client-based attributes necessary for evaluating if a client is the right fit for a particular firm.

Different Programs for Different Organizations

During the process of evaluating whether a client is the right fit, it is initially important for a firm to understand the specific audiences or **publics** that the client intends to target. Different goals and different publics lead to very different campaigns serving, for example, nonprofit, government, and for-profit organizations. Within the realm of for-profit businesses, one key distinction to understand is whether the potential client is considered a business-to-business company (B2B), a business-to-consumer company (B2C), or a combination of both. It is critical to identify and prioritize whether customers are other businesses, consumers, or a mix in order to adequately develop audience-focused plans, since the objectives, strategies, tactics, and tools required may be vastly different for these audiences. That said, PR agency tactics may be similar across business types. Even though disparate audiences dictate unique language and style, separate communication **channels**, and customized tools, approaches such as media relations, social media, event marketing, or digital advertising may be appropriate in many

Different Clients, Different Publics, Different Programs

The following provides hypothetical examples of potential organizational publics and goals for a variety of organizations. What agency-executed objectives, strategies, and tactics would be a good fit to accomplish these goals?

- Local Nonprofit (Animal Shelter)
  - Publics: Employees, members/donors, community members, local and state legislators
  - Goals: Achieve organizational mission—increase local cat and dog adoptions, raise cause awareness, raise funds, retain staff, add volunteers

- National Nonprofit (Disease Prevention and Research)
  - Publics: Employees, board of directors, members/donors, consumers, state and national legislators
  - Goals: Achieve organizational mission—increase research funding and decrease illness, raise funds, advocate for legislation, retain staff, grow outreach and influence

- State Government Agency (State Parks Service)
  - Publics: State residents (particularly outdoor enthusiasts), state legislators, other state and federal parks officials and organizations
  - Goals: Achieve organizational mission—balance preservation and maintenance with accessibility for residents, advocate for increased funding and support, educate publics about the value of conserving natural resources and wild places

- Small B2B Business (Local Law Firm)
  - Publics: Shareholders (partners), employees, customers, industry vendors, community members
  - Goals: Achieve organizational mission—increase profits for shareholders, grow/improve reputation, attract top attorneys

- Large B2B Business (Global Auto Parts Manufacturer—Public Company)
  - Publics: Board of directors, shareholders/stockholders, employees, customers (other automotive manufacturers), industry leaders, governments/regulators, local communities, vendors
  - Goals: Achieve organizational mission—increase market share, decrease regulatory burden, improve efficiency, hire and retain top employees, maintain positive relationships with shareholders

- Small B2B/B2C Business (Local Bakery)
  - Publics: Employees, corporate customers, individual customers, community members, vendors
  - Goals: Achieve organizational mission—increase profits through a focus on corporate orders and large individual orders, grow awareness within the community

(Continued)

(Continued)

- Large B2C Business (Video Game Design— Privately Held Company)

  ○ Publics: Employees, customers, industry leaders, community members (near headquarters)

  ○ Goals: Achieve organizational mission— increase sales, attract top design and programming talent, drive innovation, increase market share

- Large B2B/B2C Business (Cellphone Service Provider—Public Company)

  ○ Publics: Board of directors, shareholders/ stockholders, employees, corporate customers, consumer customers, government regulators, community members (in major markets)

  ○ Goals: Achieve organizational mission—increase business and consumer market share, improve consumer reputation, create and promote new products and services, improve hiring and training of staff

different situations—with the right targeting and focus. As **audiences** drive the project objectives, it can easily multiply the opportunities, as well as the workload, to ensure that all target groups are covered.

Business to Business (B2B)

Individuals new to the PR field tend to underestimate the scale and importance of—as well as the market for—B2B PR efforts. There are far more B2B transactions made in the U.S. economy than B2C transactions,[2] largely because the supply chain in a given industry consists of multiple steps in the design, development, and manufacturing of a product before it is available to the consumer as a final sale.

For example, in agriculture, farmers must purchase land, buildings, seeds, heavy equipment, fertilizer, insecticide, and other materials before growing crops and selling their yields. These crops are initially sold to distributors, who, in turn, sell them to grocers, who finally sell them directly to their consumers. It is this final step—the sale to the consumer—that defines the B2C transaction. Each transfer of goods that leads up to this final sale to the consumer is part of the B2B transaction chain. It is important to understand that each service provider (vendor) in a specific B2B supply chain is focused on communicating its own message to its specific customer base. This example highlights a single branch in the greater supply tree or matrix. Each organization within a supply chain may also benefit by working

---

[2] Sandhusen, R. (2008). *Marketing* (4th ed.). Hauppauge, NY: Barron's, p. 520.

with an agency to add significant value to its business and help achieve its strategic goals.

Many small business leaders might view a media placement in the *Wall Street Journal*, *Forbes*, or *Inc Magazine* as the best possible coverage and exposure. Using our agricultural example, it may be evident that these publications, while read heavily by entrepreneurs, business leaders, and investors, are most likely not subscribed to by the target farmer or agricultural industry leader. The agricultural community may be much more likely to read *Farm Progress*, *Modern Farmer,* or the *Farm Journal*. While the circulation numbers of each of these periodicals will most definitely be smaller, a seasoned agency professional would know that it's not about volume; rather, it is about getting the direct hit: The right story told to an appropriate audience holds more value than the best-possible story told to an uninterested audience.

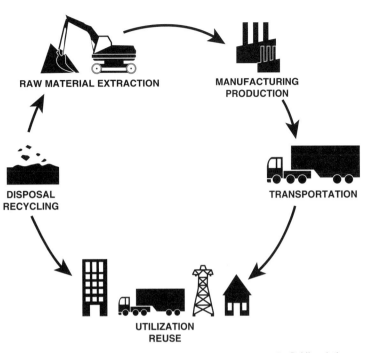

RAW MATERIAL EXTRACTION

MANUFACTURING PRODUCTION

TRANSPORTATION

DISPOSAL RECYCLING

UTILIZATION REUSE

Public relations adds value at every step in the life cycle or supply chain of a product or service (consumer or business-to-business).

Business to Consumer (B2C)

Public relations is more commonly associated with B2C communication; that is, messages created by organizations targeting a broad consumer audience using tactics ranging from earned media outreach to traditional paid mass media. B2C public relations can support brand awareness, product marketing, and sales efforts but may also include advocacy communication and community relations efforts. Approaches can target a public's opinion on specific issues critical to a business's client base.

Outreach to consumers today can be accomplished in more ways than ever before, highlighting the communication possibilities and challenges of attention fragmentation. In addressing this challenge, modern agency practitioners use, for example, multiple direct-to-consumer channels at much more reasonable cost than traditional broadcast media advertising. This allows clients the opportunity to more easily supplement PR media outreach with social media, search engine optimization, and other digital advertising methods. From targeted social media content and advertising to **blogs** and e-newsletters, the availability and scalability of tactics has made direct communication easier than ever for organizations of all sizes.

B2B and B2C

As distinct as these two approaches to public relations can be, B2B and B2C companies are often not wholly separate. There are countless organizations, both large and small, that transact on the business and individual consumer levels. Just as a B2C transaction targets a specific type of consumer, a company focused more on B2B markets may also have significant interests in cultivating a positive image toward certain individual customers. For example, the field of community relations works to strengthen the local perception and impact of a corporation both as an employer and as a good neighbor rather than directly driving business results. Many B2B companies enjoy the benefits of strong community connections despite never selling products directly to consumers in their region. And manufacturing companies can, of course, develop both consumer and industry-only products.

Publics are not always aware of such distinctions. For example, strong coverage in a media outlet or market targeted for a business audience can be easily shared with consumers (and vice versa). As an organization's ability to share its own story through **owned media** content (such as its website, blogs, and company social media channels) has grown, the benefits of positive media coverage in any market have multiplied. Manufacturers of consumer products are selling direct to consumers—rather than through third-party retail outlets—and providers of services are selling, often via digital means, to both consumers and businesses.

From a business and communication perspective, all signs point to continued convergence of these audiences and channels. For the agency professional, this means that there will become fewer differences and barriers between B2B and B2C public relations and a more diverse and complex media landscape to consider when developing strategies for clients.

Types of PR Expertise

The process of identifying the right clients should draw heavily from an agency's collective expertise. All agency leaders should be strategic thinkers, but some develop a particular knowledge of an industry, a region, or a specific tactic (such as media relations, investor relations, or crisis communication) that sets them apart. PR agencies may focus on one or more industries or identify with specific types of campaigns within a single industry, including product launches, advocacy outreach, or consumer events. They may also base their value on relationships with journalists, social media influencers, or community leaders.

It can be useful, particularly for new professionals, to seek out a specific industry or two to focus on and develop a deep understanding of the business and common strategies. This narrowed focus allows practitioners to acquire a core practice area that maximizes relationships, allows for efficient media monitoring,

Blend Images/Alamy Stock Photo

Blend Images/Alamy Stock Photo

and permits more time for executing outreach rather than continuously learning the structure, practices, and terminology of new industries.

Some top professionals and agencies maintain a narrow or single industry focus. Others are motivated by the challenge of learning about new companies, industries, and business models amongst their perpetually growing list of clients. Both approaches can be rewarded in an agency environment.

Similarly, the integration of communication and PR tools and tactics means that no individual and few agencies are excellent at everything. For example, expertise in handling crisis communication within the food service industry or consumer electronics product launches are both extremely valuable services. Many agency professionals could perform these tasks, but few would consider themselves true experts in those niche areas. PR agencies able to carve out a specific focus—and serve clients in need of these services—can be extremely successful. Even firms with a more open structure or broader aims for growth benefit from drawing some boundaries for their expertise and client development.

Clients Large and Small

Simply put, organizations come in all shapes and sizes. Nearly all businesses could benefit from an improved level of communication as well as from additional outside counsel, but this does not mean that working with these businesses should be approached in similar ways.

Client Contacts

Large: When working with larger organizations, agencies typically report directly to managers, directors, or vice presidents in the marketing, PR, or communication departments.

Small: The main client contact in a small organization may be the chief executive officer (CEO), chief operating officer (COO), or vice president of sales or marketing.

Scope of Work

Large: Agencies working with a larger, more hierarchical organization often take on a more specialized focus. These businesses have more internal expertise and strategic oversight as well as more internal capability and staff. They are more likely to hire separate agencies to handle PR, advertising, social media, and creative productions. Companies with multiple locations may retain the services of a larger national or international agency as well as multiple local agencies, depending on their needs.

Small: The small, privately owned business or local nonprofit organization may place increased value on strategic insight and appreciate the skills required to implement a wider variety of tactics. The smaller business is less likely to walk in the door of an agency knowing what its needs are, or it may have an incomplete perspective on the role of public relations for its business.

Division of Labor

Large: As these organizations have more internal expertise, individual projects may be completed with close interaction between agency and client teams. Additional layers (and schedule delays) for approvals may be necessary. Larger businesses are also more likely to take responsibility for specific elements of the design, marketing, writing, and distribution of collateral materials based on their internal expertise.

Small: Once a level of trust between the agency and the small business client is established, these organizations often prefer for the agency to take responsibility for the majority of the work, gathering insights and setting strategy at the beginning of projects and then pushing forward with limited oversight. This approach can introduce its own challenges but, when executed properly, allows for significant efficiencies within the agency environment and increased cohesiveness with the client.

Measurement and Reporting

Large: The project-related objectives and milestones of a larger organization can (and should) be tied to specific events, issues, messages, and competitors. Reporting of each should be detailed, including insights written for professionals in the field, as well as be able to be summarized, browsable, and clear enough to be easily reported to leaders within the organization who may not have backgrounds in public relations.

Small: Project objectives of a small organization are more closely tied to brand awareness and growth as well as to sales. Reporting and measurement should be tailored to the client's sophistication level and include an appropriate level of depth, reflecting the information that is most important to them.

In both types of organizations, the agency professional must learn to communicate results at multiple levels, both internally and externally, within the company structure while also including the right amount of substance based on the specific audience.

Client Types, Obstacles, and Solutions

The challenges that PR practitioners may face on a daily basis are as diverse as the clients themselves. These may include, but are not limited to, miscommunication or misunderstanding of goals or deliverables, objectives that are constantly shifting, or personality conflicts within teams. Unfortunately, there are also some PR professionals who commonly deflect personal responsibility for oversights or missing deadlines and blame the client directly rather than first considering how to improve their own processes.

If you ask a seasoned agency practitioner to describe the demands associated with his or her problem clients, most indicate that they fall into relatively predictable categories. Some clients can simply be unreasonably demanding or have unrealistic expectations of an agency's efforts. It falls on the firm and the practitioner to set boundaries in how to most appropriately deal with this type of client. In these instances, it is worth considering best practices for working with clients entering the relationship with a variety of predispositions. Practitioners can diffuse conflicts by approaching these clients with the right perspective, setting clear expectations, and quickly identifying challenges and solutions.

Client issues are always unique and should not be based on stereotypes, but grouping together some of the potential personalities and situations can be useful to understanding how to solve them strategically. Taking the time to properly examine any client specific issue can be helpful in understanding and **diagnosing** issues, helping improve the relationship and the agency deliverables.

The Overly Demanding Client

Within the service industry, it is commonplace to expect that clients or customers will inherently ask, even demand, something more than what they have actually paid for. Life in a PR agency is no different. Clients commonly request more media coverage, additional meetings with their agency executive, or increased face time with the agency partners. In supporting these clients, a PR practitioner can feel as though the amount of work that they do is never enough. Common techniques in dealing with an overly demanding client include the following:

- **Be clear and descriptive** with respect to the actual deliverables and what is included in the price of the requested agency services.

- **Set program/campaign expectations and educate the client when necessary.** When clients, especially those without significant PR experience, don't know the usual process and outcomes of PR work, they are much more likely to be confused or concerned with the results.

- **Develop a clear understanding of the client's business objectives** and exactly how and why the agency will support them. The best way to showcase the value of the agency is to directly connect deliverables (event attendance, web traffic, brand awareness) with the agreed-upon strategies and tactics.

- **Ensure rhythm and consistency along the way.** Outline how to deliver a steady stream of media coverage, social media successes, or improvement in public sentiment rather than establishing a "feast or famine" environment. This strategy highlights the value of consistent, ongoing coverage (particularly for retainer relationships).

The Unresponsive Client

A common challenge for public relations practitioners is navigating appropriately when a client does not react at the same speed as the journalist or creative project time line requires. Practitioners commonly begin to question their own tactics: Should I email them again? Will they be annoyed if I leave another voicemail? In evaluating and troubleshooting the relationship with an unresponsive client, consider the following:

- **Each process and touchpoint should be made as simple as possible** for the client.

- **When possible, ask *yes or no* questions** to the client with appropriate follow up. The harder and more complicated the question, the longer it often takes to receive the answer.

- **Provide "final" versions for approval,** rather than working drafts for review.

- If a client commonly responds to requests slowly, **avoid media opportunities that require rapid turnaround** (same day or within hours).

- **Be very consistent and fully responsive with all agency deliverables,** including maintaining a meeting pulse and regular client interaction. Do not expect more from the client than what is being provided to them.

- **Set clear, realistic, and achievable deadlines** on all projects.

- **Avoid being in a position of needing a response too quickly.** Plan internal deadlines appropriately and ensure that media opportunities are not missed due to delayed responses from the client.

The Unsophisticated Client

There are some clients that enter a relationship with a PR agency without knowing the slightest bit about the process or expected outcomes. They may have misconceptions about what public relations is and what an agency can accomplish for them. Agencies team members have a responsibility to educate each client about the basic functions, processes, and results of public relations, including the

Understandably, organizational leaders take their brand identity and reputation very seriously. It often takes multiple drafts to come to agreement on important language.

benefits, expectations, and potential challenges of specific strategies and tactics. When educating the unsophisticated client, practitioners should ensure that they do the following:

- **Clarify each objective, strategy, and tactic, particularly as they relate to costs**. While practitioners may have a clear understanding of, for example, the difference between paid and earned media, clients may not. Every PR firm has a different cost structure, and so it is important to overcommunicate. This should become part of the practitioners' standard operating procedure.

- **Take the time to prepare the client for media opportunities.** Practice the interview with the client. Do not assume that the client knows the right way to behave with reporters, the importance of meeting media deadlines, or what the reporter needs to take away from the interview.

- **Reinforce the expectations, process, and desired outcomes before each project, campaign, event, and media opportunity.**

The Perfectionist Client

It is important to keep in mind that every word matters. As public relations counsel, understanding the importance and responsibility of managing a company's public image and reputation is paramount. However, there are always clients who prefer to intervene in ways that are counterproductive. In managing these clients, it is imperative to set various expectation early, including that press releases are not works of art. While every word does matter, some have a greater significance than others. Not every social media follower will share every post. Media coverage is not always perfect, and the most visible media stories are often less product-centric. Helping a client learn the realities of public relations from the beginning of the process promotes a stronger relationship from both perspectives. Some useful considerations in managing this type of demanding client are as follows:

- **Do not simply *do*. Help the client to understand the *why*** behind an approach before, during, and after **implementation**.

- **Clearly set client expectations in alignment with the expected level of success.** It is easy to say that everything will be perfect every time, but that's not how public relations works.

- **Set objectives and key messages first, and then follow through by incorporating them within the strategies and outcomes.** Weaving in key messages, audience-friendly examples, and objective-focused calls to action are unassailable ways to demonstrate to the client that agreed-upon priorities are being achieved.

- **Avoid simple mistakes.** Agency professionals should utilize their talented teammates to proofread all content in order to avoid as many errors as possible before sending out for review and approval. This is particularly important when working with a perfectionist client.

The Best Friend Client

Common in the professional service industry is the ideal of promoting a friendly, positive working relationship with individual client contacts; however, it is also important to understand there is a line where "too friendly" can have a negative impact. Excessive demands on a practitioner's time and expertise, whether based on a real or imagined friendship, are unprofessional and complicate the counselor/client relationship. The following techniques can be useful in establishing an appropriate level of friendship within a professional relationship:

- **Set boundaries with agency work and with clients.** Decide the frequency and timing of appropriate client communication. Introduce workflow time lines and ensure that they are frequently referred to and followed. Keep personal communication separate from work communication.

- **Make efficiency and effectiveness a priority.** All professional time should be focused on alignment with client goals and project scope.

- **Ask yourself: Am I spending extra time on this client? Is it justified?**

- **Ultimately, if the client contact relationship does develop into a particularly friendly one, consider shifting the account management to a different person within the agency.**

The Down-on-Their-Luck Client

Economic cycles lend themselves to recurring prosperity as well as financial strain for certain organizations at certain times. As PR agencies are on the service side of the business relationship, it is not uncommon for a client to expect the support of a PR firm even when the firm's retainer is not being paid in full or on time. While a certain degree of agency-determined flexibility can be both strategic and admirable, these situations often end up with unpaid retainer fees, frustrated team members, and an overall negative situation. It is important to consider the following when determining the viability of a new (or existing) client encountering financial difficulties:

- **Vet the financial health of any potential client before entering into a relationship**, particularly one with a long-term contract retainer. Identify any red flags regarding the success of their company. Has this organization grown far faster than seems reasonable? Are they prone to flash over substance in their own business?

- **Never forget that the PR firm is also a business**. While some arrangements can be made, it is professionally unfair to paying clients for agency staff to spend time on those that are behind on retainers.

- **Include specific financial language within contracts, and follow established processes related to billing procedures and notifications.** Ensure that an attorney reviews the standard client contract from the perspective of remedying a delinquent account.

The "Cause" Client

Passionate clients can be considered a blessing and a curse, often at the same time. These clients bring energy, direction, and purpose to the relationship, but they are also prone to unrealistic expectations for agency engagement and results. Small business owners and nonprofit leaders are most likely associated with this category of clients, as their well-placed ambition often outpaces their resources. Each client relationship, especially those including a reduced or waived retainer (such as **pro bono** clients), should have extremely clear and well-monitored boundaries. Common techniques when working with a "cause" client include the following:

- **When evaluating the scope of a project, the budget should always be a part of the conversation.** Big project and campaign ideas should only live within what's financially possible.

- **Discuss and agree on a clear project plan, both internally and with the client, before initiating a project.** Emphasize that any change that deviates from the project plan may change the overall cost.

- **It is better to say "no" earlier rather than later,** even if the client has their heart set on a certain approach (large event, broadcast advertising campaign, etc.). If they cannot successfully execute a desired tactic on a shoestring budget, this should be communicated up front.

- **One common approach used for pro bono clients is to set an internal cap or hours retainer for their work.** Whether the associated support is at a discounted rate or being executed for free, the agency should track the associated time as if it was for a standard paying client.

Even the best client can introduce challenges when negative financial circumstances arise. Oftentimes, as PR professionals, this is outside of our control. Crises can happen for a business without much warning. A strong, healthy relationship with a PR firm and its account manager can be tested and strengthened during trying times, but it can turn irreconcilable just as quickly. The best agency professionals leverage the challenges of working with clients under adverse conditions to build their deepest connections and show the true value of strategic PR counsel to help organizations reach their goals.

Reflect and Discuss

1. What factors can influence whether a client will be a good fit for your agency?

2. How might an agency draw its boundaries and focus its expertise?

3. Why would becoming too personally close to a client contact make the professional relationship more difficult?

4. Why is setting clear expectations for clients such a critical part of avoiding challenges?

Valerie Stachurski

Valerie Stachurski is the founder and president of Toronto-based PR agency, Charming Media. After establishing herself as a writer, influencer, and tastemaker in fashion, beauty, and lifestyle, Valerie combined her media contacts with her knowledge of influencer marketing to create a fresh PR agency providing services to an established roster of clients such as Sketchers, Turkish Airlines, Oxford Properties, and several designers on the World MasterCard® Fashion

Week seasonal calendar under client THE COLLECTIONS™. Charming Media executes strategic campaigns with a combined focus on both traditional and online media relations as well as consumer marketing initiatives.

What are your responsibilities and duties at Charming Media?

As the president and founder of Charming Media, I am involved with business development, hiring new employees, overseeing what the employees are doing day-to-day, making sure we get the right interns, and making sure we're doing the right strategies. Really, I'm in charge of everything and oversee everything, but all of the employees here have their own responsibilities, so I make sure they're on the right track and talk to them periodically to make sure that we're meeting the clients' expectations.

How large is Charming Media?

Charming Media is a small agency with four full-time people and two interns.

Do you consider yourself a niche agency? Do you service a wide range of clients?

We serve a wide range of clients with a specific lifestyle focus. Under the lifestyle category, we service fashion, beauty, travel, and food and drink. We work with a range of large corporate companies and smaller independent brands.

Regarding choosing a client: Are all clients the right client? And how do you make the decision to work with someone?

It's been a learning process for me. The company is three-and-a-half years old and when we first got started, it was very important to work with as many people as we could in order to see where our strengths were. Until you're really in it, it's very difficult to realize, "Oh, I really do like working with fashion" or "I'm not particularly interested in working with fashion."

I try and associate what I like to do and personal interests and bring that to the types of brands that I like to work with. I always encourage our staff (who are involved with coming up with new ideas for potential new clients) to do

this. I say to them, "Well, what types of brands do you like? What would you like to be working on?" When it comes to business development, we try and focus on brands that interest us and that we feel like we can stand behind; we believe in their story, and we see a strategy in that going forward.

Do you work with consumer companies versus B2B? Do you look for large companies or smaller companies? Does it matter? What process goes into taking on those kinds of clients?

We like consumer brands with good distribution. We work with brands like Sketchers and a few beauty brands. These are brands that have a name behind them, and then there's also great brands that nobody has heard about and it's on us to make people hear about them—that's another challenge we really like as well. We don't do too much B2B and focus mainly on consumers.

What is your best approach to handling an overly demanding client?

It's very important to manage expectations with time and results. It's important for us to address situations as early and be as up front as possible, so we can tell clients what we're available for and express what we can do for them. If there comes a time where the relationship begins to seem unhealthy because demands are getting too high, we wouldn't take that type of behavior.

What is your best approach to handling an unresponsive client?

These are difficult because you don't know why they are being unresponsive. In my early days, I would think, "They must not like us; they
(Continued)

(Continued)

must not be happy." You have to put yourself in their shoes and consider why they are being unresponsive. Either they're really busy or they don't see that they need to get involved in our strategy right now. It's very important that you do get them on the phone at some point and make them agree to relay certain information to you by the deadlines.

What is your best approach to handling unsophisticated clients?

It's important to see if they have a spokesperson in their company that might like to represent them in interviews. It doesn't matter if they're unsophisticated if they aren't on camera and don't see it being a factor in our personal relationship. If they are going to be doing a lot of broadcast interviews, it is important to address the situation. That's why they're hiring you—to put "your best you" forward. Clients come and go, but your media contact is the most important thing. You have to address situations gently.

What is your best approach to handling perfectionist clients?

That could be very tough. The client's approach to their brand can be very insightful for us; we learn more about their brand; we learn more about their passion. They can be difficult, and sometimes, you actually have to give them deadlines. It's important to respect their passion about their brand; sometimes they aren't always perfectionists, sometimes they're just passionate and protective of their brands so it's important to respect them.

What is your best approach to handling the best friend client?

You can start to feel very close to them and when a decision does need to be made, you feel like it can be a personal thing. It's important to create distance. If they're asking you to meet up after work or on the weekend (unless you're comfortable with that and it's within policy), it should always be "no." Keep it limited. Keep it to lunches instead of dinners, coffee instead of a drink.

What is your best approach to handling a down-on-their-luck client?

Provide them with words of encouragement; often give them insight as to what your outreach has resulted in; always be optimistic in looking toward the future; and be a beacon of hope. Offer yourself up as a listening ear and just be there. They're hiring you for their consultation, so if they do open up and ask for guidance, I think that's more than appropriate.

What is your best approach to handling a "cause" client?

Set expectations as to what you are offering and what you're bringing to the table so that they're not hoping you go above and beyond that. Most people respect that because they know you're doing it pro bono. Come to it with a formal contract in place and say, "for this pro bono work, we're only going to offer X number of hours."

Top 5 Skills Every PR Pro Should Know

1. The ability to brush things off quickly and move on.

2. The ability to take responsibility when something has gone wrong.

3. Good writing skills: Some people are strong speakers and some are stronger writers, so it's important that you can fall back on your writing skills.

4. Empathy: Empathize with your client and what they're going through. Also take the media's role into consideration.

5. Smile. I see a lot of straight-faced PR people and if it has stopped being fun, then it's not what it should be. What we're doing is serious, but if you can't smile, then you shouldn't be doing it.

Top Must-Haves

- **Must-download app**: Instagram. It's great to showcase what we're doing. On my personal account, I show the behind-the-scenes on what we're doing and on the business account, we show the results of that. It's a way to show the behind-the-scenes of Charming Media.

- **Must read**: I read marketing magazines every day that have industry news: PR news, what agency just got the latest account, what brands are coming to the country, what companies just launched a campaign, and who in the industry is changing companies. Industry news is the most important thing.

- **Must-use tool**: Sprout social. It's an app we use to manage all of our social media for all of our clients, monitor mentions of our clients on Twitter, and generate reports.

CHAPTER 3

Starting Off on the Right Foot

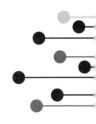

Negotiating with a potential client, building a plan, and executing a contract only scratch the surface of developing rapport between the client and the agency. Those first interactions and meetings take on critical significance in setting the cadence, tone, and expectations for a successful relationship. Agency professionals can make their lives immeasurably easier by asking clarifying questions that lead to concisely crafted, measurable objectives. Following these practices leads to a clear understanding of the client needs and overall scope of work, both of which are important to achieve success.

The Initial Client Kickoff Meeting

One cannot overstate the importance of preparing and planning for the initial client kickoff meeting, but far too often, agency professionals are misguided into believing that it is their responsibility to come to these meetings with all of the answers in hand. In reality, the true value of these meetings should be in the opportunity to further explore the client's industry and setting, understand the marketplace, and present a clear plan and process for moving toward the defined objectives. Being able to determine which of the following questions are relevant within the conversation entails significant research, much of which should be completed in the early stages of the proposal process.

Author Patrick Lencioni highlights the approach of proposing clarifying questions in his business fable, *Getting Naked*. He notes that the value of a true **counselor** is not in having all of the answers, but knowing the right questions to ask.[1] The remainder of this chapter

Objectives

- Organize an effective first meeting with a new client.

- Understand critical questions to ask during the beginning of a client relationship.

- Develop the skills to effectively set client expectations.

- Envision the long-term client-development perspective.

---

[1] Lencioni, P. (2010). *Getting naked: A business fable about shedding the three fears that sabotage client loyalty* (1st ed.). San Francisco, CA: Jossey-Bass.

- **Client organizational goals**: Organization-wide short-term and long-term goals should be discussed and clarified.

- **Client industry environment**: Identify major competitors and industry trends.

- **Client strengths and weaknesses**: Define organizational value to the publics of interest, members, and stakeholders. Internal/external threats should be identified and noted.

- **Client communication successes**: Share strategies, tactics, and programs that have led to previous successes.

- **Client communication challenges**: Define gaps in perceptions and awareness for key audiences.

- **Client reporting structure**: Determine the main client contacts, executive contacts, and day-to-day partners.

- **Client–agency communication**: Set the timing, cadence, and structure for all anticipated communications (formal meetings, informal check-ins, reporting, etc.).

- **Client approvals**: Identify the appropriate personnel responsible for signing off on external content.

- **Agency capabilities**: Highlight the services that the agency offers.

- **Agency philosophy**: Take the time to share the agency/practitioner's approach and perspective to the deliverables being requested.

- **Agency cost structure**: Clearly detail all anticipated (retainer or fixed) costs to the client and the frequency in which they will be billed for services.

will focus on the process of kicking off a client relationship using this idea of structured inquiry.

When considering adoption of this approach, it is important to understand that initial interactions are not merely confined to the first meeting; rather, initial concepts should realistically account for the first several meetings. The exact timing or number of meetings is less important than establishing the groundwork during the initial interactions of the new relationship.

Deliberate Processes

At the start of any relationship, the commitment to following all agency processes, building from strategic planning, and executing on deliverables can rapidly establish trust with the new client. The earlier in the relationship that this happens, the more smoothly the account will run, and the easier it will be to overcome any unanticipated challenges.

Proper management of the initial meeting(s) often require a delicate balance encompassing a dedication to the process and a degree of open-endedness. Each client has a unique story, situation, and industry; however, veteran practitioners often note that organizational challenges are generally categorized by their similarities, which further define the appropriate information-gathering approach. In some cases, there are very clear competitors, structural and institutional obstacles, or industry trends pointing toward a strategy that has the greatest potential of success. In other cases, a more open-ended approach may be necessary to ensure that the root causes of challenges (including solutions) are properly identified and evaluated.

©iStock.com/Artist's Member Name

Agency practitioners should take advantage of in-person client meetings to demonstrate their organization, passion, and strategic acumen.

It is also essential for an agency to properly define and embrace an accepted set of assumptions that will support all subsequent contributions. Ensuring that the agency is not forming strategies or planning deliverables based on incorrect or incomplete assumptions is vital. The initial client discussions should provide validation/rebuttals to any prior research that the agency has conducted and fill in any gaps or establish additional connections that may not have initially seemed related. More importantly, an initial meeting should help define and prioritize each of the outputs.

This chapter positions these questions and processes for integration within an initial series of meetings. It is important to understand that it is not realistic to ask, let alone answer, all of these questions in a single sitting. Agency leaders strive to answer as many questions that they can on their own and rely on these early meetings as a verification/clarification tool. Remember that the outcomes from these initial meetings generally raise many new questions and that the success of a PR practitioner comes in situating these questions as part of a holistic yet directional discovery process rather than simply diving deeper into client specifics.

Face Time With Leadership

The outset of any new client relationship provides a valuable opportunity for a public relations firm to ask for the full, undivided attention of some or all of a client's leadership team. Face time with the leadership team may either happen in a single, larger engagement or (and sometimes preferably) over the course of several smaller meetings with various departments.

Agencies should request input and attendance at a kickoff meeting from a broader cross-section of the client organization. Executive leadership and the internal communication/marketing/PR team(s) are essential attendees, with representation from human resources, sales, product development, customer service, fundraising/development, membership, and event planning teams, as appropriate. The broader the team, the better perspective an agency will acquire related to the challenges and opportunities that the client faces.

The following questions are not meant to be exhaustive or applicable to all circumstances, but they can serve as a reference point when working to define the critical elements during the initial phases of a new relationship.

What Are Your Organizational Goals?

Effective public relations does not happen in isolation. Specific goals for public relations should reflect and be directed toward supporting a significant portion of the larger organizational goals and objectives. Agencies that position their communication or campaign objectives in the larger context of supporting and driving organizational goals tend to have greater success over the long term. Agency professionals must align their success with the organization's success. This begins with the first question in the first meeting and should be reinforced throughout the research/diagnosis, objective-creation, strategy, tactics, implementation, and reporting/evaluation processes.

What Are the Most Critical Trends in Your Industry?

Agencies may have extensive, moderate, or little experience in a given client industry. Whether or not the practitioners have worked in the industry before, it is important to keep in mind that the firm is the expert in communication and your client is the expert in their discipline. This delineation provides the firm with an opportunity to draw on client expertise and perspective first, before proposing solutions to a given problem.

By separately situating PR expertise around issues of communication, **relationships**, and perception, a broader base can be realized in establishing the tone for the working partnership. For example, clients should be asked to review all technical content for the appropriate language and terminology utilized within their industry. While a smart agency team will become increasingly proficient at internalizing and writing clearly in the voice, tone, and technical specificity required for a specific industry, those clients who live and breathe within a specific business arena should be ultimately responsible for providing input and feedback on the appropriateness of content and language.

Who Are Your Most Important Competitors?

While an agency should always come be prepared with a basic understanding of a particular field ("Google-level" depth), most executive organizational leaders bring decades of industry knowledge that may be invaluable to others across the table. Discussions related to the state of a given industry or the history of an organization's competition prove to not only be a useful window into the field of interest but also to provide an organization-wide perspective on the larger business sector.

As counselors, PR practitioners have a responsibility to share an outsider's view on the answers to this question. While some organizations may be acutely aware of their direct competitors, a collection of new information that external, unbiased research uncovers can be extremely valuable to present to a client.

What Do You See as Your Organization's Greatest Strengths and Weaknesses in the Marketplace?

One cannot underestimate the importance of obtaining leadership insights on the strengths or weaknesses of an organization or brand relative to competitors. These insights are significant for the agency in developing the best-possible strategic messaging and positioning. The resulting discussions often provide a historical perspective on how an organization captures market share, how they are differentiated from their competitors, and areas wherein they may be vulnerable. In a 2006 *Harvard Business Review* article, Anderson, Narus, and van Rossum define three types of organizational value propositions. These are commonly categorized from the simplest to the most nuanced: all benefits, favorable points of difference, and resonating focus.[2]

Oftentimes, PR agencies require an increased level of granularity and understanding related to the organizational value proposition within a particular market. For-profit organizations tend to be categorized with one of the following value-based descriptors as it relates to their position in the marketplace:

- Best product: An organization offers the most complete, robust, or high-end solution within their marketplace.

- Best value: The organizational mix of functionality and price make their product attractive to potential customers.

- Unique value: The organization offers a product, feature, or service that is not offered by any of its competitors.

- Lowest price: A specific organization may not necessarily provide the best product, but it is sufficient for customer needs and less costly than any of its competitors.

- Strength of relationships/contracts: The success of an organization does not necessarily depend on a superior value proposition but on previously completed work that solidifies their position with key customers or contracts.

---

[2] Anderson, J. C., Narus, J. A., & van Rossum, W. (2006). Customer value propositions in business markets. *Harvard Business Review, 84*, 90–99.

[3] Ibid, p. 93.

©iStockphoto.com/alvarez

Addressing internal communication challenges (including communicating to team members, donors, or shareholders) can be a key part of a PR agency's efforts.

By understanding how their clients are positioned within a particular industry, agency professionals can provide additional research to highlight how the client is perceived externally. Knowing how current and potential customers view the client allows agency practitioners to, for example, create additional awareness around any perception gaps.

Since strategy should consistently be a part of each communication and interaction, the agency and the client need to work together to better understand how or whether current positioning continues to be appropriate in the marketplace. This analysis can be completed using a variety of formal and informal market research methods, with the results pointing toward core elements of organizational objectives, strategies, and tactics.

What External Communication Challenges Have You Faced?

The value of a client can be realized by more than simple economic measures. The relationships between agencies and clients can also highlight important information about the competitive marketplace and uncover potential changes to the economic, political, and media climates that impact both communication and organizational goals. Discussion related to these topics may result in defining new tactical or strategic approaches, such as the increased use of social media to counter the efforts of competitors, or leading the organization in a new strategic direction, including brand or messaging shifts or repositioning.

Discussions related to the identification of external obstacles can also demonstrate what an organization should *not* do. Outcomes from these conversations may result in directing organizations to commit an excessive amount of resources toward communication efforts with new audiences when it may be more effective to focus on improving communication with existing audiences.

What Internal Communication Challenges Have You Faced?

An often-underutilized tactic that integrated agencies leverage to unlock additional internal value begins with an upgrade of internal communication programs. Organizational **stakeholders**, from employees and board members to patrons and donors, should not be overlooked when developing strategic communication plans. Public relations scholar James Grunig notes that internal communication is "one of the most important contributors to organizational effectiveness—it helps organizations define their goals, values, and strategic constituencies." Grunig goes on to state, "Systems of internal communication are part of organizational structure and culture; however, they also contribute to the creation of structure and culture."[4]

Agency professionals can provide perspective in understanding current or potential internal communication disconnects, ensuring that overlooked functions are represented in future strategic planning. Depending on the size, structure, complexity, and geographic disparity of an organization, internal communication strategies provide a significant opportunity for PR agencies to demonstrate measurable value and impact.

Completing a review and identification of any internal communication gaps often points to a focus on more controlled channels of communication, assigning success more directly to the agency and client professionals rather than to external media, competitive, and environmental factors. An organization's commitment to a successful analysis of internal communication fosters improved internal relationships and employee commitment, creates a feeling of belonging, provides perspective about the organization and its environment, and promotes a strong internal understanding of the reasons for change.[5]

What Industry Publications Do You, Your Customers, and Your Potential Customers Read?

Although executive leaders are commonly tasked with providing organizational leadership and defining the overall strategy, these individuals are also extremely valuable resources in understanding the larger trade media landscape within a particular industry. An organization that devotes resources to the development of positive relationships with trade media can realize positive outcomes as a result. Probing client executives on what, when, and how they stay up-to-date on industry trends is a valuable indicator of the best approaches in reaching other like-minded professionals.

Keep in mind that each industry approaches information gathering differently. For example, the preference within a particular field of industry may rely predominantly on print over digital channels, while others may realize a significantly greater social media focus. It is important to understand that all industries include a mixture of both top-tier and second-tier media outlets, allowing the organizations to connect with targeted audiences through a variety of channels, including print, web, e-newsletters, social media, events, and so on. Client responses to this question can help practitioners prioritize their efforts in identifying and pursuing specific audiences of a particular publication or media channel.

---

[4] Grunig, J. E. (Ed.). (1992). *Excellence in public relations and communication management.* Abingdon, UK: Routledge, p. 532.

[5] Welch, M., & Jackson, P. R. (2007). Rethinking internal communication: A stakeholder approach. *Corporate Communications: An International Journal, 12,* 177–198.

Questions for the Communication Team

While engaging the executive team can be invaluable on a strategic level, it is also important for agency professionals to request communication-centric clarifications directly from the client's internal communication, marketing, or PR teams. These resulting insights are useful in identifying prior roadblocks, reasons for program successes and failures, and any additional resources that may be available.

What Are the Biggest Communication Challenges You've Faced?

In discussing the greatest communication challenges experienced by clients, an agency team can gain important insights into internal and external perceptions of an organization. For example, a client may be interested in analyzing the impact of a new competitor on its growth goals, ultimately leading to a strategic, management-level integration of their work into the organization as a whole. Alternatively, this discussion may identify something as simple as resource deficiencies preventing an organization from sustaining its initiatives or lead to an obvious disconnection between departmental and leadership goals. The process of identifying and navigating the intraorganizational challenges faced by clients is essential in the cultivation of a fruitful agency–client partnership.

What Communication Strategies and Tactics Have Succeeded/Failed in the Past? Why?

This question presents the clearest opportunity for a client to elaborate on specific tactical insights; the strength of their external relationships; and perspectives on the behaviors, needs, and inclinations of their intended publics. Seemingly simple obstacles can derail the eventual success of a strategic campaign. A deeper understanding of each strategy and tactic can provide agency professionals with an opportunity to learn from a client's organizational history.

What Are the Largest Events and Projects on Your Calendar for the Year?

The process of mapping out a client's major events and activities over the course of the year provides an agency professional with a list of priorities and a supporting timetable. Understanding the event schedule allows the PR team to identify any redundancies or gaps and focus on any areas that may not be covered. This exercise also provides agency professionals an opportunity to play the role of counselor from the outset.

The details and insights realized from this line of questions can sometimes lead directly to the holy grail of client understanding: defining the true organizational priorities. However, these are often only found through intuition and often run deeper than even executive leaders are willing to communicate during a first meeting. With that being said, a series of initial meetings can provide an unparalleled opportunity for an agency team to formulate many of the strategic communication elements that will support future organizational success. Although it may sometimes appear cumbersome and challenging to define a client's organizational priorities, the overarching process is not complicated. Listen carefully to what is said and what is not said in these initial meetings. Gauge enthusiasm and understand clearly what has been said. Ultimately, the process encompasses a holistic approach toward evaluating an organization and its environment as well as identifying where opportunities for communication expertise can create the greatest impact.

Setting Expectations

One of the single most important determinants contributing to the success of a client relationship is taking the time to communicate a distinct, well thought-out set of expectations. When both parties clearly understand and agree upon the expectations of both teams, each is more comfortable and confident with the other. When defined expectations are communicated and achieved from the start of the relationship, trust is built more quickly.[6]

This idea of setting expectations is particularly important when communicating with a client that is not only new to a specific PR agency but to agency relationships in general. From the proposal stage through the initial months of the partnership, clearly defined expectations go a long way in easing the fears of apprehensive organizational leaders. Conversely, agencies may also be in the position of reorienting clients who may have experienced a less-than-productive partnership with a different agency. Overcoming this challenge should not be underestimated. Leveraging many of the questions listed above in a relationship such as this can provide significant insights into the challenges of past external experiences and help in diagnosing internal constraints. While a more comprehensive strategic approach will be covered in the following chapters, this initial overview underscores the areas that should be managed immediately.

Many PR agencies use time-tracking software so that practitioners and agency leaders can identify how much time is being spent on particular clients and projects. Whether used directly for billing purposes or not, careful tracking generates invaluable insights that can improve time management and workflow.

---

[6] Croft, A. C. (2006). *Managing a public relations firm for growth and profit* (2nd ed.). New York, NY: Haworth Press, p. 159.

One important question that requires attention is, "Why are these factors so important?" As communication counselors, PR practitioners help clients to tackle some of the largest and most difficult challenges that their organization may face. These are not simple topics to discuss or debate, let alone easy problems to solve. Many executive leaders take these challenges very personally. In the role as a counselor, it is important to not underestimate the responsibility of facing these challenges and offering well-vetted, valuable insights. Building this trust begins with setting clear expectations.

Communication and Time Management Expectations

In a traditional agency–client relationship, the largest financial components of an agreement tend to be tied to the agency's professional time. With this in mind, both parties should have a clear understanding of time estimates for all tasks within the scope of the agreement, including face-to-face meetings, check-in calls, and any time required to support such activities (research, report development, strategic planning, writing, media outreach, etc.). In most cases, the vast majority of this time may not be obvious to the client, so it is important to discuss these topics and set the expectation from the outset.

It is also important to schedule regular communications with the lead contact or contacts, such as a weekly call or biweekly in-person meeting. These recurring communications provide an opportunity for both teams to deliver any updates, discuss any strategic plan revisions, deliver research results, or identify any challenges in outreach. Creating and distributing a standard agenda and regular topics for discussion helps to promote a more efficient and comfortable meeting.

Of course, these recurring, prescheduled meetings should not be the only contact that agency professionals have with their clients. In general, practitioners are communicating with their client counterparts on a daily basis using email, texts, chats, and phone calls. Identifying the appropriate channels, pace, and depth of communication while also executing on client deliverables is a challenge in and of itself. The best agency professionals are able to anticipate questions, conduct efficient meetings, and leverage informal communication channels to address client needs proactively.

Client Involvement Expectations

Agency professionals must also ensure that they make clear the degree and type of involvement desired from the client for the relationship to succeed. Particularly for organizations that have limited experience working with PR agencies, the importance of timely and responsive communication, the prioritization of "hot" media inquiries, and the level of necessary engagement in varying projects must be clearly defined.

Timeline and Approval Expectations

As is the nature of communication, decisions and approvals specific to PR activities must move much more rapidly than typical organizational processes. Since media time lines often require responses within 24 hours, rather than weeks or months, agencies can educate and prepare their clients appropriately by defining the types of opportunities that may require immediate responses or communication. Some clients will be able to take advantage of short-turnaround inquiries, while others may have additional hierarchical layers and approvals required prior to outreach or response. By defining these limitations, agencies are empowered to create strategies that reflect the client's organizational strengths but avoid placing their clients in uncomfortable situations.

Proactive and Reactive Expectations for Media Engagement

Within each organization, a defined structure and process for approving internal and external communications should be in place. PR practitioners should help clearly identify and discuss the approval structure with each client and define the process and expectations early in the relationship. Agency professionals should make clear to clients that the time lines for responses to a media opportunity will always be clearly defined and communicated and that the most critical timing element for these opportunities is the initial agreement and scheduling. Creating a unique way of separating and prioritizing these types of requests for clients can provide a significant boost to successful media outreach.

Crisis Preparedness Expectations

In its simplest meaning, the word *crisis* tends to promote a sense of immediate attention and responsiveness. Crisis situations often elevate high-priority external outreach activities to an even more critical level. Agencies need to set clear expectations related to any organizational crisis situation, requesting that they will be made aware of the situation and brought in early in order to provide strategic insight in support of the work needed to overcome the crisis.

Crisis PR planning should be a part of any onboarding process for retainer clients. Largely, this work involves the identification of all key organizational stakeholders who will be responsible for planning and responding to a crisis situation and underscoring the key organization-wide actions required for dealing with media and other external publics. The details of these processes will be covered more in-depth in later chapters, but the skeleton of this process should be constructed with the client at the beginning of the relationship—hopefully, well before any such crisis occurs.

Client Contacts and Reporting Relationships

The majority of agency–client relationships commit time to developing a clear reporting structure responsible for overseeing the contracted deliverables. On the client side, this structure may be complex or as simple as a single individual with day-to-day authority. It may be a team and include a **C-suite** executive, such as the chief marketing officer, or a tactical-level employee. Additionally, it is important to understand that certain individuals may be given the *responsibility* to oversee an agency's work but not the *authority* to make decisions regarding these efforts. As you can see, this can quickly become one of the most challenging aspects of the agency–client relationship if the roles and functions are not clearly defined and agreed upon.

In the instances where agreements have been made regarding expected roles and responsibilities, agency professionals should always be mindful of potential shifts in a client's oversight structure. Changes in a client organization may be deliberate and clear, unplanned and vaguely understood, or fall anywhere in between. Veteran agency professionals often develop a sixth sense in identifying these client and relationship changes, but all practitioners should maintain a basic awareness. Keep in mind that client reorganizations are not necessarily negative for an agency, but they often constitute significant extra effort to build/rebuild a relationship and to educate a new manager about the agency's practices and expectations.

Designating Reporting and Approval Chains

Within the process of identifying the appropriate points of contact (POCs), both the client and the agency generally appoint a project or account leader that will handle a significant portion of the responsibilities. The client's project/account leader has the responsibility of not only ensuring that the agency is remaining on task and executing their deliverables effectively but also has the added duty of explaining to organizational stakeholders the value of the project.

If this client representative played an instrumental role during the agency search process, including developing the request for proposal, interviewing multiple agencies, and reviewing potential strategic plans, this individual should already be invested in the success of the relationship. Unfortunately, this is not always the case. As an example, let's say that a vice president of marketing unilaterally selects an agency without input from others and then assigns a PR manager who was not part of the search process to the position of overseeing their work. One can already envision many potential challenges within the agency–client relationship even before the first meetings are scheduled.

Agencies generally do not have control over the selection of a client contact; however, they can be instrumental in ensuring that both organizations clearly understand the approval process needed as part of executing strategies and tactics. Best practices suggest that an organization's leadership team should be involved in creating and approving a strategic plan. Then, the responsibility often shifts to the organization's communication team to direct specific items for approval as needed. For example, a press release may be requested highlighting the annual earnings for the organization. The communication team should ensure that the specifics contained within this press release were previously reviewed and approved by both the accounting department as well as the executive teams. By leveraging the client contact, agency professionals can create a clear contact structure to aid in communication with the functional areas necessary for reviews and approvals. As an agency representative, it is critical to reinforce with the client that they are responsible for identifying each of these functional stakeholders or anyone else responsible for approving various tactical items.

Whatever the circumstances, agencies should continually review, adjust, and tweak these reporting processes to ensure that pertinent information is shared with project/relationship managers, company leadership, and other relevant stakeholders.

The Pace of Change and Communication

Developing a sense for the fluidity and openness to change within a client organization is an extremely valuable skill to foster as a PR practitioner. Some organizations move at a rapid pace while others work tirelessly to avoid change altogether. Either way, agencies are rarely brought in to maintain the status quo: They are designed to drive change, in some form, for an organization. Agencies and practitioners are not always in a position to select the type of client that they will work with, but they can ensure that they communicate and execute at a pace that is sympathetic to the client's existing norms. They must clearly communicate this change and avoid making too many assumptions about what organizational leaders perceive. For day-to-day contact, make sure to communicate expectations related to anticipated response times, and define when your client prefers emails, phone calls, texts, and in-person contact. Generally, the best approach is a mix of methods based on client preference.

Kickoff Meeting Attendance

In preparing for the kickoff meeting, agency representatives should invite all previously identified client-facing team members and executives assigned to the account. It should be requested that the client attendees include all key communication team members and functional leaders—including identified executives. The meeting itself should always be led by a seasoned agency practitioner. Providing an opportunity for these groups to meet together—and then again separately, if possible—can be valuable from the perspective of gaining independent insights for the agency team. It can be easy to overlook the impact that organizational hierarchy can have on many of the details that clients are willing to provide. As an agency counselor, the more accurate the information, the more effective the strategies will be.

It is also valuable, especially from an agency perspective, to have representatives from various public relations and integrated communication disciplines attend a meeting of this nature. Experts who can provide insights into media relations, social media, internal communication, branding, or digital design, for example, support a consultative approach that values the entirety of a client's challenge over a specific solution.

Location

The location for the kickoff meeting can vary depending on the needs and resources available for the project. Consider the goals of the meeting before deciding whether a more intimate arrangement supports the main priorities or if it would be advantageous to involve a larger group in a larger space. A comfortable agenda should be reflected in a comfortable space and arrangement, as should a fast-paced crisis situation.

Additionally, if geography and budgets allow, face-to-face kickoff meetings are vastly preferable to help set the tone for a positive relationship. Technology can help to involve additional participants but should never be a distraction from the personal dialogue that is critical in cultivating a new relationship. Ideally, within the first several meetings, have both the client and the agency host face-to-face meetings. This can help demystify the organizations and create a deeper relationship.

Timing and Length

When determining the timing and duration of the kickoff meeting, consider the objective and priorities for the meeting. Some clients prefer a short kickoff meeting, allowing the agency to begin work quickly and ask more questions as details arise. In contrast, a deep-dive initial meeting may be the only time that some key client decision-makers are available to attend. Successful account managers make the most of each opportunity by using the planned attendance to drive the agenda. Both timing and duration choices should balance these factors.

Agenda

Attendees of a kickoff session should walk in the door with a clear idea of the topics and goals of the meeting. A properly constructed agenda should include an outline of the meeting date and duration, all relevant objectives, discussion points, and key takeaways. If possible, the agenda should be sent to all participants prior to the meeting so that they can provide appropriate feedback and arrive prepared.

Agency leaders must be prepared to be flexible during the kickoff meeting but also ensure that key questions are answered. Creating an official agenda can help to build in some flexibility and allow each discussion to progress naturally. It is important to be realistic about the number of items being covered when setting up the agenda, but it is also critical to set the expectation that an agency professional prioritizes goals and topics for the sake of everyone's time.

Billing for Services

Within the framework of initial contract negotiations, discussions specific to the costs associated with PR services should be included, further reemphasized, and explained in detail at the start of the relationship. Communication should be explicit as it relates to the anticipated billing structure, frequency, and what services will and will not be included in a retainer. The fewer financial surprises, the better the situation for both sides.

Agencies often use the concept of *billable hours* to represent the required professional time committed to a particular task or project. Billable hours have long been a standard approach in the legal profession and other professional services (including accounting, business consulting, and public relations) and help both firms and their clients to better understand the value of time spent on specific projects. Although billable hours are not universal across all agencies, they are widely utilized in the agency environment.

As you might expect, entry-level professionals tend to have the lowest rates per billable hour while agency executives have the highest rate. These rates are broadly reflective of the amount and quality of work that individuals at these levels are able to accomplish. The hourly rates that are set by a firm are largely based on job titles rather than individual performance. Time tracking reports, which can be recorded in a little as 10- or 15-minute increments, are filed by each professional within an agency. Each individual's report contains both billable and non-billable time.[7] Agencies should account for time spent on both internal projects as well as client-specific work. This information allows agency leaders to ensure they have a clear understanding of *who* is doing *what* and *for whom*. In addition to helping determine client costs, billable hours are an important metric to help a firm assess and evaluate the amount of professional time that goes into researching, planning, executing, and reporting PR campaigns.

Project Clients Versus Retainer Clients

Within an agency environment, it is common to assign resources to support specific short-term or fixed-term project-based clients or longer-term monthly retainer clients. In either case, billable hours can be used to estimate and evaluate the time involved in completing work for an individual client.

---

[7] Ibid, p. 165.

Uses for Tracking and Billing

The methods in which an agency tracks and bills time associated with projects vary almost as broadly as the countless variations of agencies that exist in the marketplace. However, the tracking of billable hours is also an important internal tool that agencies commonly use when reviewing their own teams. Spending an excess of time to accomplish straightforward client work or not accruing enough billable time can become a significant issue. In general, most successful agencies track hours to ensure that project and retainer clients are being treated fairly and equitably.

Tracking hours can also act as a resource in proactively identifying structural problems and workflow challenges. When a client requests support that is beyond the project scope and will require additional hours to complete, the tracking can be helpful in explaining the limitations of a retainer agreement. With this in mind, there are also disadvantages of tracking billable hours. Agencies that report hours to their clients may find themselves in a situation wherein they have completed all of their assigned deliverables without meeting their contracted hours. In this case, financial restitution or other arrangements may need to be explored.

The Diminishing Importance of Billable Hours

The majority of PR agencies still use the billable hours structure, and university-level student-run agencies have started to incorporate this tracking system within their capstone service-learning courses, but its influence may be waning.[8] In a 2011 study involving 83 student-run agencies, only 32.6% actually tracked billable hours.[9] This may be reflective of the PR industry as a whole deemphasizing the billable hour within the business model. A strong movement is currently gaining traction toward diverting away from strict adherence in the legal world,[10] and public relations may find itself following suit. That said, tracking time, whether narrowly related to billing or not, should play an important role in agency workflow and evaluation, both internally and in relation to client projects.

With the movement toward public relations encompassing more integrated marketing communication strategies and tactics, the barrier to entry for starting an agency or working as an individual practitioner is lower than ever before. Traditional PR firms may be encouraged to look to alternate models to ensure that clients remain satisfied.

---

[8] Swanson, D. J. (2011). The student-run public relations firm in an undergraduate program: Reaching learning and professional development goals through 'real world' experience. *Public Relations Review, 37*, 499–505.

[9] Bush, L., & Miller, B. M. (2011). US student-run agencies: Organization, attributes and adviser perceptions of student learning outcomes. *Public Relations Review, 37*, 487.

[10] Turow, S. (2007). The billable hour must die. *The ABA Journal, 93*, 32.

Key Takeaways

The process of initiating a new client relationship may seem quite overwhelming and process driven. In many ways, it is. For this reason, it is uncommon that PR practitioners graduate from college and look to start their own PR agency right away. The following points should be considered in order to place the client management experience into perspective. Contributing to freelance or pro bono opportunities in public relations can be valuable in gaining experience and developing the necessary skills valued within an agency environment. Client management can be one of the most rewarding yet challenging aspects of agency life. Any opportunity that a practitioner is afforded to develop skills supporting this area of agency life will set a budding practitioner apart from other entry-level associates.

- **Start small.** Short-term projects are easier to manage than most ongoing retainer relationships.

- **If you can, practice your PR and client management skills separately.** It is not necessary to take on a new task *and* a new type of relationship at the same time. If you have created collateral materials for a student group in the past, this may be a good place to start for a community pro bono project, rather than a media relations campaign.

- **Remember that no one gets everything right the first time.** At some point, every agency practitioner will be responsible for guiding a lost client or will lead an unsuccessful project due to a miscalculation. Agencies exist, in part, because this type of work is best done in teams. One significant benefit of such an arrangement affords practitioners the opportunities to collectively support each other.

Reflect and Discuss

1. What do you see as the biggest strengths and biggest gaps within your client management skill set?

2. How can you work to prioritize the most important client questions?

3. What collegiate or postcollegiate experiences can help you prepare for client interaction?

4. How do you see yourself as a counselor or consultant? What traits could you strengthen in this area?

5. What is your personal value proposition as a practitioner? How would you bring value to your next PR agency?

Heather Sliwinski is the PR lead at 6SensorLabs, a San Francisco–based tech startup creating greater food transparency and empowering consumers to make healthier decisions. She has managed the corporate and product communications programs for the tech industry's most innovative companies, including Samsung, salesforce.com, VMware, and more. Sliwinski graduated from the University of Wisconsin–Madison with a BA in journalism and mass communications and a certificate in business.

Agency Life: What You Need to Know About Working at a PR Firm*

Upon graduation from college, I noticed a common trend among entry-level job descriptions for which I was applying: Public relations agency experience was preferred and sometimes even required. I had held a number of jobs and internships in the industry throughout my college career, but none were with an agency. I didn't understand why working at an agency was put on a pedestal, but I knew that getting that experience would be an important step in my career.

After working in marketing for a couple of years, I decided to make the switch to PR agency and have gained experience at a handful of agencies since then. I've found that agency life poses its own unique challenges, and new professionals should learn to expect a few commonalities among agencies once joining their ranks.

Learn to Juggle

The ability to multitask is not only crucial, but it is the crux of your job. Most agencies will have a team dedicated to a handful of clients. These clients may all be in the same industry, such as consumer products or health care, or they may run the gamut of industries. New professionals in agencies will quickly have to learn multiple clients' businesses, products, and services inside and out to communicate effectively and in an educated way.

One of the biggest differences between agency and in-house positions is how you prioritize. At an agency, you can't prioritize one client over another. They all need equal attention, and if your five clients each have a last-minute project at 5 p.m. on a Friday, the work needs to get done for all five clients. Be prepared for long hours but great client relationships and invaluable experience as a result.

Learn to Accept Every Opportunity

New professionals at agencies will gain experience in almost every PR task—building media lists, media monitoring, pitching reporters, drafting press releases, managing social media accounts, and creating PR plans. Nothing is off-limits for an entry-level PR professional.

*Source: Reprinted with permission from Sliwinski, H. (2015, September 29). Agency Life: What You Need to Know About Working at a PR Firm. Retrieved from https://apps.prsa.org/Intelligence/Tactics/Articles/view/11222/1116/Agency_Life_What_You_Need_to_Know_About_Working_at#.WqFCH4JGOk8.

Take advantage of this opportunity. While it might seem overwhelming at first to try and master everything an agency has to offer, doing is the best way of learning. When I first started, I would volunteer to tag along on a Saturday morning to a radio station to observe a client interview or come up with pitch ideas from breaking news. Within the first year, there weren't many skills I didn't try. Not only do you build your skill set, but you become the go-to person on the team when questions arise—no longer just a worker bee, but an invaluable member of the team.

Learn to Speak Up

When I first started at an agency, I was apprehensive to speak up as the greenest person in the room of experts. However, I learned that not only was sharing ideas encouraged, it was expected! You won't be making copies forever. Agencies want to see their staff grow into strategic thinkers and creative minds. Senior leaders like new professionals who take initiative and share their ideas, whether it's for a client project or proposing a more efficient way to get the work done.

It's also extremely important to keep your career goals in mind. Don't keep it a secret if there is a specific project on which you want to work. Not only does asking for specific projects show passion, but it allows you to share your unique interests and skills. Just because you are a new professional doesn't mean you have nothing to bring to the table. Since my prior position was in marketing, I had experience in redesigning websites. When one of our clients was looking to redesign their website, I jumped at the chance not only to use my past experience but also to lead a project I really enjoyed. I now have two company website redesigns under my belt and a happy client. Don't be shy in asking for what you want!

While switching to an agency was overwhelming at first, the experience has had so much to offer. If you take advantage of the wealth of opportunities agencies offer, you can build an amazing foundation for the rest of your PR career.

Top Must-Haves

- **Must-download app:** For me, it's PicsArt. I love all the editing functions it has. Is it lame to say Facebook? Love it or hate it, it's a huge part of our lives.
- **Must-read book, blog, or media outlet:** I've been living in San Francisco for more than two years and working in tech public relations for a bit longer. Techmeme.com gives me all the breaking tech news for the day, so I can read the headlines and see who's writing about what.
- **Must-use tool:** Cision—I've been using it since my first agency job and still need it to find emails and new publications. But beware—always do your research before pitching a reporter. Don't just spam from Cision! It's not always up to date.

Strategies and Tactics

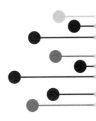

CHAPTER 4

Managing Projects, Meetings, and Client Communication

E very agency professional has had *that day*. A reporter calls needing a photo on deadline. The print shop can't match the necessary shade of red for a brochure. A client's website inexplicably stops working using their preferred browser. The sixth draft of a crisis statement fails to meet a discerning chief executive officer's standard. It happens. Some challenges are inevitable with the volume and complexity involved in practicing agency public relations. At the same time, many of these obstacles can be avoided if the appropriate planning is followed. Should the client have already provided the photo to the agency team? Were the right questions asked of or by the print shop before accepting the project? Did the website developer run sufficient tests using different browsers? Had the agency discussed with the client the processes and expectations (particularly immediacy) required for a crisis response prior to the event occurring? Regardless of

Objectives

- Understand the role and perspective of project management in agency work.

- Define the steps necessary for success before, during, and after client meetings.

- Anticipate common challenges in communicating with clients.

- Clarify best practices for client reporting.

©iStockphoto.com/Sidekick

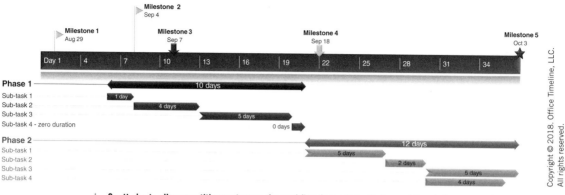

| Gantt charts allow practitioners to map the workflow for each tactic in a public relations campaign.

where the responsibility falls or if these situations were preventable to begin with, challenges such as these often fall on the agency professional.

Clients, outside **vendors**, reporters, and publics simply do not possess the perspective that agency professionals bring to situations, projects, and decisions. Practitioners see the way their clients function and the way that other external partners function based on a wide variety of experiences. This perspective carries both opportunity and responsibility: the ability to see what others cannot but the expectation of using that vision to anticipate and avoid challenges whenever possible.

As a result, veteran practitioners have become increasingly efficient and effective as much through their **project management** skills as through their public relations acumen. The most relevant priorities of any agency professional are to deliver projects on time, on budget, and within scope.[1] This does not happen without clear team communication, effective project leadership, and expert use of meetings and **reporting tools**. These individuals must anticipate and solve problems before they happen and cultivate a project pulse, tone, and energy that advances projects rather than holding them back. The overarching goal of appropriately connecting these skills is to build and maintain strong relationships with internal and external team members. This endeavor is never easy or black and white; however, strong relationships build trust that cannot be overvalued in terms of client, project, or agency success.

The Project Management Institute (PMI) defines projects as both temporary and unique, with a specific desired outcome not achievable through everyday organizational operation.[2] Project management is an art form in and of itself, one that even the most experienced professionals must continually adjust depending on clients, time lines, and campaign goals. Client and project management involves extra effort

---

[1] Morris, P., & Pinto, J. K. (2011). *The Wiley guide to project organization and project management competencies.* Hoboken, NJ: John Wiley & Sons.

[2] PMI. (2016). *What is project management?* Retrieved March 1, 2015, from http://www.pmi.org/en/About-Us/About-Us-What-is-Project-Management.aspx

to decode—or ideally, anticipate—obstacles, with various important factors to consider when building successful project teams.

Setting Expectations for Success

Teams generally function much more effectively when the expectations have been clearly communicated at the start of a relationship or as each project or campaign initiates. This also encompasses overall communication and operational processes, including the anticipated results.[3] In PR campaigns, these often take the form of SMART objectives: specific, measurable, achievable, realistic, and time bound. Objectives serve as expectations for all project-related activities, but there should be structure instituted throughout the process, including project phases, deadlines, meetings, and additional communication. The more clearly the process expectations are defined, the more likely that all team members will stick to them. Keeping team members informed and up-to-date on projects goes a long way toward building trust and enthusiasm.[4] By painting a well-defined picture of a project's progress for a client, agency practitioners demonstrate that they understand the path to completion. It clarifies expectations and defines what the client must provide to enable an agency team to achieve shared goals.

Dividing and Distributing Work

Many PR projects and campaigns can seem overwhelming at the start, even for the most seasoned agency teams. The process of breaking each component of the campaign down into its individual parts and then assigning those parts to the appropriate team members empowers everyone and makes the larger project seem more achievable. In this way, practitioners are able to make the most of each individual on a team.[5] Often, the first step is assessing the skills and abilities of team members in order to identify the project elements best suited to them.[6]

Clarity and Accountability

It is also important to understand that there are a number of potentially problematic factors. Many of these stem from a lack of understanding about the issues, expectations, and processes at hand. Such challenges often faced by teams include

---

[3] Croft, A. C. (1996). *Managing a public relations firm for growth and profit*. New York, NY: Haworth Press, p. 159.

[4] Newsom, D., VanSlyke Turk, J., & Kruckeberg, D. (2000). *This is PR: The realities of public relations* (7th ed.). Belmont, CA: Wadsworth, p. 442.

[5] Slevin, D. P., & Pinto, J. K. (2011). An overview of behavioral issues in project management. In P. Morris & J. K. Pinto (Eds.), *The Wiley guide to project organization & project management competencies* (pp. 1–19). Hoboken, NJ: John Wiley & Sons.

[6] Delisle, C. L. (2011). Contemporary views on shaping, developing, and managing teams. In P. Morris & J. K. Pinto (Eds.), *The Wiley guide to project organization & project management competencies* (pp. 39–69). Hoboken, NJ: John Wiley & Sons.

a lack of overall motivation, an unclear definition of success, a lack of common vocabulary, or an incomplete perspective or context for the project.[7] Effective project delegation involves setting clear standards and holding each individual accountable for their piece of the puzzle.[8] Leadership is about conveying a clear project vision to both agency and client teams so that each individual understands how their efforts contribute to the larger project.[9]

Timing and Pacing

A significant part of planning and developing appropriate expectations comes down to timing. Agency practitioners must make the most of the time devoted to each client while accomplishing as much as possible for the agency as a whole. Long-term clients tend to repeatedly return to agencies not only because of success but also due to having a positive experience in completing a project. An organized, well-paced process demonstrates excellent management and mastery of every part of a campaign.

When initiating a new client relationship, agency professionals should focus on setting the expectations for individual tasks, including prioritization and client preferences. For example, some clients request that all pressing matters be handled over the phone rather than via email, while others prefer a text message and the opportunity to respond using the communication medium that they choose. Finding the correct channels for distinct levels of priority is crucial for establishing clear project communication. Adopting these communication norms leads to fewer missed deadlines and a clearer understanding of the priorities within a project.

Best Practices for Project Management

Creating and maintaining an evenly paced workflow, setting clear expectations for agency and client team members, and sticking to internal deadlines does not simply happen by accident. Each is a result of foresight, project planning, and continuous communication. Day-to-day project management can make or break the quality of a client's agency experience. A series of poorly run projects, even those realizing successful results, can influence a client's decision on whether to seek out other agencies or move a project in house. As with any business, the customer experience is critical, and the organization and effectiveness of that experience with an agency is largely determined by the quality of project management.

Furthermore, clients will regularly remind you of their desire for consistency, efficiency, and effectiveness. These are much more likely to happen when there

---

[7] Ibid, pp. 60–64.

[8] Croft, A. C. (1996). *Managing a public relations firm for growth and profit.* New York, NY: Haworth Press, p. 159.

[9] Thomas, P., & Kerwin, J. J. (2011). Leadership of project teams. In P. Morris & J. K. Pinto (Eds.), *The Wiley guide to project organization & project management competencies* (pp. 70–88). Hoboken, NJ: John Wiley & Sons.

is a mutual understanding of the goals and objectives for specific projects. When both parties understand and agree on the focus for their combined efforts, there is a shared sense of purpose and priority. In this way, agency professionals have the ability to measure their performance and adjust their work accordingly.

Client Communication

Often, organizations function with a *cc* culture, an understanding that certain individuals should be included (or *carbon copied*) on most or all digital communication to ensure they are in the know. Including a variety of client contacts on updates and communications can often be positive. With more team members included, the entire unit can become increasingly efficient and avoid "third-party interpretation syndrome." With this in mind, there can also be a potential downside to this inclusive strategy. Too much information, particularly for senior executives, may slow down processes or lead team members to ignore emails from the agency. Practitioners should have open discussions with client teams regarding when and how inclusion on communication is necessary for different projects and different team members.

Balancing the information requirements of all team members should never be taken lightly. Communication should be as jargon free and concise as possible.[10] Agency practitioners should be flexible and transparent regarding project communication, including a thorough understanding of what has or has not worked for their organization in the past. They should also frequently provide clients with an opportunity to make suggestions about processes and project communication.

Blend Images/Alamy Stock Photo

Pacing Progress

From a project- or campaign-planning perspective, practitioners should work backward from final deadlines and establish internal milestones in order to ensure that each of the components comprising the larger project is completed. Each deadline should be clearly assigned to an individual or the small group assuming

A clear, concise agenda sets expecatations for all meeting participants, particularly clients.

---

[10] Beard, M. (1997). *Running a public relations department*. London, UK: The Institute of Public Relations and Kogan Page, p. 37.

responsibility for its completion. Particularly important are the time lines for project components that build upon each other. If one piece of this puzzle falls behind, it can easily drag the entire project behind.

To this end, successful projects often have internal milestones and achievements that ensure that progress is realized over the course of the project. This could include establishing and achieving project checkpoints on a regular basis and providing frequent recognition for individual contributions. Everyone appreciates an environment that clearly values their effort and establishes the link between individual contributions and group success.

Agency and Client Meetings: Before, During, and After

Pulling off a successful meeting occurs in part because the objectives and expectations of the meeting were preplanned, including anticipation of discussion points and relevant topics. Agency professionals can and should manage these responsibilities for meetings with clients. Conducting an effective meeting often entails a degree of foresight and preplanning, but it saves the larger team significant time in added efficiency and productivity: If all participants are aware of the expectations and can consider issues prior to the meeting, they become more effective contributors. These instances also provide an opportunity to demonstrate many of the organizational and communication skills that agencies use when working with the media on their clients' behalf. In this way, they contribute to the continued development of building trust within the relationship.

Many professionals are subjected to a variety of painfully unorganized, unproductive, and inefficient meetings on a regular basis. Running useful and engaging meetings distinguishes agency professionals from the crowd.

Pre-Meeting Planning and Communication

First, agency practitioners must determine the appropriate timing for a meeting in order to address the most pressing objectives. Far too often, practitioners schedule and conduct unnecessary and unproductive meetings that ultimately contribute to meeting fatigue and undermine the credibility of an agency. Meetings should be viewed as an opportunity for agency professionals to demonstrate their understanding of the audience (in this case, the client) and what that audience finds valuable. Practitioners should ask themselves, "Is a meeting the best way to address an issue, reach consensus, or define an objective? Will a meeting be a more effective channel for achieving this goal over other types of communication?" Meetings allow for simultaneous, dynamic discussion, which can be extremely productive but also quite messy. The amount of work to be accomplished in a specific meeting must be clearly defined and understood by the leader as well as by the participants. A meeting with objectives that are too broad can easily devolve into questions related to organizational goals or specific agency partnerships. In general, these meetings do not accomplish objectives that move organizations forward toward achieving their goals.

Useful meeting topics include defining a clear project scope for a specific campaign, updating an agency team on significant changes within a client organization (such as a reorganization, personnel transitions, or shift in business priorities), or reviewing past efforts to identify potential areas for improvement. In each case, a sizeable portion of the content to be covered during the meeting should be forwarded to all participants prior to the scheduled discussion so that they can arrive with a clear perspective to share. This way, the meeting can begin with all participants on the same page: discussing ideas that can improve a campaign plan, addressing concerns about onboarding and workflow, or defining and prioritizing lessons learned for future campaigns. More specifically, **meeting objectives** (with definable outcomes) would *not* include outlining/drafting a campaign plan (too broad), writing specific messages (too complex/time intensive), or assigning tasks for an upcoming project (too simple). It would be more productive to *review and critique* a campaign plan, *prioritize* prewritten messages, or *discuss* the challenges of assigned tasks from a prior project.

These activities, when managed efficiently, support the core values that agency practitioners want to reinforce: creating a shared sense of purpose with clients, allowing all participants to provide input and perspective, and building consensus on potentially divisive issues such as prioritization and objectives. As these are all complex concepts, providing team members with the appropriate information prior to the scheduled discussion allows time to reflect, do additional investigation, and distill opinions. Those who put in the most effort beforehand to comprehend and synthesize the content are in the best position to contribute and are generally rewarded for their efforts.

Practitioners are also responsible for identifying the desired audience for a specific meeting. Once the meeting topic and objectives are defined, practitioners must decide which members of the agency and client teams should be invited to participate. As a reminder, attendees can be full participants or simply observers. Particularly in the case of executive team members, some may find it useful to participate in several, but not all, stages of a campaign. Keeping these individuals *cc*'d on communication helps them to decide when they should participate and when they can let others report back as necessary. Agency practitioners may prefer that leadership is present at certain meetings due to their decision-making ability. Basic considerations when deciding who should attend a meeting should focus on whether a potential participant's perspective would be integral to the discussion, how deeply involved they would be with executing decisions made during the meeting, and how difficult it would be to convey information to them if they did not attend.

Setting the Agenda

Once the overarching topic, objectives, and participants are set, the agency leader can develop the specific agenda. This exercise defines the anticipated path that the meeting will follow from the start (objectives, materials shared, perspectives provided by the attendees) to the conclusion. The leader of the meeting should understand what the final outcome looks like, whether it be an agreed-upon list of campaign priorities or a mutual understanding of revised project goals. A clear path and an intuitive connection among the starting point, objectives, activities, and expected outcomes encourage buy-in and participation. While the format of the outcome should be defined, it is imperative that the content grows from and is open to the activities and the discussion of the meeting itself. Attendees should feel that their participation serves a purpose, and making the range of potential outcomes too narrow or rigid negates the value of their attendance and input.

A clear agenda uses language that can be easily understood by all parties. This can sometimes be challenging, as agencies and clients may have a number of different terms and acronyms for the same processes or vocabulary. Agendas should avoid constantly introducing new concepts, issues, and processes. Practitioners should strive to make agendas familiar and consistent for clients.

A well-developed agenda balances the inclusion of an appropriate amount of detail to ensure that the attendees feel a sense of progress with enough open-ended perspectives to generate valuable discussion. It demonstrates that a variety of ideas and opinions are valued.[11] This is, of course easier said than done. The correct balance shifts from group to group and with different meeting objectives. The more complicated or divisive a particular issue might be, often the narrower the agenda's focus, in order to encourage productivity.

Tips for Executing the Meeting Successfully

A successful meeting, from an agency practitioner's perspective, includes providing the agency team with a clear plan of action for resulting work, aligning agency and client objectives and priorities, and allowing client team members to participate. To accomplish these objectives, one must manage discussion effectively. Agency professionals should think of themselves as **facilitators** rather than lecturers. The responsibilities of a facilitator include maintaining a friendly and efficient pace, encouraging all stakeholders to contribute, and knowing how much off-topic discussion is acceptable in order to allow healthy conversations to conclude. They put themselves in the shoes of the audience: the project team.[12] Measuring yourself based on these factors allows for a productive meeting environment and encourages attendees to contribute.

- **Successful meetings start and end on time.** This demonstrates respect for all participants and sets the tone for an efficient meeting.

- **The objectives, language, and strategic context should be clear.** Practitioners must ensure that all participants begin with a clear understanding of the topic and terminology at hand. This often means avoiding PR- or marketing-specific language and acronyms as well as contextualizing the meeting's objectives as part of larger organizational goals. If everyone can speak the same language and understand the meeting's strategic purpose, facilitators have a much clearer path to productivity.

- **Productive meetings are not inflexible.** Planning or leading discussion in a way that is too rigid makes attendees feel disconnected from useful discussion and devalues their opinions and insights. Flexibility in managing discussion allows all participants to contribute and ensures that organic and original concepts can emerge. Effective agendas and meeting facilitation maintain a balance so that groups stay focused, while avoiding predetermined conclusions.

- **The best facilitators seek out multiple perspectives.** There are times when groups are fully in agreement, but, more often, louder voices can intimidate some individuals into staying silent, creating a false sense of consensus. Skilled facilitators encourage all participants to engage in the

---

[11] Ibid, p. 95.

[12] Ibid, p. 37.

conversation and attempt to bring out diverse perspectives from multiple stakeholders, departments, or organizations involved in a project.

- **Flexibility is paramount.** No useful meeting has ever gone exactly as planned. Successful facilitators continually gauge the sentiment of the room, listening for agreement, dissent, hesitation, enthusiasm, confusion, comprehension, reservation, or reiteration. They respond to these shifts in tone from all participants—agency and client—in order to better understand and address issues and disconnections or to build on agreement and enthusiasm.

- **Speaking the truth should be rewarded.** Agency counselors can and should bring up delicate, difficult-to-discuss client issues. This outside perspective is one of the most valuable services an agency can provide, but it does not make such conversations easy. It is helpful to show admiration and support for those who make the most difficult or critical statements. In this way, agency practitioners empower the process of open discussion related to the deepest organizational challenges; this may prove to be the necessary first step in solving a client's core issues.

- **Clients are the experts on their industry.** It is a good practice to always regard the client as the business and industry expert. The client should be a valued part of decisions made in terms of positioning messages, products, or organizations within an existing group of competitors. This approach provides the client with necessary and distinct—but not all-encompassing—authority within the larger decision-making process. It also involves treating clients with respect and deference regarding their industry knowledge.[13]

Meeting Follow-Up

Conducting effective meetings does not end when the room empties or when everyone disconnects from the conference call or video chat. Agency practitioners should provide a recap or summary of the key takeaways for those in attendance and others who would find value in the information. Summaries should clearly articulate actionable items, identifying the specific individuals from the larger team responsible for a particular task, including the anticipated deadline. Meeting recaps can also express appreciation for the group's input and provide an update as to the next meeting or expected communication.

By following up with the broader team, practitioners can provide some level of closure to the meeting and ultimately ensure that client team members understand exactly what to expect as the project and the agency relationship progress. Meeting summaries also allow for participants to address key points, clarify any misunderstandings, or note any changes of direction that may have occurred after the meeting. Since agency–client

---

[13] Croft, A. C. (1996). *Managing a public relations firm for growth and profit.* New York, NY: Haworth Press, p. 160.

communication is a continuous process, meeting-specific communications serve a vital role for providing updates and clarification to the team members involved.

Reporting to the Client

Concise, clear, and easily shareable project updates and reports go a long way toward strengthening agency–client relationships. Functional, specific reporting allows clients to see at a glance what value agencies provide. These communications should deepen a client's understanding of public relations, connect organizational priorities to agency strategies and tactics, and show a clear understanding of the industry and the client's internal needs. Ideally, reporting documents should be developed in such a way that the information contained within can be immediately distributed to the executive leadership team if requested, taking advantage of the opportunity to share insights with a broad client audience.[14]

Reporting Documents

Many agencies follow a customizable reporting format that ensures that certain agency-wide structures and values are front and center, while allowing differentiation for the range of client projects and priorities. The format of these documents is critical, serving both as a checklist for inclusion of all relevant information as well as a template format that is simple to scan and understand from the client's perspective. The best reports make it easy to identify the most important takeaways but also provide additional details to those interested. Recipients will most likely not read every word, but different sections may be of more importance to certain individuals or departments within a client organization.

As a result of the myriad of potential audiences, one of the most challenging tasks for the agency team becomes contextualizing the content for readers with varying degrees of PR knowledge. As is often the case within the meetings themselves, many client team members have valuable perspectives to share, but they may not have experience with, for example, proactive earned media outreach, social media community building, or search engine optimization (SEO) tactics. Agencies should provide context in order to highlight success on each of these fronts. How is the client doing relative to the campaign's objectives and expectations? How does it rank among competitors? What does success look like? The agency should appropriately paint this picture for the client.

Showing Success

Ultimately, clients are primarily interested in understanding the results of tasks that are being performed on their behalf. Distributing a press release is not an end in itself, but as a key process step, it becomes important to ensure that clients are aware of drafting, approval, distribution, and follow up. Particularly early in a

---

[14] Beard, M. (1997). *Running a public relations department*. London, UK: The Institute of Public Relations and Kogan Page, p. 55.

client relationship, it is valuable to overcommunicate the successful completion of each of these steps to help build trust with the agency team. The culmination of this process comes in **summative evaluation**, where agencies can demonstrate the short-term and long-term benefits of a project.[15]

Success, much like organizational objectives, never follows a cookie-cutter approach. Reporting success, or client "wins," should reflect a balance between what is important to the client and where an agency wants to demonstrate its greatest value. This means that certain metrics, media outlets, or events of particular importance should absolutely be highlighted; however, agencies should not hesitate to educate clients on more impactful measures based on the projects goals and objectives. Ideally, the important metrics should have been agreed upon at the objective stage of campaign planning, and the same approach can be taken at smaller levels within a project.

Outlining Strategies for Improvement

An important and often forgotten value of reporting documents is that they can also serve as a tool to improve day-to-day work. These documents can include reminders about requested information or approvals, suggestions for updating workflow or processes, or even mid-campaign recalibrating strategies and tactics. While there should always be face-to-face discussion related to significant items, there can be value in putting recommendations in writing. Remember that reports as documents often have a wider client audience that meeting conversation and email do not.

Reporting and implementing strategies for improvement create space for productive communication regarding challenges and opportunities. They reinforce the energy put behind constant improvement of projects and processes. Most importantly, they demonstrate the commitment and understanding that drives many veteran agency practitioners: The long-term success of a client organization and the client–agency relationship is more important than specific steps within an individual project.

Reflect and Discuss

1. How does having project management skills enhance a PR practitioner's professional contributions?

2. How should agency professionals decide which client team members should participate in specific meetings?

3. What strategies were discussed that outline how to plan effective business meetings?

4. How should practitioners report back to clients after a meeting?

---

[15] Bobbitt, R., & Sullivan, R. (2009). *Developing the public relations campaign.* Boston, MA: Pearson, p. 181.

Mike Driehorst

Mike Driehorst is a PR strategist and project manager for Weaving Influence, a digital marketing communications agency specializing in book marketing.

After an early career in journalism, Mike has worked in public relations for more than 20 years and traces his professional social media roots to 2006. During his career, Mike worked with a range of local and national organizations, from publishing and nonprofit to automotive, construction, manufacturing, and retail.

How do you build a strong professional relationship that requires a deep understanding of the clients' day-to-day work, their roadblocks, frustrations, and aspirations?

Any good agency–client relationship starts with the agency personnel having at least two key qualities: A strong curiosity about pretty much everything (or at least the ability to fake it) and a level of empathy. I often say that there are relatively few things at which I'm an expert. However, I know at least a little about a whole lot. I can talk on the surface about topics such as comparing the pros and cons of pyrolytic-versus sputter-coating glass manufacturing, the value a funeral director offers a grieving family, and different approaches to business coaching.

Having a strong curiosity and asking questions allows practitioners to dig in and get not only to know clients' products and services but also to ask about their business goals and other operational issues that you'll need to address, or at least know about, in working with media.

Similarly, you have to have a level of caring—not only the quality of your work but about the success of your clients. If the client is successful and you can show your contribution, then you and your agency will be successful as well.

It's like what the career counselor advises in talking with students about post-college life: Focus on doing what you enjoy and what interests you and the income will take care of itself. Focus on the clients' needs, and odds are they'll stick around for a long time.

What does it mean to provide strategic counseling to clients? Can you give an example?

No business or organization should hire an agency unless that agency is filling a hole or adding value. While agencies can provide tactical support, their biggest strength is providing an objective outsider's view based on its communications focus (PR, advertising, social, etc.) and its work with other clients. That perspective and experience can be a huge asset in providing strategic counseling when combined with a deep understanding of the clients' goals, market(s), and at least a surface understanding of strengths and weaknesses.

With that combination, agencies can develop a plan—a roadmap—of how clients can achieve their goals. Strategic counseling can really take many forms. It can be a weekly or monthly meeting in which agencies act as a coach, providing feedback, a valuable outsider's

(Continued)

(Continued)

perspective, and rough recommendations on strategies to try.

Deeper, it can look like a short- or long-term plan of action, complete with brand positioning, what PR tactics to employ, what media to target, if there should be an internal communications component and how that looks, and other facets of communications that public relations entails.

One critical skill necessary for understanding a client better is learning to ask questions in order to gather the appropriate information. Are there specific questions you ask clients that help build a solid relationship?

Though agencies are essentially nothing more than a vendor, they have to act as if they're another department of the client's organization. Ideally, agencies should have the mind-set of the client, but with an outsider's perspective. Therefore, questions to ask—once you get on the same page as to the overriding goals—deal with the following:

- *Past*: What has worked for you before? What didn't work?

- *Present*: What are the strengths and weaknesses of our product/service? (Also, often, agencies will survey customers to get this same feedback and see if clients' perception is the same as the marketplace's.) What about your business keeps you up at night? Who are your competitors and how do you fare against them?

- *Future*: What events or situations could impact your business (pending government policies and regulations, evolving technology, your business buying or getting bought, etc.)?

Creativity, ideation, and brainstorming— what do those mean to you with respect to the work you do for clients?

Any type of process such as brainstorming produces best results with a focus on what you're trying to achieve: What are you starting with (if there are any concrete barriers) and what do you want to achieve? The leader should keep people on track, and someone should be responsible for keeping notes, no matter how crazy the ideas are.

Back to the question, the process is about trying to develop a fresh way to achieve a client need. The best brainstorming meetings I've been a part of allow for a free flow of ideas, almost a stream of collective consciousness where those involved build off each other.

What does customer service mean in the PR agency (or corporate) setting?

At the very least, it means meeting expectations. Those expectations are best met by educating the client. Whether you work in an agency or in-house, educating your clients, your boss, or your colleagues in another area is an ongoing process. It's not about talking down to or lecturing them. It's about making them aware of at least the basic *whys* behind a particular approach or a particular recommendation.

Too often, PR professionals will toss out huge numbers around circulation or talk about a high number of media hits. In reality, that type of reporting does clients no good as it usually doesn't accomplish business objectives. If clients are aware of why you're taking a certain tactic and have an idea of what the end result looks like—an ongoing awareness among the targeted audiences, a certain message being reported in clips, and so on—then clients will know what to expect, which will reinforce their trust in you.

And it'll be easier to show when you exceed expectations if clients understand what they are.

Top 5 Characteristics Every PR Professional Should Have

1. Writing. A strong command of English, knowing your grammar, and being able to convey a thought is a must-have foundation for everyone in public relations.

2. The ability to take notes quickly and clearly (so that you can understand them later).

3. Curiosity.

4. Self-discipline to do what's right and not be one of those relatively few who give the PR profession a bad reputation through stretching the truth, trying to fool your audience, or providing clients with results that don't help their goals.

5. An understanding that, often, it's not a 9-to-5 job.

Top Must-Haves

- **Must-download app:** For relationship-building with media, it's Twitter. It's great for following their stories, for engaging with them when I don't need anything (i.e., not pitching), and finding other prospective media outlets. Feedly also is a good tool to keep track of blogs and media outlets.

- **Must-read book/blog/ media outlet:** PR-wise, Jeremy Pepper is a PR blogger and pro I've read and connected with since I first became involved in social media around 2004 on a personal level. He always provides an insightful, often against-the-grain take on a situation or the general state of PR affairs. His blog is at http://pop-pr .blogspot.com/. Other sites I've found helpful in helping me keep perspective while providing other insights are
  - ○ Harvard Business Review: https://hbr.org/ topics
  - ○ PFSK: http://www .psfk.com/

- **Must-use tool:**
  - ○ SimilarWeb.com: Free third-party tool that I've found that is relatively accurate in measuring site visits.
  - ○ Awesome Screenshot: Free browser add-on for screen captures of an entire page, a selection, or just what you see on the screen.
  - ○ Cision or a similar tool for researching media and developing media lists.
  - ○ Brandwatch or a similar comprehensive social media monitoring tool. They provide great help with tracking crisis communications situations.

Corporate Communications

A Look at Crisis Communication and Media Relations

W hat happens when a city of more than 100,000 people is unexpectedly exposed to a well-documented health risk and, as a government official, you are being held responsible for the decisions that endangered the health and livelihood of these unsuspecting residents?

You hire two public relations agencies.

This scenario is not only real, it also highlights some of the decisions that Michigan Governor Rick Snyder faced when dealing with state-related economic short-falls. Imagine being the agency professionals fielding this call on what may have been an otherwise uneventful Thursday afternoon. Within minutes, your team would be running full tilt into the center of national media firestorm.

The majority of agency–client relationships do not begin during a crisis, but it is not uncommon for organizations, from small businesses to major corporations and government entities, to ask for help when the media spotlight shines in their direction.

A little historical framework for this particular scenario should be helpful. For more than a year, residents of Flint, Michigan, complained and publicly protested to draw attention to the poor quality of water provided to them by the local municipalities. Eventually, concern from around the nation took hold as celebrities, politicians, and even presidential candidates brought increased public awareness to the toxic tap water provided to the city.[1]

In the midst of a financial downturn and budget constraints, the state of Michigan, under the direction of Governor Snyder, elected to switch Flint's water supply from

Objectives

- Recognize the role corporate communication plays at an agency and within an organization.

- Illustrate how crisis communication is an integral part of the public relations planning process.

- Explain the importance of media relations and recognize how to cultivate strong relationships with journalists.

- Understand the evolution and changing role of media relations.

---

[1] McLaughlin, Eliott C. (2016, January 21). Flint's water crisis: 5 things to know. *CNN*. Retrieved December 12, 2017, from http://www.cnn.com/2016/01/18/us/flint-michigan-water-crisis-five-things/index.html

Michigan Governor Rick Snyder testifies before Congress in 2017 during the Flint Water crisis.

A Flint, Michigan, resident holding contaminated water during the scandal that left residents with no clean drinking water.

Lake Huron to the Flint River as a cost-saving measure. Following the April 2014 change, residents began complaining that their water looked, smelled, and tasted funny.[2]

One of the many challenges with this change was that the water now being supplied to Flint residents was highly corrosive. According to a class-action lawsuit, neither the local water authority nor the state Department of Environmental Quality (DEQ) treated the water for corrosion, in accordance with federal law.[3] The combination of older, lead-based pipes and the oversight of treating the water appropriately contributed to iron leaching into the water supply for the city's residents. By the time the city decided to revert back to water from Lake Huron, the damage was already done. What began as a cost-cutting measure quickly turned into a public health and public relations crisis. The state's slow, measured response only exacerbated the public outcry against the governor and the DEQ.

In response, Governor Snyder hired two PR firms to help his office deal with the Flint water contamination crisis: Mercury Public Affairs of Washington, D.C., and Finn Partners, a New York–based firm which also has offices in Detroit.[4] As you can imagine, news of the governor using

[2] Hanna, J., Wolf, Z. B., Castillo, M., Botelho, G., Tran, L., & Ganim, S. (2016, January 21). Flint's water crisis: 5 things to know. *CNN*. Retrieved February 1, 2016, from http://www.cnn.com/2016/01/18/us/flint-michigan-water-crisis-five-things/

[3] Smith, L. (2015, October 18). State admits Flint did not follow federal rules designed to keep lead out of water. *Michigan Radio*. Retrieved December 12, 2017, from http://michiganradio.org/post/state-admits-flint-did-not-follow-federal-rules-designed-keep-lead-out-water

[4] Oosting, J. (2016, January 22). Snyder hires two PR firms amid Flint crisis. *Detroit News*. Retrieved February 1, 2016, from http://www.detroitnews.com/story/news/politics/2016/01/22/snyder-hires-two-pr-firms-amid-flint-crisis/79201468/

public funds to hire multiple PR agencies was not well received. In fact, using Twitter, U.S. Representative Dan Kildee called out Governor Snyder directly.

Rep. Dan Kildee ● @RepDanKildee · 22 Jan 2016   ⌄
Governor Snyder, **the #FlintWaterCrisis is an ongoing public health emergency, not a public relations problem.**

> **Beth Fouhy** ● @bfouhy
> Gov. Snyder has retained PR firm Mercury to help manage #FlintWaterCrisis, per @tonydokoupil. "Lead in the water, Mercury in the politics"

💬 34   ↻ 332   ♡ 298

Representative Kildee was not the only individual taking to social media to point blame: Filmmaker Michael Moore, a native of Flint, Michigan, created a petition demanding Snyder be arrested for his actions, noting that the governor "effectively poisoned, not just some, but apparently ALL of the children in my hometown."[5] Democratic presidential candidates Hillary Clinton and Bernie Sanders each criticized Governor Snyder for his nonchalant attitude regarding the situation. Clinton accused the governor of not caring about the children of Flint, while Sanders called for the governor's resignation.[6] Snyder's office took to social media and tweeted back: "Political statements and finger pointing from political candidates only distract from solving the Flint water crisis."[7]

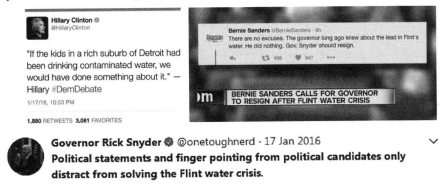

Governor Rick Snyder ● @onetoughnerd · 17 Jan 2016   ⌄
Political statements and finger pointing from political candidates only distract from solving the Flint water crisis.

💬 2.4K   ↻ 291   ♡ 300

[5] Moore, M. (2016, January 30). Michael Moore: 10 things they won't tell you about the Flint water tragedy, but I will. *EcoWatch*. Retrieved February 1, 2016, from http://ecowatch.com/2016/01/30/michael-moore-flint/

[6] Chambers, F. (2016, March 7). Fire him! Clinton and Sanders call for the head of Michigan Governor Rick Snyder as Hillary declares it is 'raining lead' in Flint during Dem debate—but he reminds voters they 'Won't be staying to solve the crisis . . . I will' in live-tweet defense. *Daily Mail Online*. Retrieved December 12, 2017, from http://www.dailymail.co.uk/news/article-3479780/Fire-Clinton-calls-GOP-governor-Michigan-resign-declares-raining-lead-Flint-Sanders-calls-water-crisis-disgrace.html

[7] Rosa, C. (2016, January 19). Cher, Michael Moore and more celebrities react to the Flint water crisis in Michigan. *VH1*. Retrieved February 1, 2016, from http://www.vh1.com/news/237610/flint-water-crisis-celebrity-reactions/

Even after hiring two PR agencies to help manage the crisis, Governor Snyder and his office continued to lay blame on the employees of the state DEQ, specifically for failing to require Flint to add corrosion control chemicals that may have prevented lead from leaching into the water supply.

Did the beleaguered governor hire the right agencies? One would want to look for specific skill sets when hiring an agency to take care of crisis communication efforts. The best agency–client relationship exists when the agency team's experience contributes to a greater understanding of the strategic challenges at hand. Expertise and specialization in certain tactics such as media relations, crisis communication, social media, or branding may also factor in. The agency's prior relationships with local media, production partners, and community leaders can also make a significant impact. In this case, the governor hired a firm specializing in timely crisis communication (Mercury) and an agency with a local Michigan footprint (Finn Partners).

As an agency professional, it is important to understand that you will sometimes be called upon under the most difficult circumstances, when mistakes have already been made. It is here, during the heat of these moments, that research and strategy play a critical role. Taking a long-term approach and providing clear-eyed, honest counsel to clients can improve the quality of support, resources, and information given to those most at risk during a crisis and help organizations and their stakeholders begin to rebuild trust—even when it must begin from the ground up.

The Role of Corporate Communication and Agency Partners

Let's consider why a governor would need to hire a PR agency during this situation. After all, most governors have a full staff of employees, and Snyder had an eight-member communication team in place.[8]

Corporate communication is a management function or department within most companies, similar to the marketing, finance, or operations departments. The corporate communication department works closely with company executives and key constituents to execute the corporate strategy and develop messaging for a variety of purposes both inside and outside of the organization.[9] *Corporate communication* can refer to internal and external communication for a variety of organizations.

Corporate communication was once nearly synonymous with *public relations* or *public affairs*. However, the corporate communication function has realized an increased level of importance in the 21st century as a result of better integration among marketing, advertising, PR, and social media teams. By overlapping functions, agencies have capitalized on the idea of having teams with expertise

[8] Official State of Michigan contact list. (2016, February 3). Retrieved from https://www.michigan.gov/documents/snyder/Phone_377483_7.pdf

[9] Cornelissen, J. (2014). *Corporate communication: A guide to theory and practice* (4th ed.). Los Angeles, CA: SAGE.

across multiple disciplines, providing value to organizations unable to keep up with the increasing complexity of communication strategies and tactics.

A corporate communication, PR, or organizational communication department is generally responsible for the oversight of communication strategy, media relations, crisis communications, **internal communications, employee relations, reputation management, corporate social responsibility (CSR)**, investor relations, government relations, and, at times, **marketing communication**.[10] However, instances will inherently arise when a company does not have the internal resources or specialized expertise to execute these tasks. This is the time when they call in an agency to assist. The Flint water crisis was far too large in scope for Governor Snyder's communication team to handle alone. Ultimately, the governor's office made the decision to bring in outside council.

When faced with a scenario wherein an organization does not have the resources to manage appropriately, it is important to know what type of support an agency can offer. Services that are most frequently desired from an outside agency include some or all of the following corporate communication functions:[11]

- Strategic and campaign planning
- Research
  ○ Market research
  ○ Message testing
  ○ Competitive analysis
  ○ Campaign measurement and evaluation
- Media relations
  ○ Proactive media strategy and outreach
  ○ Media list building and research
  ○ Crisis communication
- Events creation and execution
  ○ Corporate and/or media-focused events
  ○ Special events designed for public outreach
  ○ Oversight and management of event and trade show sponsorships
- Internal communication

---

[10] Chandra Guru, M., Sanjeevaraja, N., Gopala, N., & Parashivamurthy, M. (2013). *Corporate communication for organizational management: A perspective.* Retrieved December 12, 2017, from http://gifre.org/library/upload/volume/121-126-vol-2-4-13-gjcmp.pdf

[11] Wynne, R. (2013, April 10). What does a public relations agency do? *Forbes.* Retrieved January 11, 2016, from http://www.forbes.com/sites/robertwynne/2013/04/10/what-does-a-public-relations-agency-do/

- Speech writing

- Copy writing and blogging for the web (internal and/or external sites)

- Social media management, including positive and negative responses to opinions online

In this chapter, we will focus on two critical and overlapping areas of interest: crisis communication and media relations.

Crisis Communication

Trust is a fundamental requirement in any relationship and an important consideration when identifying an outside agency to represent your company or brand in any capacity. This is especially true when faced with the need to partner with an agency while in crisis mode, when media relationships become more important than ever. Every photo, quote, commentary, or misstep can be accessed on the social sphere forever.[12] Few can forget when former U. S. House Representative Anthony Weiner tweeted lewd photos of himself during a lengthy sexting scandal that ultimately ended with him losing his job,[13] or when BP chief executive officer (CEO) Tony Hayward, on the front lines of his company's battle to contain the massive Gulf of Mexico oil spill, commented to reporters that he wanted "[his] life back."[14]

Crisis communication is the dialogue between an organization and its public prior to, during, and after the negative incident, while **crisis management** is the process of strategic planning for a crisis or negative incident.[15] Effective crisis management includes crisis communication. While some agencies choose to specialize in crisis situations, all veteran agency practitioners have, at some point, sat across from clients and worked through the strategic details leading up to, during, and after a crisis.

Former Congressman Anthony Weiner pled guilty in Federal Court for sexting and was sentenced to 21 months in jail.

[12] Giancontieri, D. (2008). *Master media relations: The complete guide to getting better press coverage.* New York, NY: IUniverse.

[13] Resnick, G. (2014, February 19). Anthony Weiner, disgraced over sexting scandal, still tweeting. *The Daily Beast.* Retrieved January 23, 2016, from http://www.thedailybeast.com/articles/2014/02/19/anthony-weiner-disgraced-over-sexting-scandal-still-tweeting.html

[14] Bergin, T. (2010, June 2). BP CEO apologizes for thoughtless oil spill comment. *Reuters.* Retrieved January 23, 2016, from http://www.reuters.com/article/us-oil-spill-bp-apology-idUSTRE6515NQ20100602

[15] Fearn-Banks, K. (2008). *Crisis communications: A casebook approach.* New York, NY: Francis & Taylor.

01 Preparation
- Anticipate what risks business could face (Business Impact Analysis)
- Design, test & implement controls to address risks
- Identify constituents & most effective communication tools for each
- Prepare measures such as chain of command, asset inventories, contingent lines of credit, etc.
- Form response team of internal & external personnel; assign responsibilities
  - Identify crisis manager & spokesperson
    - Revisit & test plan to make adjustments & identify new risks & weaknesses

02 Response
- Assess situation & needs quickly
- Ensure team covers all bases, including preventing additional damage
- Assess public message against potential litigation & other risks; test
- Deploy necessary personnel
- Respond to media, identify constituents & retain crisis communications firm if necessary
- Identify regulatory restraints on action & manage government relations
- Identify additional measures needed
- Prevent crisis from lingering

03 Stabilization
- Perform legitimate inquiry or investigation
- Consider use of special board committee to conduct investigation
- Preserve attorney-client privilege
- Assure constituents
- Deal with wrongdoers, if any
- Monitor situation & response, assess whether additional measures are needed

04 Recovery
- Complete investigation & determine how to handle information
- Consider necessary personnel or structural changes; review composition on board & involvement
- Evaluate compensation & incentives
- Determine what ongoing monitoring or controls are needed
- Reconsider crisis management & business plans

This four-step process illustrates how PR professionals can mitigate damage during a time of crisis.

Source: © Sage Publishing, Inc.

Preparation is the most important phase of any crisis response plan. According to an International Association of Business Communicators (IABC) survey, only 67% of companies have a plan for what to do when a crisis hits.[16] Crisis planning services most frequently offered by an agency include the following:

- Risk assessments

- Crisis communication strategy development

- Crisis plans

- Crisis response manuals

---

[16] IABC survey: Only 67 percent of companies prepared for the next crisis. (2006, February 23). *IABC.* Retrieved February 1, 2016, from https://www.iabc.com/iabc-survey-only-67-percent-of-companies-prepared-for-the-next-crisis/

- Crisis management training and simulations

- Media training

- Message development (statements, press releases, articles, and more)

- Social media management and online reputation management

An agency's outside perspective can provide invaluable support when an organization needs additional expertise, time, and fortitude.

However, every misstep does not necessarily lead to a crisis and not every crisis ends in disaster. A crisis can be a time for "meaningful and positive change" that makes organizations and communities more resilient.[17] There are times when an organization can avoid or navigate a potential crisis by partnering with a communications agency to research audiences and better understand their needs. Watching for patterns in customer service complaints, seeing spikes in negative social media conversations, or monitoring public opinion around key issues can all contribute to organizations making informed decisions within and beyond the communication department. Subtle changes in action and messaging might be all that is required to avert a problem.

Media Relations

Many PR firms working in media relations leverage both media and audience research to identify proactive/reactive communication strategies in an effort to cultivate strong relationships with journalists. Successful agencies continue to refine, reassess, and reiterate messages to connect with journalists and their readers, viewers, and listeners. While media relations can oftentimes be at the center of a PR practitioner's expertise, it is only one strategic approach. The PESO model introduced by Gini Dietrich includes *paid* media, *earned* media, *shared* media, and *owned* media and should be considered alongside traditional media relations efforts.[18]

Although research/diagnosis, objectives, strategies, tactics, implementation, and reporting/evaluation (ROSTIR) ground all successful integrated PR campaigns, clients often only desire to see the results; they are often unaware of the delicate dance that happens between a PR professional and a reporter. Far too frequently, the PR professional is requested to deliver headlines on an expedited schedule rather than building a foundation that will provide long-term value. Fairly or unfairly, PR professionals are commonly measured by the number of media hits that they score for their clients. Agency practitioners should take the time to set clear, measurable, and reasonable objectives and expectations with clients using metrics that are more closely related to overall campaign value.

Press releases are another tool long associated with the day-to-day work of a PR agency professional. In today's information-driven environment, the press

---

[17] Sellnow, T. L., & Seeger, M. W. (2013). *Theorizing crisis communication.* Chichester, West Sussex: Wiley-Blackwell, p. 76.

[18] Dietrich, G. (2014). *Spin sucks: Communication and reputation management in the digital age.* Indianapolis, IN: Que Publishing.

release is becoming more of a formality and less of a source for media to publish news. A release may be a necessary component of executing a campaign and distributing a message, but it is often insufficient on its own to generate earned media coverage. If you wait for the next company press release to help secure that feature article for a client, you may be waiting a while.

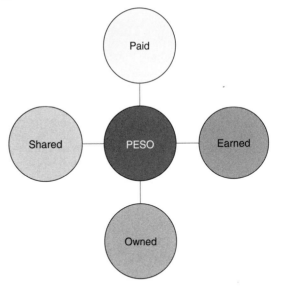

The majority of respected publications are not interested in regurgitating company news.[20] From a media perspective, reporters seek out *scoops* or first-reported stories that will garner more attention and recognition than their competition. Journalists research and write about newsworthy topics of genuine interest to their readers. They are interested in conveying how organizations are incorporating new technology, handling the latest trend, or tackling new challenges. If a reporter receives a press release, they assume that other media outlets have received it as well, thus diminishing its value.

PESO is a multi-channel communications model developed by Gini Dietrich. PESO incorporates paid media, earned media, shared media, and owned media.

---

[19] Newman, N. (2015). Executive summary and key findings of the 2015 report. *Digital News Report.* Retrieved January 23, 2016, from http://www.digitalnewsreport.org/survey/2015/executive-summary-and-key-findings-2015/

[20] Bobbitt, R., & Sullivan, R. (2009). *Developing the public relations campaign.* Boston, MA: Pearson, p. 119.

In order to establish a strong relationship with journalists, PR professionals should keep four areas in mind when looking to generate news for a client: industry trends and challenges, customer motivations, potential customer objections, and company strengths.[21] As a note, agency professionals commonly value individualized media pitches more than a mass distribution of press releases. A successful pitch occurs when the practitioner has a deep understanding of the client's content and can translate that information appropriately into the required media outlet's format, structure, and constraints. Practitioners should always prepare by researching the specific client and the broader industry, with the goal of understanding and communicating the client's specific value in the industry in a format that is valuable to the reporter/publication. Take the time to understand the reporter's needs, focus on the messaging, and clearly define the benefit and impact of the story that you are pitching.

Understand Reporter Needs

Every time that you sit to write a press release or pitch an idea to a reporter, ask yourself, "So what? Who cares? Why is this newsworthy?" While this exercise may seem trivial, many professionals do not ask these questions and end up sending subpar pitches as a result.[22] PR professionals should know what they are trying to convey before reaching out to reporters. Consider the following when drafting the message: *Why is this new or different? What makes our announcement important outside of our organization?* Newsworthiness is based on how, whether, and to what extent the story will affect a specific audience as well as being the best fit for that specific reporter or editor to cover.[23] A topic is not interesting simply because we, as PR professionals, say that it is. Not everything is newsworthy. For this reason, media outreach planning must identify the impact for the intended reporter and their audience.[24]

Focus on Messaging

Ask yourself: Who is the audience that the message of the press release is trying to reach? Is a certain industry, region, or demographic the target? Sending a blanket press release to every contact on your media list will most likely not provide you with the result that you had hoped, especially in the minute-to-minute news environment that we currently live in. It is critical that PR professionals focus and adapt their messages. Target your message to the publication and to the reporters of interest. Customization and personalization, when feasible, are the most effective ways to demonstrate your knowledge and build trust with media professionals.

---

[21] Moran, K. (2012). Getting ink. *Bulldog Reporter.* Retrieved January 25, 2016, from https://www.bulldogreporter.com/getting-ink/

[22] Luttrell, R. (2013, February 28). 5 questions to ask when writing news releases. *My PRSA Productions.* Retrieved December 12, 2017, from http://apps.prsa.org/Intelligence/Tactics/Articles/view/10097/1074/5_questions_to_ask_when_writing_news_releases

[23] Ibid.

[24] Ibid.

Outline the Benefit or Impact

Reporters are interested in knowing what their audience will gain from the information provided in the press release or pitch. Each time that a journalist receives information from PR practitioners, they want to know that it will benefit their readers, listeners, or viewers. Make sure that the press release or pitch addresses the needs of publications' audiences.

Capitalize on Trends

Identify industry trends and then hone in on how your client addresses these issues. Consider taking a national event/topic and brainstorm how your client can localize its impact for a reporter's audience. For example, a guest post on an influential industry blog or a bylined article regarding the topic might result from following the important trends in your client's industry. Such opportunities have the added benefit of increasing the volume of content and traffic to a media outlet's website without taking up the reporters' time. Not all outlets accept bylined content, but it is often worth investigating potential opportunities in both consumer and trade media outlets.

Ultimately, there isn't a formula for successful media relations planning. Understanding how news will impact your client, its stakeholders, and the media will go a long way toward helping connect them with their most important audiences and build public credibility.

Five Client Questions for Agency Practitioners

The opportunity to support an organizational media relations function should be an exciting and empowering experience. The right PR firm is knowledgeable about industry trends, understands the ins and outs of a client's products, and connects to media influencers.[25] Juliet Travis, founder and Principal of Travis Communications, notes that there are five questions every agency should be prepared to answer from a potential client:[26]

1. *How does the client think?* PR agencies should be a natural extension of their client. They should get inside their client's head and think through each stage of news-driven activity down to how to map the client's PR program back to their business and overall marketing goals. Be prepared for the client to expect the agency to understand their products and services, but also their company culture.

(Continued)

---

[25] Bobbitt, R., & Sullivan, R. (2009). *Developing the public relations campaign.* Boston, MA: Pearson, p. 97.

[26] Travis, J. (2016, January 21). Why hiring a PR firm is like finding that perfect pair of jeans. *Muck Rack.* Retrieved January 23, 2016, from http://muckrack.com/daily/2016/01/21/why-hiring-a-pr-firm-is-like-finding-that-perfect-pair-of-jeans/

(Continued)

2. *Do you have the latest tools and technology to support our business?* Public relations is about connecting strategy with overall goals. Today's practitioners are responsible for the integration of media relations, marketing, and social media following PESO strategies. Practitioners need to amplify their efforts using timely content marketing and industry-focused outreach. Clients want to know their agency has the ability to support their needs.

3. *How deep do your media connections run?* Agencies are known to have deep databases of media contacts supporting any move in a different direction or new market. This data also provides the ability to conduct additional research in order to uncover new contacts in various other markets.

4. *Is there excitement?* Chemistry matters. Agencies work with clients that are aligned with their area of expertise and vice versa. Clients will be an extension of the agency; when possible, choose clients with whom you get along well.

5. *Can we agree and disagree, but still work well together?* Good agencies will push their clients. They ask tough questions. They may disagree and challenge their clients, but ultimately, it is the job of the agency to understand why their client is doing what they are doing and to come up with strategic plans that direct them toward mutual success.

Reflect and Discuss

1. What is corporate communication and how does it play a role in agency life?

2. The chapter examined both crisis communication and crisis management. What are the differences between the two?

3. What has social media done to crisis situations?

4. What questions would you ask an agency if you were hiring them to handle your media relations? Would you ask them different questions if they were handling your crisis situation? If so, what questions would you ask?

5. Do you see yourself going into media relations or crisis communication? If so, what traits or skills must you possess or develop?

Joe Sloan

Joe Sloan, a young professional works as a managing director for 30 Miles North out of Santa Monica, California. The agency is a small, boutique PR firm specializing in a blend of digital and traditional public relations. They work on projects that include branding consultation and creative work as well as traditional public relations for the technology startup industry. Joe is responsible for business development, client account management, creative copy, pitching, and story development.

What advice do you have for students interested in public relations?

Put yourself out there. After graduation, I continued to do internships. I used my connections to get an internship in California. I uploaded my resume to the Silicon Valley Facebook page, then someone referred me to 30 Miles North, and before I knew it, I got the job. A lot of my success has been because of networking. Don't give up and don't be intimidated. Don't let intimidation or lack of self-confidence control your decisions.

What are the salary expectations for PR professionals?

Salary expectations vary from company to company (Joe works on a percentage of client retainer fees). When we get a client, I get 30% of the monthly retainers. Our typical retainers range from $4,000 to $7,000 a month, depending on what we do for the client. When accepting a job offer, factors come into play other than salary. I like my boss's attitude; I like our client focus, and the fact that I can wear flip flops and shorts in the office. I was willing to accept this retainer fee-based salary because of the other benefits that came with the job. If I didn't have the strong feeling that it was a great fit for me, I probably would have asked for an actual salary.

How would you describe life around the office?

Unpredictable. I generally have a to-do list for the week and within an hour into my workday, it completely changes, depending on what the client needs and whatever comes up. I look at what is going to benefit my client most in the short term and intersperse that with long-term development.

What are your media relationships like?

The majority of my job revolves around working with journalists. And I just love media relations. I will write an email specific to that journalist with a pitch about why they should write about my client and the product/service that has to do with my story idea. I will usually include a press release (not in an attachment) and follow up within a few days.

(Continued)

(Continued)

Top 5 Characteristics Every PR Professional Should Have

1. Phenomenal writing skills

2. Propensity to digest complex information and reiterate it for the everyday person

3. Aptitude to multitask

4. Perseverance

5. Confidence

Top Must-Haves

- I can't live without Google drive. The communication of documents between people is so much easier.

- The Google search bar is a helpful asset. I'm always conducting research, reading, or seeing what's trending.

- My email is always accessible on my phone.

CHAPTER 6

Social Media

A Comprehensive Look at What Companies Need

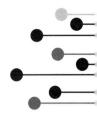

Organizational Social Media for Clients

Any organization that is actively building or sustaining a brand understands that they should be using social media to interact with their customers. But for those who are not, where should a company even begin? Snapchat, Twitter, Facebook, YouTube, LinkedIn, Pinterest, Instagram . . . the list of social platforms just keeps growing. Social media management can be overwhelming. It's no wonder that a recent American Express survey of small business owners revealed that *social media expert* was the most commonly listed position they were seeking to fill.[1] Companies reach out to agencies for assistance with social media for a variety of reasons: because they do not have the appropriate internal expertise, because they are faced with a crisis, because they are working on a specific project, or because they simply do not know where to begin.

In this chapter, we answer the recurring questions asked by organizations seeking to develop a social media strategy. According to Mike Bal, author of *Marketing Apocalypse: The Brand Survival Guide*, clients want to know:[2]

- What makes social content different from the other content that companies create, such as websites, brochures, or media alerts?

- What goes into developing a social content strategy?

Objectives

- Explain the different networks and channels that make up social media.

- Describe the function and usage of social media for organizations.

- Understand that an influential social media strategy must deliver a compelling message.

- Anticipate some of the challenges and opportunities for agencies engaging in social media outreach and community building for their clients.

---

[1] Vanderkam, L. (2014, August 6). Should you outsource your social media? *Fast Company*. Retrieved January 10, 2016, from http://www.fastcompany.com/3033989/the-*future*-of-work/should-you-outsource-your-social-media

[2] Bal, M. (2014, December 26). How to design a social content strategy that converts. *The Daily Egg*. Retrieved January 9, 2016, from http://blog.crazyegg.com/2014/12/26/social-content-strategy/

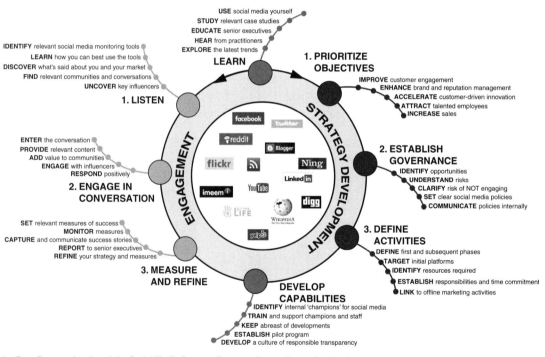

Ross Dawson developed the Social Media Strategy Framework to guide professionals through developing effective social media campaigns.

Source: Reprinted from Dawson, R. (2009). Social Media Strategy Framework [Digital image]. Retrieved March 9, 2018, from https://rossdawson.com/frameworks/social-media-strategy/.

---

[3] Wong, D. (2014, January 29). 11 critical content creation tips. *HuffPost.* Retrieved December 14, 2017, from https://www.huffingtonpost.com/danny-wong/11-critical-content-creat_b_4681265.html

- What tools are needed to be successful?

- How does social strategy evolve through monitoring, evaluation, and research?

Running social media for an organization is very different than managing personal channels. While they may share the goals of a distinct, consistent voice; compelling content; growth in followers and engagement; and participation in real conversations with other users, the path to these ends is very different. Organizations need significant planning and structure to create and maintain a strong social media presence. They need teams of people (often both internally and externally at agencies) balancing the strategic planning, idea generation, content creation, and approval as well as daily posting, monitoring, and responding. The complexities grow when multiple social media channels are added to the mix.

Although many companies hire recent college graduates to bolster their social media teams, fluency in the language of Instagram and Snapchat does not necessarily translate to a successful career managing social media for organizations. To get there, agency practitioners must bring strategic perspective and a desire to stay ahead of the fast-moving nature of social channels and networks. They should cultivate the ability to write exquisitely, to research thoroughly, to understand the approach behind sound decision making, and to nurture the unique relationships of individuals and brands built through social media.

©iStockphoto.com/laflor

Content Creation and Curation

Content is the currency of the modern social sphere. Companies use content to earn trust, gain attention, increase engagement, and garner a variety of actions from users around the world.[4] Organizations accomplish this by generating original content as well as curating content: finding, repackaging, and distributing content created by others. Creating and sharing social content engages fans and customers. Companies should recognize that the primary goal is to develop stronger relationships between an engaged audience and a brand.

In PR, brainstorming brings people together to share ideas, creatively solve problems, and join forces to work toward client goals.

---

[4] Bal, M. (2014, December 26). How to design a social content strategy that converts. *The Daily Egg*. Retrieved January 9, 2016, from http://blog.crazyegg.com/2014/12/26/social-content-strategy/

Content is everywhere on the social sphere and forces organizations to think and act as publishers rather than as marketers or advertisers. This change in dynamic often leaves leadership frustrated. Companies are accustomed to selling products and maximizing advertising and marketing efforts; after all, it is about the bottom line, right? Developing content that your intended audience is interested in reading, watching, or listening to is drastically different from producing content that you, the company, would like people to read.[5] It's a different way of thinking, and some C-suite executives are moving to support it. Agency professionals contribute by using their outside perspective to recommend content strategies and tactics reflective of both audience preferences and organizational needs.

Your content is anything that your target audience, clients, and customers see online when they are researching and interacting with your brand. This can be simple text, such as videos, images, **memes**, blog posts, or **GIF**s, or as intricate and detailed as **infographics**, e-books, and white papers. To capture attention, it is critical that your content provides value to social media fans and followers.[6] This applies equally to original and curated content. Content can be customized and shared across numerous social media platforms, so defining the channel-specific audience and purpose of the message is crucial. A reasonable question to ask prior to content development may be this: *What does the organization want the content to do?*[7] Develop and link **key performance indicators (KPIs)** for individualized content tracking during implementation.

According to Doreen Olson, owner of Social Imagineering, much of the content that companies will either create or curate for social media profiles will be classified in one of three categories: goodwill, audience centered, or call to action.[8]

Goodwill

Goodwill arises when companies curate and share thoughts and ideas from other profiles, businesses, or industry influencers. This process also helps strengthen industry relations. Content sharing is contagious, and camaraderie is built between organizations when information is disbursed. Readers appreciate when a business shares content other than their own. Social Media Examiner contributor Jamie Beckland wrote that "when you reference someone else's content, you'll credit them, driving traffic back to the original source material. Promoting other people's great work is the best way to make the people you respect into your newest fans." Peer advice,

---

[5] Ibid.

[6] Ibid.

[7] Brown, R., Waddington, S., & Wilson, R. (2013). *Share this too: More social media solutions for PR professionals.* Hoboken, NJ: John Wiley & Sons.

[8] Olson, D. (2016). Social media archives—social imagineering. *Social Imagineering.* Retrieved January 10, 2016, from http://www.socialimagineering.com/category/social-media/

affinity networks, circles of trust, consistency, and strategic advocacy are crucial when spreading goodwill and establishing formidable, trusted relationships.[9]

Audience Centered

Natural and meaningful conversations conducted within the social sphere should reflect conversations in real life. Over time in our non-virtual lives, relationships develop and trust is earned. A similar occurrence happens on the web. When we listen to what others are talking about, we build and deepen connections with them—the same principles should apply to online relations.[10] When brands adopt a likable, friendly rapport with an audience, a trusting, two-way relationship begins. Every company needs likeable content in order to engage the audiences that they would like to get to know most. Richard Sedley, author of *Winners and Losers in a Troubled Economy: How to Engage Customers Online to Gain Competitive Advantage*, defines the purpose of this interaction between a business and its customer: "Strengthen the emotional, psychological or physical investment a customer has in a brand."[11] Likeable social media content draws from a clear organizational voice while anticipating and responding to an audience's expectations, needs, and desires. It is relevant to broader news and conversations of interest to followers and should be engaging and valuable for them.

Call to Action (CTA)

Call-to-action (CTA) messages are a critical component of digital content that an organization can create and post on social media profiles. CTAs are targeted phrases that encourage an audience to act.[12] They may include downloading a white paper, following the company on Twitter, registering for a webinar, signing up for an e-news blast, or sharing company content with a friend or colleague. By developing and incorporating CTAs, the audience has the opportunity to further engage with the organization. When consumers are given the option of learning more, signing up, or sharing with others, they often do so. For example, at the end of a blog post, you might consider including a CTA that directs readers to download a case study. An example might look like this: *For more ideas, examples, and case studies exploring the ups and downs of event planning, download Michelle Weaver's*

---

[9] De Clerck, J-P. (2014). Developing a content strategy for customer engagement. *ISCOOP*. Retrieved January 11, 2016, http://www.i-scoop.eu/content-strategy-customer-engagement/

[10] Brown, R., Waddington, S., & Birch, D. (2013). *Share this too: More social media solutions for PR professionals.* Hoboken, NJ: John Wiley & Sons.

[11] Perks, M., & Sedley, R. (2008). *Winners and losers in a troubled economy: How to engage customers online to gain competitive advantage.* London, UK: CScape.

[12] Deshpande, P. (2013, July 17). 5 tips every content curator needs to write better calls-to-action. *Content Marketing Institute*. Retrieved November 5, 2017, from http://contentmarketinginstitute.com/2013/07/tips-content-curator-write-better-calls-to-action/

Event Planning Essentials. To make your company's CTAs as effective as possible, identify the objective as, for example, downloading an e-book or template, sharing a post, or registering for an event. CTAs should be short and actionable.

While they are important, CTAs generally represent a small percentage of content. Much like a friend who only asks for favors—and never seems to worry about what you need—brands should include CTAs thoughtfully alongside the other two content types. Therefore, most content does not include a CTA, but when it does, it should be strategic and purposeful. The correct balance is different for every brand. Consider the following useful tips from authors Rob Brown, Stephen Waddington, and Robin Wilson of *Share This Too: More Social Media Solutions for PR Professionals* to strike the appropriate mix when developing content:[13]

- **Be remarkable:** Attempt to produce content that is compelling and targeted toward your audience but also contributes to company objectives.

- **Be valuable:** Think about the audience and what they will find useful. Get out of the habit of simply posting what the company wants to post.

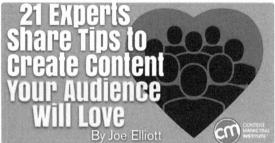

Aaron Orendorff @ @iconiContent · 4 May 2017
Writing #content is only **20% of the job; the** other **80% is** promotion, says @TaliaGw. buff.ly/2p1gvwc via @CMIContent

Create Content Audiences Will Love: 21 Experts Share Tips
21 content marketers share their best tip to create content their audience will love – Content Marketing Institute
contentmarketinginstitute.com

💬   ↻ 6   ♡ 13

- **Build trust:** Foster relationships by treating your audience as human beings. This includes acting with transparency (such as agency practitioners disclosing when they are sharing client content through personal channels) and with a genuine desire to build mutually beneficial relationships with audiences.

- **Talk with consumers, not at them:** Respond to interactions on your social channels and let your customers know you are listening and are interested in engaging with them. The organic nature of social media rewards content of real value and interest to audiences and buries messages that are narrowly about an organization.

- **Avoid the hard sell:** We all work with the boundaries of business objectives and return on investment (ROI) demands, but no potential

> Content creation is about balancing organizational messages and audience engagement. PR professionals should cross-pomote social media content among multiple channels.

---

[13] Becklan, J. (2011, April 1). How to grow a following with other people's popular content. *Social Media Examiner.* Retrieved August 17, 2017, from http://www.socialmediaexaminer.com/content-curation/

customer wants "BUY NOW!!" messages filtering through their social feeds. This is a turn-off and customers will go elsewhere.

Many of the standard planning practices apply for agency professionals building social media content strategy for a client. Consider overarching organizational goals, what your customers care about, and how your brand wants to interact with the audience online. Developing a strategy that integrates these key elements will go a long way in cultivating rewarding relationships. Combining strategic planning with an agency's perspective connects social media outreach with a core objective: multiplying and improving relationships with stakeholders.

Building the Right Relationships

Organic Social Media Versus Paid Social Media

In the early days of social media development, networks were purely organic. If an organization wanted consumers to interact with content, they only needed the content to be interesting, informative, or newsworthy. Today, most social networks contain some degree of sponsored content that allow organizations to advertise to additional social media users.[14] Most organizations can benefit from utilizing a mix of boosted, paid, and organic content, depending on the message, time line, and objectives.

Organic social media maintains customer loyalty, resolves customer issues, and provides a connection between a brand and its followers. According to Krista Neher, organic social media assumes that you have to earn your way into the newsfeed using great content that will resonate with a target audience.[15] Most organic social media posts stay away from directly selling products or services, as touting an organization's goods rarely drives engagement. The premise of organic social media content is permission based, meaning that your social posts must be good enough for people to opt in and want to hear more.

When handled well, organic social media permits brands to recruit ambassadors and cheerleaders, also known as influencers, who have the ability to reach more people and add more credibility than with paid efforts. Organic content continues to play a significant role in social media, but paid strategies are seen as a way to maximize a company's content reach while at the same time generating actions that lead to revenue. A variety of options for paid social media provide a growing array of selections for organizations to target their efforts and expand their followers.

---

[14] Comcowich, W. (n.d.). Paid, organic and sponsored: The social media marketing trifecta. *CyberAlert Blog*. Retrieved January 12, 2016, from http://www.cyberalert.com/blog/index.php/paid-organic-and-sponsored-the-social-media-marketing-trifecta/

[15] Neher, K. (2014, October 27). The future of social media: Paid vs. organic. *ClickZ*. Retrieved November 5, 2017, from https://www.clickz.com/clickz/column/2377715/the-future-of-social-media-paid-vs-organic

The main objectives governing paid social media reside with the creation of posts that both grab attention and stand out in the cluttered social media landscape but, more importantly, also build a company's brand.[16] According to Ryan Schram, chief operating officer of IZEA,

> whether a company calls it "paid social," "native advertising," "content marketing," "influencer marketing," or "sponsored posts," the paid social media category has redefined what digital word-of-mouth—sometimes called "word of mouse"—can be for public relations practitioners and their clients. Consumers are not only forming business relationships with the brands they love, but they are also creating and sharing brand-sponsored content with their personal social following. The ramifications of this trend are astonishing, and highly transformative, to the over-arching landscape.[17]

According to research conducted by The Halverson Group and The Right Brain Consumer Consulting, paid social media continues to demonstrate its value within the social sphere and among influencers. Their findings note that 52% of companies now have a stand-alone sponsored social media budget for their brand and find sponsored social media as one of the top three most effective marketing investments that they make.[18]

The Evolution of a Company's Social Media Strategy

In today's cutthroat corporate environment, the success or failure of any organization's social strategy hinges on the strength of the strategy itself. A company cannot create content without a plan, but the plan must also be revisited and revised regularly. Social strategies are malleable and evolve over time. The fact is, new social channels pop up frequently. As a result, so do new approaches to reach key company stakeholders, investors, consumers, employees, and members of the community.[19]

---

[16] Neher, K. (2014, October 27). The future of social media: Paid vs. organic. *ClickZ*. Retrieved December 14, 2017, from https://www.clickz.com/the-future-of-social-media-paid-vs-organic/29078/

[17] Schram, R. Personal communication, November 15, 2015.

[18] Murphy, T. (2015, November 15). *The 6th annual "state of sponsored social" report shows sponsored social posts as effective as TV commercials.* Retrieved November 5, 2017, from https://www.slideshare.net/tedmurphy1/2015-state-of-sponsored-social-54686207

[19] Matthews, L. (2010). Social media and the evolution of corporate communications. *The Elon Journal of Undergraduate Research in Communications, 1.* Available at http://www.elon.edu/docs/e-web/academics/communications/research/02matthewsejspring10.pdf

SOCIAL MEDIA AUDIT

SITE	LINK	PROFILE NAME	FOLLOWERS	DATE OF LAST ACTIVITY	FREQUENCY OF POSTS	MONTHLY REFERRAL TRAFFIC	% OF CHANGE (LAST YEAR)	% OF CHANGE (LAST MONTH)	CLICKS PER POST	CLICKS PER POST (LAST MONTH)	CLICKS PER POST CHANGE	FACEBOOK REACH	% OF CHANGE (LAST WEEK)	FOLLOWERS (TODAY)	FOLLOWERS (LAST MONTH)	FOLLOWERS CHANGE
FACEBOOK												0				0
INSTAGRAM												0				0
TWITTER												0				0
LINKED-IN												0				0
GOOGLE+												0				0
SNAPCHAT												0				0
PINTEREST												0				0
TUMBLR												0				0
YOUTUBE												0				0
OTHER												0				0
OTHER												0				0

Social media audits should be conducted to assess which platforms are working and where an organization can improve. Tables can help to quickly organize and present the results of an audit, as well as to track ongoing progress.

An early step in building an organizational social strategy is identifying the correct channel or channels. Companies must pick and choose the social media platforms that best match their audience, their content, and their communication goals. As internal and agency teams always have limited time, they must balance the needs of channel monitoring, content creation, content distribution, and organic engagement and participation. Successful agency practitioners focus on the channel(s) they can execute effectively rather than attempting to build a presence everywhere. Organizations should only take on the project of creating a presence on a specific channel if they have the resources and time to maintain it. In addition to guiding these decisions, a significant part of an agency practitioner's role is to stay informed about and engaged with emerging social media platforms. Through this work, they can constantly evaluate and reevaluate whether specific platforms add value for individual clients and their audiences.

A social media strategy presents businesses with the opportunity to earn trust, showcase expertise, and meet potential customers.[20] When businesses lack a clear social media strategy, they struggle to garner the desired customer engagement levels, insights, and conversions that they are looking for. Every comprehensive social media strategy needs to include the following:[21]

1. an audit of the existing social media presence

2. specific, measurable, achievable, realistic, and time-bound (SMART) social media objectives

3. development of a content creation strategy, calendar, and process

4. ongoing measurement and refinement research

5. proper review and adjustment of the overarching strategy

---

[20] Create Social Media Strategy. (n.d.). *Hootsuite*. Retrieved January 15, 2016, from http://socialbusiness.hootsuite.com/rs/hootsuitemediainc/images/Social-Media-Strategy-Guide.pdf

[21] Ibid.

Only after an organization identifies the topics that will resonate with their audience and support their objectives can they begin to adjust their social media strategy accordingly. Tweaking a social media strategy should be a continuous process that clients frequently request of their agency partners. Evaluation happens through the execution of a social media campaign. As is often the case, agencies will leverage analytics and feedback to guide their clients through these updates.

Reflect and Discuss

1. Discuss the differences between *content creation* and *content curation*.

2. What are the three areas in which most practitioners will curate content?

3. Every comprehensive social media strategy should include which elements?

4. The chapter outlined methods for creating strategic and purposeful content. What were they and why were they so important?

5. If you were hired at an agency to run the social media for clients, how would you organize yourself? What did you learn from this chapter that would assist you in becoming an exemplar social strategist?

Darryl Villacorta

Darryl Villacorta is the social media manager at Sprout Social. He has a background in digital media and loves all things related to tech, social media, and video. Outside of the office, his favorite things include acting, songwriting, and writing teleplays. Sprout Social is a platform for social media analytics and a software tool used by many public relations agencies; it is tasked with offering social media engagement, advocacy, and analytic solutions for leading agencies and brands, including Hyatt, Uber, Zendesk, Microsoft, and Zipcar. Sprout's social media engagement platform enables brands to more effectively communicate on social channels, collaborate across teams, and provide an exceptional customer experience. Bambu by Sprout Social, a platform for advocacy, empowers employees to share curated content across their social networks to further amplify a brand's reach and engagement.

In the article, "Complete Checklist for Social Media Managers," originally written for *AdWeek*, Darryl suggests breaking down the management and curation of social media by developing daily, weekly, monthly, and quarterly strategies:[22]

Daily

- Respond to inbound social messages.
- Monitor and respond to brand mentions.
- Create conversations with brand advocates.
- Find and engage with potential customers.
- Research the social media industry.
- Preload your social editorial calendar.
- Post three to six times on Twitter.
- Post one to two times on Facebook.
- Post one to three times to Instagram.
- Post one to two times to LinkedIn.
- Study your products and services.
- Monitor the competition.
- Work on a personal blog post.

Weekly

- Engage with thought leaders.
- Engage with marketing partners.
- Discuss tactics with your team.
- Run your social media analytics.
- Encourage sharing through employee advocacy.

Monthly

- Audit your strategy.
- Attend local events.
- Detox from social media.
- Collaborate with other departments.

Quarterly

- Assess key performance indicators.
- Adjust quarterly goals.
- Gauge team needs.

Having had the opportunity to interview Darryl further, he also offered these insights:

Imagine you are student right out of college and you've just landed yourself a great job in the social industry. What should you expect? How should you prepare?

Expect to hit the ground running right from the start. Responsibilities will vary by role, but the one constant across the board is the organization's trust in your social knowledge and expertise. Set guidelines and educate your cohorts that trial and error is part of the job. Another way to prepare is to learn to say "no." Individuals can maximize their efforts (and keep their sanity) by working smarter, not harder. Lastly, keep the lines of communication

(Continued)

---

[22] Villacorta, D. (2015, July 1). A complete checklist for social media managers. [Infographic.] *Adweek.* Retrieved August 17, 2017, from http://www.adweek.com/digital/a-complete-checklist-for-social-media-managers-infographic/

(Continued)

open. Social media within an organization shouldn't live in its own silo.

What goes into strategic social media campaigns?

A lot of planning! Before starting any campaign, it is essential to identify specific goals and target audiences. Also, prepare for the unexpected with ample resources before, during, and after any campaigns—it's better to be safe than sorry!

What is the best and most effective way to manage and curate social media?

Have a streamlined workflow that can be scalable. There isn't a right or wrong way to manage and curate content for social media consumption; however, the process should be able to be replicated by others in a manner that is streamlined to generate maximum efficiency.

What is your opinion on organic social media versus paid social media? Pros/cons? Why should a company care about both/either/neither?

I've said this before and I'll forever keep saying it: social media has never been free. You may own your time and content, but you're working on rented land. Simply relying on organic methods can only take you so far. If you're a serious marketer, you need to ask yourself which social networks provide the most benefit to your brand.

Any final thoughts to share?

This can be applicable to any industry: "Never stop learning."

Top 5 Characteristics Every PR Professional Should Have

1. Great improvisational skills
2. Close attention to the details
3. Up to date with current social trends/pop culture
4. Great time-management skills
5. Sociable online and offline

Top Must-Haves

- **Must-download app:** Feedly! It's a great app for staying up to date with news from all industries. Also, it is customizable and integrates with many social media management tools.
- **Must-read book/blog/news outlet:**
  - **Book:** *No Bullshit Social Media* (Erik Deckers & Jason Falls)
  - **Blog:** Sprout Social Insights, Social Media Examiner, The Next Web, TechCrunch, SocialTimes
  - **Media:** Entrepreneur, Inc.
- **Must-use tool:** Sprout Social—I'm obviously biased.

CHAPTER 7

Marketing

Marketing in a Public Relations Agency

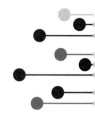

What happens when public relations and marketing work together? Well, they can accomplish a lot. By focusing on larger concepts, events, powerful visuals, solid research, insights, and outreach, today's campaigns can generate results that drive marketing. Marketing and PR tactics can complement each other in achieving organizational and communication goals and objectives.

For example, British Airways offers more direct flights to the United Kingdom from the U.S. west coast than any of its competitors, yet research indicates that British Airways is perceived as out of touch with Silicon Valley's entrepreneurial spirit. In an effort to combat this image, the company launched a campaign dubbed "UnGrounded," centered on innovation. According to Simon-Talling Smith, executive vice president of American–British Airways, the strategy was simple: Do what British Airways does best—connect people, communities, and ideas.[1] Working with Ogily, American–British Airways set out to help solve problems facing businesses worldwide, the airline invited more than 100 technologists, company founders, academic leaders, and entrepreneurs to an "innovation lab"–style hackathon flight scheduled to fly from San Francisco to London.[2] Upon landing in London, the UnGrounded flight team presented their findings to the United Nations–sponsored Decide Now Act (DNA) Summit and the Secretary General of the United Nations International Telecommunications Union.[3]

Objectives

- Explain the roles public relations and marketing play within an agency setting.

- Describe how public relations and marketing are interrelated and how they can work together.

- Explain the primary objectives of public relations and marketing.

- Apply marketing and public relations tactics to a strategic communication plan.

---

[1] Meza, S. (2014, March). WELOVEAD. *British Airways*. Retrieved August 3, 2016. http://www.welovead.com/en/works/details/b5cweutAi

[2] Meza, S. (2014, March). Ungrounded: An innovation lab in the sky. [video]. *British Airways*. Retrieved August 3, 2016, from http://www.welovead.com/en/works/details/b5cweutAi

[3] Shapiro, T. (2014, August 16). 5 crazy brilliant PR campaigns. *Stratabeat*. Retrieved August 3, 2016, from https://stratabeat.com/5-crazy-brilliant-pr-campaigns/

The combined effort was publicized and maintained via a multifaceted campaign that included the following elements:[4]

- launch event with influencers from the technology and innovation arenas

- a delegate selection process, in which the UnGrounded board selected the appropriate innovators to participate on the "flying innovation lab," which included the founders of GoogleX and Craigslist

- a Mashable contest, whereby readers could win a seat on the flight

- Google hangouts with influencers and British Airways senior representation

- a kickoff press conference with the governor of California, dubbed "Virgin Airlines, Eat Your Heart Out"

- journalists from outlets such as *Wired* and *TechCrunch*

- presentations at the United Nation's G8 Summit

As a result, this campaign increased premium business departing from the San Francisco International Airport by 20% year over year. What's more, revenue from small and midsize businesses increased 10% while twenty-six concepts and four winning ideas were realized from the hackathon. More than ninety unique articles were published in top-tier media outlets about British Airway's UnGrounded inventive flight, thanks to coordination with media relations teams. This is an excellent example of how efforts between two adjacent functions—public relations and marketing—can complement one another. Through integrated marketing approaches, PR practitioners can amplify media relations and social media efforts as well as engage with new audiences. Marketing tactics often prove effective in areas where traditional PR and media relations efforts tend to fall short, such as programs with tight deadlines and timing challenges, or messages that are too sales-focused for earned media coverage.

Transcending the Public Relations and Marketing Divide

Public relations and marketing are increasingly working together. In fact, many agencies today try to emphasize the similarities and interconnections between public relations and marketing, often strengthening the role and impact of public relations.[5] However, this has not always been the case.

[4] Meza, S. (2014, March). WELOVEAD. *British Airways.* Retrieved August 3, 2016. http://www.welovead.com/en/works/details/b5cweutAi

[5] Smith, B. G., & Place, K. R. (2013). Integrating power? Evaluating public relations influence in an integrated communication structure. *Journal of Public Relations Research, 25,* 168–187.

Economic, political, and social uncertainty and upheaval during the 1970s and 1980s brought about vast changes within our industry.[6] During this time, many PR and advertising agencies merged, with the ad agencies often taking the lead, resulting in a distinct divide between agencies exclusively practicing public relations, public relations/advertising firms, and marketing specialties. Ultimately, the PR sector continues to grow because consumers, as well as agencies, took notice of the strengths that public relations presented.[7] By the 1990s, digital technology began to connect the world as never before. Communication became even more important; however, the gulf between public relations and marketing grew. The two sides often argued about which discipline was more influential, which contributed more to their

Table 7.1 Perspectives of PR & Marketing		
	PR	**Marketing**
Primary Purpose	Relationship building with publics	Increase product/ service demand
Tactics (Priority order)	- Earned media - Owned media - Shared media - Paid media	- Paid media - Owned media - Shared media - Earned media
Cost	Primarily earned/shared (lower cost)	Primarily paid/owned (higher cost)
Audience Definition	External & internal: Publics	External: Target market
Media Types	Primarily uncontrolled	Primarily controlled
Scope	Broad: Organizational interests, reputation, engagement with society	Narrow: Product- and sales-driven approach aimed at target audiences

organization's overarching goals, and which department should receive more internal resources, funding, and strategic influence. As public relations and marketing evolved, the two entities began to experiment with new strategies to expand their communication activities and target specific audiences. Even though their work appeared similar to someone not familiar with the activities associated with public relations or marketing, practitioners knew that the two disciplines were conceptually very different.[8] Ray Simon, of The Raymond Simon Institute for Public Relations, noted in his book, *Public Relations: Concepts and Practice,* the differences between public relations and marketing: "Both are major external functions of the firm and both share a common ground in regard to product publicity and consumer relations. At the same time, however, they operate on different levels and from different perspectives and perceptions."[9] Public relations is often associated with building relationships between internal and external publics in order to gain trust and acceptance of the organization's activities, while marketing generated sales of goods and services and directly contributed to the company's bottom-line profits.

[6] Newsom, D., VanSlyke Turk, J., & Kruckeberg, D. (2007). *This is PR: The realities of public relations* (9th ed.). Belmont, CA: Thomson Wadsworth.

[7] Ries, A., & Ries, L. (2002). *The fall of advertising and the rise of PR.* New York, NY: HarperBusiness.

[8] Tourney, M. (2016). *Welcome to practicing public relations.* Retrieved July 5, 2016, from http://www.practicing publicrelations.com/

[9] Simon, R. (1980). *Public relations: Concepts and practices.* Columbus, OH: Grid.

The overarching purpose of public relations is to build relationships with stakeholders by observing and listening to customers, interpreting emotional responses and conversations, and creating meaningful content or experiences from these findings. In contrast, marketing is tasked with gathering and analyzing customer data based on concentrated marketing-related efforts and then to make conclusive decisions as a result.[10] Both marketing and public relations should be constantly aware of and responsive to their publics. PR and marketing efforts are cyclical and intertwined. PR professionals understand how to create and place content that communicates core messages without reading like advertising copy, while marketing professionals excel at developing content designed to sell.[11] Marketing measures its success in sales, while public relations measures its achievements in relationships and reputation. By working together, both teams have better stories to share that resonate with targeted audiences.

Historically, in many organizations, public relations and marketing have been separate. The PR teams work to build community relationships, direct internal and external communication strategies, manage crises if they arise, and secure media coverage, while marketing works to drive revenue through sales and point of purchase initiatives. Today, more agencies have recognized the benefits of integrating these areas of expertise and are staying one step ahead by continually combining the efforts of PR and marketing professionals in order to deliver the best strategy for their clients. USC Annenberg's 2017 Global Communications Report predicts convergence of marketing and public relations. In fact,

> almost half of PR professionals and more than 60% of marketing executives believe that their two disciplines will become more closely aligned in the next five years. Some think PR will dominate. Others think it will be dominated. Perhaps the reality is somewhere in between.[12]

It should be clear that public relations and marketing must work together to be as complimentary and efficient as possible. These teams should always look to sit together at the strategy table.[13] Together, the two can unlock useful insights and develop successful communication strategy by working together.

---

[10] Iliff, R. (2014, September 25). How marketing and PR should work together to reach customers. *Mashable*. Retrieved July 13, 2016, from http://mashable.com/2014/09/25/marketing-pr-art-science/#T2SmyAV61SqB

[11] Lustig, B. (2014, October 15). 5 reasons CMOs need their PR team for content marketing plans. *Bluetext*. Retrieved July 13, 2016, from http://www.bluetext.com/cmo-pr/

[12] Annenberg, USC. (2017). *Global communications report 2017*. USC Annenberg School for Communication and Journalism, University of Southern California. Retrieved November 6, 2017, from http://annenberg.usc.edu/sites/default/files/KOS_2017_GCR_Final.pdf

[13] Spurlin, R. (2017, August 3). Convergence: The intersection of marketing and PR. *PR Daily News: Public Relations News and Marketing in the Age of Social Media*. Retrieved July 13, 2016, from http://www.prdaily.com/Main/Articles/21048.aspx

Two Is Better Than One

As the fields of public relations and marketing continued to expand their scope and range of activities, as well as adopt communication techniques that had previously been considered the expertise of the other discipline, lines between the two functions have blurred. With this convergence of PR and marketing services, agencies have unlocked solutions that make strategic efforts more efficient and effective for both the agency and for the client.

Gini Dietrich's PESO Model in Action

Agencies need to be more than a liaison with the media. Unfortunately, many agencies are plagued with the reputation that media relations are all they know how to do. Nowadays, they need to be brand ambassadors, content creators/curators, listeners, managers, and strategic partners. When planning, it should become common practice that PR tactics can support marketing activities. Earned media is most often associated with public relations, while paid media aligns with marketing. If planned and executed correctly, neither the client nor the customer should be able to identify exactly where one strategy begins and the other ends. PR and marketing efforts should align with integrated communication supporting the organization's higher purpose. While this may sound challenging, clients appreciate the success when this has been accomplished. The **PESO model** (paid media, earned media, shared

---

Five Key Questions in Strategic Communication Planning[14]

1. What does your organization hope to accomplish?

2. Who is your target audience or demographic and what motivates them to use your product/services?

3. What are your human and financial resources?

4. Is your current PR and marketing mix delivering results?

5. What qualifies as success?

---

[14] Guthrie, M. (2010). 10 questions to ask as you build your marketing plan. *Beneath the brand.* Retrieved December 17, 2017, from http://www.talentzoo.com/beneath-the-brand/news/10-Questions-to-Ask-as-You-Build-Your-Marketing-Plan/14959.html

media, and owned media) is one example of an approach that helps practitioners from both sides integrate a suite of strategies and tactics that fit the situation, instead of sticking to the artificial barriers between PR and marketing departments.

Earned Media

From a marketing perspective, media relations efforts can be seen as raising awareness, improving credibility, and strengthening customer (and potential customer) relationships. Earned media has wide distribution that pulls customers into your media channels. Customer engagement reaches its peak when earned media appeals to your prospective and current customers and transitions them into brand advocates and influencers. This can also be considered a return of classic word-of-mouth marketing, but with a modern twist. Media relations successes can be shared through social media and other channels to reinforce their impact with key audiences. For example, customer reviews on sites such as Yelp can be considered a form of earned media. In this way, earned media works more effectively when paired with other strategies. Earned media and marketing tactics to promote it should become a component of a client's integrated communication ecosystem.

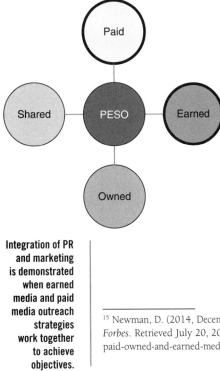

Paid Media

Paid media, in its simplest form, is essentially publicity gained through paid channels such as advertising. Companies spend money with media outlets, search engines, and other services to promote their business, product, or service. In addition to traditional advertisements on radio and TV, in print, or on billboards and other displays, digital advertising has grown to include Google AdWords; Facebook, Twitter, and Pinterest ads; search engine marketing (SEM); and pay per click (PPC).[15] While a thoughtful media plan for purchasing and executing paid media strategies is important, it also needs to include compelling messaging to be effective. As we discussed earlier in the text, calls to action driven largely by customer benefits.

Integration of PR and marketing is demonstrated when earned media and paid media outreach strategies work together to achieve objectives.

---

[15] Newman, D. (2014, December 3). The role of paid, owned and earned media in your marketing strategy. *Forbes.* Retrieved July 20, 2016, from http://www.forbes.com/sites/danielnewman/2014/12/03/the-role-of-paid-owned-and-earned-media-in-your-marketing-strategy/2/#6a3902ff7dd3

For example, Olympia Outdoor Flashlights hired the creative agency, Seed Factory, to increase awareness and sales through the purchase flashlights, headlamps, and portable solar battery power. Seed Factory developed a multifaceted approach, leveraging both earned and paid media efforts. By primarily using press releases, Seed Factory targeted journalists that focused on outdoor sports, travel, hunting, women's lifestyle, men's lifestyle, and general interest.[16] To complement their media relations efforts, they also created a print advertisement campaign to appear in one of the leading outdoor publications. Within six months, Olympia Outdoor realized dramatic growth in its social media metrics and generated significant media interest. Their integrated PR and marketing efforts yielded strong results:[17]

- Followers on Facebook increased by 30 times their base number, while their Twitter followers increased by 2,987%.

- Media coverage in variety of publications, including *Competitor*, *Outdoor Life*, and *Runner's World* magazines garnered more than 1.1 million media impressions.

- Social media efforts increased overall traffic to Olympia Outdoor's website.

There was a time when earned media and paid media could stand on their own as separate successful strategies. However, as times have changed, consumers have evolved beyond simply responding to publicity and cleverly written commercials or jingles. Customers are more interested in building relationships with the brands that they trust and seek increased involvement with those brands on a regular basis. Authentic brands strive to look and feel the same on the outside as they do on the inside while resisting the temptation to follow the latest trend.[18]

The Ecosystem of Earned and Paid

Many agencies recommend that their clients focus on creating holistic strategies that utilize a mix of earned media and paid media driven by the campaign or

---

[16] Gardella, S. (n.d.). Olympia Outdoor: Social. *Seed Factory*. Retrieved July 22, 2016, from http://www .seedfactorymarketing.com/project/olympia-outdoor/

[17] Ibid.

[18] Burch, D. (2013). *Share this too: More social media solutions for PR professionals*. Chichester, UK: Wiley, Chapter 2.

challenge at hand. By creating engaging, customer-oriented content using both owned and paid media, it is easier to place the content strategically and to earn the audience's trust and support. Every PR and marketing agency has a variety of tools at their disposal to achieve their desired results, and many have identified a smaller subset of go-to strategies.

Building a Marketer's Tool Kit

PR and marketing campaigns should always consider long-term results that use media to deliver strategic, cohesive, planned messages focusing on an idea or concept.[19] Developing a standard set of tools across an agency helps to efficiently cultivate consistent PR and marketing content. It also helps promote a clear and consistent vision and definition for PR and marketing initiatives to clients.[20] According to Kathy Hanbury, Founder and Principal at E3 Content Strategy, the following traditional marketing tools have proven useful for many agency PR practitioners executing integrated campaigns:[21]

- **PR and marketing playbook:** A detailed overview of the PR and marketing tactics that your client is using in their campaign. This should include descriptions of content products or services, their purpose, key platforms, targeted audiences, resource requirements, and how each is being used in the campaign.

- **Brand brief:** A one-page, high-level description of the client's corporate brand, voice, and personality. Individuals have different roles on a project, therefore it is important that everyone correctly understands the client's overarching brand.

- **Style guide:** Style guides are created to identify the official usage of a corporate color palette, approved typefaces, photo guidelines, and preferred ways to refer to products, services, and the company itself. This helps to ensure brand consistency. Large organizations often have their own style guides that incorporate brand voice/language considerations as well as visual design elements. Agencies should move clients toward a more cohesive, standardized brand through creating and institutionalizing the use of style guides.

---

[19] Blakeman, R. (2015). *Integrated marketing communication creative strategy from idea to implementation* (2nd ed.). Lanham: Rowman & Littlefield.

[20] Hanbury, K. (2011, July 12). Creating a content marketing toolkit. *Content Marketing Institute*. Retrieved July 20, 2016, from http://contentmarketinginstitute.com/2011/07/creating-a-content-marketing-toolkit/

[21] Ibid.

- **Article submission brief:** This is a form that summarizes information from content contributors who are submitting an idea for an article.

- **Article template and checklist:** A short template with an easy-to-populate format that aids in the development of effective content. This should include key concepts and a high-level checklist about the client and the campaign strategies.

- **Proofreading checklist:** Prior to publishing content, it should be reviewed for accuracy and style. Create a checklist verifying that all facts, spelling, grammar, keywords, URLs, and other pertinent details have been proofread.

- **Image library:** Gather images from across the organization that accurately and positively represent a client's product or service. Having preapproved, organized, and labeled images saves time and minimizes mistakes.[22]

- **Opportunities calendar:** Create a calendar that includes all upcoming events such as trade shows, product introductions, industry conferences, social media opportunities, the release of study findings, or community events. There are various scheduling tools and free templates online available that can help plan your clients' posts in weekly or monthly segments.

- **Measurement outputs:** Website visits and social engagements are useful metrics to track, but they do not provide enough information on the ultimate success of marketing tactics. For the best results, determine what's most important to your clients (Sales? Awareness? Opinion change? Behavior change?), and close the loop with relevant measurement results. The International Association for Measurement and Evaluation of Communication has developed a free interactive evaluation framework for professionals to use. You can find it online (http://bit.ly/AMECframework).

While this list is not a comprehensive inventory of every tool, it provides some of the most common within the industry. It is not necessary to use each tool when developing strategies and identifying deliverables; start with what is appropriate for the task. Most agencies also have a defined set of combined PR and marketing tactics to use when building an integrated campaign.

---

[22] Hoppe, M. (2012, July 13). 9 tools for your content marketing toolkit. *Weidert.* Retrieved July 20, 2016, from https://www.weidert.com/whole_brain_marketing_blog/bid/107230/9-Tools-For-Your-Content-Marketing-Toolkit

Kelly Fletcher

Founded in 2007 by Kelly Fletcher, Fletcher is an award-winning, national agency with offices in Knoxville, Tennessee, and Atlanta, Georgia. Their expertise is grounded in the practice of public relations and content creation. Over time, the agency has expanded their service offerings out of the need to be more involved in the creation of the core marketing strategies that were driving their clients' PR efforts. Today, Fletcher works with a wide range of companies to define, execute, and measure individual marketing strategies. They combine their passion for content creation with a sophisticated approach to marketing, PR, and social strategies that drive women to take action.

Explain to me your agency setting—what's it like inside the walls of Fletcher public relations?

Having a background in marketing and coming from Jewelry Television, I understood the varied demographics of women. So, when I started my business in 2008, I decided that my agency was going to specialize and own the market in identifying ways to reach and resonate with women. Women are busy—we raise babies and have careers; we volunteer. My agency focuses on how we can reach women where they are by cutting through the clutter and developing messages that they will hear. The agency started with myself and two clients, and we've grown organically from there.

What services does your agency offer?

We started out as what I call a "pure plate" PR firm and then, over time, we morphed into a content marketing firm that used public relations as one of its tactics. In 2014, we rebranded to Fletcher Marketing/PR (http://www.fletchermarketingpr.com/) because we are focused on the integration of marketing and public relations to produce a more holistic result. Generating content is so much a part of marketing and public relations these days that much of what is produced is a combination of sponsored, paid, native, and direct pitch.

This chapter focuses on the interconnectedness of public relations and marketing. Can you speak to how the two are connected?

I wrote my own definition for the integration of marketing and public relations. I call it #marketingpr and it reads as follows:

> #marketingpr: public relations activities focused on specific products or aspects of marketing campaigns that deliver integrated, journalistic-style content across multiple platforms.

Practitioners today are using journalistic-style content, but they are pitching and publishing it in a wide variety of traditional and digital spaces. Sometimes it's paid and sometimes it's earned, other times it's repurposed on owned media channels or shared on social platforms. We always strive to create content that can work within the PESO model. We have a rule of thumb that we try to develop content we can use at least three ways. For example, whatever content we create, we want to be sure we can use it in a blog, with a journalist, or on a social platform. The channels may change, but the idea of sharing in multiple places does not. We also always create content with at least one asset. It could be an image, a video, an infographic, or even a quiz. On average, you will get 60% more engagement with a piece of content that has at least one asset, and the more assets you have, the higher that number goes. We have to tell stories visually. We have to tell news visually. We must pitch visually.

It wasn't always an amenable relationship between public relations and marketing— what changed?

The media landscape is changing. Public relations will always have a place as part of a marketing strategy, but, for me, I don't believe it is as effective a stand-alone strategy as it once was. There is so much more competition for eyes on content. If you think about the industry just ten years ago, so much has changed. I think about the proliferation of media outlets that there are now—the uprising of citizen journalism, news coming from Twitter over the 6 o'clock news or 11 o'clock news—there is so much of a diversification of where people get their news. It's impossible to tell your story everywhere. But if you know exactly where you want to tell your story in an integrated manner using paid media and earned media, the strategy is more effective with better, measurable results.

(Continued)

(Continued)

Are there specific questions that agencies should ask clients when coming up with a PR and marketing strategy?

The first question we ask is what the client wants to achieve. Have a two-way conversation with the client. Find out what their goals are and what resources they have internally versus what they're looking to get help with externally.

What types of reports do you give clients?

We don't do anything that we can't measure. We are focused on how we are going to measure and track results from the onset. In the day-to-day as we are executing a strategy, we are also measuring in real time the success of a strategy to see if we need to readjust or not.

What is your opinion about earned media versus paid media?

I think a company really has to care about both if they want to achieve their goals. Practitioners really have to take a hybrid approach to the objective of getting our clients' content and message seen by the largest audience. Earned media is always going to be important. We are never going to stop pitching. We are never going to stop using more traditional PR efforts to get our message out there. That said, if companies are not in the paid media space, they are probably missing several opportunities. The results speak for how effective paid media is.

Top 5 Characteristics Every PR Professional Should Have

1. To be in this business, a person has to have personality. You are constantly working with clients, media professionals, and team members. Be outgoing and vibrant.

2. New graduates need to have a level of maturity. Get to work on time. Dress professionally. Develop business acumen.

3. Creativity: Today, professionals need to take whatever story they are trying to tell and divide it up to pitch to several vertical markets.

4. Writing.

5. An analytical mind.

Top Must-Haves

- **Must-download app:** Business Insider, to see what businesses are doing within the advertising and marketing areas.

- **Must-read book/blog/news outlet:** Everything! I think to really keep up with what's going on, professionals need to read every day. I try to read at least 30 minutes a day. I read publications like *Bulldog Reporter* and *PR News*. I have news aggregators that pull from LinkedIn so I can stay informed with what's happening all over. I also read good business books. Right now, I'm reading *Driven to Delight:*

Delivering World-Class Customer Experience the Mercedes-Benz Way by Joseph Michelli. It's all about how Mercedes changed the customer experience, and that's what we try to do here at Fletcher.

- **Must-use tool:** I know this sounds so basic, but I live on Google. Using Google for any kind of basic research is great. For example, if I'm working on a pitch and I'm looking for data to situate the pitch, I'll look for data to augment the points in my message.

Branding Basics

A small business owner walks into a meeting with her public relations agency team, brimming with pride about her new product. It will serve the same customers she has worked with for years but have the potential to reach outside of the existing market. It reflects the same qualities—reliability, creativity, and robust functionality—the company is known for. In her excitement, the client describes her vision: A distinct brand to represent the new product. For her and her team, this is a significant opportunity, and they are willing to invest the resources to build a new visual and linguistic brand identity to support it.

Her lead PR counsel pauses before responding. She starts by sharing her own excitement with the product and its opportunities, but she then reframes the positioning: Why expend the resources to create a new brand when this new product clearly reinforces and strengthens what's already there? A single brand, with value built up over the company's entire history, is far more valuable than any amount they could invest to boost awareness for a new product. It is never an easy conversation, but, by its end, the owner understands that the best use of resources would be to reinforce the existing brand and position the project within it rather than to build from scratch. While it is easy to get excited about a major brand change, practitioners should always look at the bigger strategic picture to evaluate and prioritize resources. Organizations can pay for advertising to increase name recognition, but there is no quick fix to establish a brand's value or build consumer trust.

Objectives

- Identify the essential elements of branding.

- Recognize that a brand is a company asset.

- Learn how to create, build, and manage a brand strategy.

- Summarize the role public relations plays in developing a brand strategy.

Brand Definition

John Williams, founder and president of LogoYes.com, suggests considering the following when defining your brand:[1]

- Examine the organization's mission statement.

- Identify the benefits and features of products or services.

- Determine what your customers and prospects already think of your company

- Pinpoint what qualities you want customers to associate with your company.

The Starbucks logo is one of the most recognizable images globally.

imageBROKER/Alamy Stock Photo

Brands are not strictly controlled by organizations. They are a reflection of what organizations really are (*behavior*), what they say they are (*communication*), and what consumers perceive that they are (*impression* or *reputation*). A brand is a company's pledge with its customers to assure consistency, integrity, and authenticity. Brands project to customers what they can expect from the company's products and services, and what's different about what this company is offering over a competitors' products.[2] Because the terms **brand** and *branding* are used so interchangeably, confusion often arises. The American Marketing Association defines a *brand* as a "name, term, design, symbol, or any other feature that identifies one seller's good or service as distinct from those of other sellers."[3] They go on to differentiate *branding* as "a customer experience represented by a collection of images and ideas; often, it refers to a symbol such as a name, logo, slogan, and design scheme." A visual brand identity frequently includes a logo, specified fonts, particular colors and/or color schemes, and icons or characters. These elements represent the implicit values, ideas, and personality of the company. The above image is one of the most recognizable logos the world over. Without hesitation, a majority of the U.S. population would instantly note the Starbucks logo. Take a moment to think about what the brand embodies beyond the logo. What feelings come to mind when you see the famous logo?

---

[1] Williams, J. (2005). The basics of branding. *Entrepreneur*. Retrieved June 30, 2016, from https://www.entrepreneur.com/article/77408

[2] Ibid.

[3] Brand. (2016). American Marketing Association. Retrieved June 24, 2016, from https://www.ama.org/resources/Pages/Dictionary.aspx?dLetter=B

Starbucks strives to enhance customers' experiences while drinking coffee. Over the years, the company managed to differentiate itself from competitors by creating a unique environment for customers. On the company website, they write,

> We're not just passionate purveyors of coffee, but everything else that goes with a full and rewarding coffeehouse experience. It's not unusual to see people coming to Starbucks to chat, meet up, or even work. We're a neighborhood gathering place, a part of the daily routine—and we couldn't be happier about it.[4]

The logo itself does not explicitly personify a company that depicts itself as a "purveyor of coffee," much less embody a "neighborhood gathering place" where people encounter a special "coffeehouse experience." Yet, we've come to know and understand these characteristics as part of the company's brand through our own experiences. This is referred to as the **brand persona** or *brand personality*. Every brand is unique. Brands often have distinct personalities with whom consumers can not only develop personal relationships with, but also define and express themselves.[5] Creating these brand personality traits does not happen overnight. It takes time and consistency in action and communication to build a brand among customers.

Creating a Company Brand

Branding Basics: Brand Strategy

Brand strategy is a long-term plan for the development of a successful brand in order to achieve specific goals. A well-defined and executed brand strategy connects the needs of consumers to the business while taking into consideration needs, emotions, and the competitive landscape.[6] Strong brands stand out in an overcrowded marketplace. An effective brand strategy aligns all communications, actions, and behaviors with a single, unifying concept. The strategy is applied across multiple communication platforms to products and services as well as provide guidance to marketing, sales, and employees. Enduring brands create equity and grow more valuable over time. The most successful brand strategies distinguish their organization so effectively that they often redirect their competitors' strategies. Brand strategies align with business tactics, promote the organizational vision, embody the company's values and culture, and represent a detailed awareness of the needs of their customers. Respected brands should also provide a distinctive value proposition, outline differentiation tactics and market positioning,

---

[4] Company information: Expect more than coffee. (2016). *Starbucks coffee company*. Retrieved June 24, 2016, from http://www.starbucks.com/about-us/company-information

[5] Wæraas, A., & Solbakk, M. N. (2009). Defining the essence of a university: Lessons from higher education branding. *Higher Education, 57*, 449–462.

[6] Gunelius, S. (n.d.). Introduction to brand strategy—Part 1: What is brand strategy? *AYTM*. Retrieved March 10, 2013, from https://aytm.com/blog/research-junction/introduction-to-brand-strategy-part-1/

and highlight points of competitive advantage that resonate with stakeholders. Organizations without a clear brand strategy tend to stumble more frequently, while survival and prosperity are largely associated with the establishment of a clear brand strategy.[7] Every so often, an organization is fortunate enough to have a visionary at the helm from the outset—such as Amazon's Jeff Bezos and Apple's Steve Jobs—while others identify a visionary leader to help redefine a broken brand with a fresh brand strategy.[8]

Branding Basics: Brand Equity

Brand Equity: The value of a brand. From a consumer perspective, brand equity is based on consumer attitudes about positive brand attributes and favorable consequences of brand use.

—American Marketing Association

To establish **brand equity,** a company must deliver reliable, dependable results to create trust with its publics. That trust then has the potential to become **brand loyalty,** which ultimately provides brands with long-term customers. *Brand equity* refers to a customer's perceptions of quality based on accumulated positive experiences with the brand. Most brands strive to achieve this status with the customer. This means that a customer is so familiar with the brand that he or she carries positive feelings and unique associations and that the brand is so well-known, they only need their logo for consumers to recognize who they are, what they stand for, or what they sell.[9] Take the Nike swoosh, for example: We regularly see the swoosh without the word *Nike* and yet we still know the company sells quality athletic apparel. Budweiser has their Clydesdale horses; Downey has a soft, cuddly bear; and Tiffany's has its iconic blue color.

Susan Gunelius, branding expert and CEO of marketing communications and strategic branding company KeySplash Creative Inc., notes that there are five stages to brand equity:[10]

1. Awareness: When a consumer becomes aware of the brand.

2. Recognition: When consumers recognize the brand and know what it offers in comparison to what competitors offer.

3. Experimentation: Consumers have experimented with the brand.

---

[7] Wheeler, A. (2012). *Designing brand identity—An essential guide for the whole branding team.* Hoboken, NJ: John Wiley & Sons.

[8] Ibid.

[9] Blakeman, R. (2015). *The bare bones introduction to integrated marketing communication.* Lanham, MD: Rowman & Littlefield.

[10] Gunelius, S. (n.d.). Brand equity basics—Part 1: What is brand equity? *AYTM.* Retrieved June 24, 2016, from https://aytm.com/blog/research-junction/brand-equity-basics-1/#sthash.mSOEMEhB.dpbs

4. Preference: Consumers like the brand so much they become repeat purchasers. At this stage, they begin to develop emotional connections to the brand.

5. Loyalty: Consumers will go to lengths to find the brand. Emotional connections increase as loyalty increases. Consumers become so connected to the brand, there is no substitute for the original.

Branding Basics: Brand Image

Brand image is what comes to mind when people think of a brand. It's the brand's public perception. A brand's image is created and maintained by what consumers think each time they encounter it. Therefore, it is vital that companies pay

Figure 8.1	Psychology of Colors in Brands	
Color	**Meaning**	**Brands**
Red	Passionate, Active, Exciting, Bold, Energy, Youthful, Physical, Pioneering, Leader, Confidence, Ambition, Power	Kellogg's, Virgin, Lego, Coca-Cola, Nintendo, Red Bull, Pinterest
Pink	Love, Calm, Respect, Warmth, Long-term, Feminine, Intuitive, Care, Assertive, Sensitive, Nurture, Possibilities, Unconditional	Barbie, Cosmopolitan, Victoria's Secret
Purple	Deep, Creativity, Unconventional, Original, Stimulation, Individual, Wealth, Modesty, Compassion, Distinguished, Respectable, Fantasy	Cadbury, Yahoo!, Hallmark, Milka
Navy	Trust, Order, Loyalty, Sincere, Authority, Communication, Confidence, Peace, Integrity, Control, Responsible, Success, Calm, Masculine	Facebook, Reebok, GAP, Tumblr
Green	Balance, Growth, Restore, Sanctuary, Equilibrium, Positivity, Nature, Generous, Clarity, Prosperity, Safety, Stable, Good Judgement	BP, Holiday Inn, The Body Shop, John Deere, Lacoste, Starbucks
Blue	Spirit, Perspective, Content, Control, Rescue, Determination, Self-sufficient, Modern, Goals, Aware, Purpose, Open, Ambition	Intel, Skype, Twitter, WordPress, Ford, Dell
Orange	Instinct, Warmth, Optimistic, Spontaneity, Extrovert, Social, New Ideas, Freedom, Impulse, Motivation	Fanta, MasterCard, Bitly, Nickelodeon, Penguin Random House
Yellow	Intellect, Joy, Energy, Optimism, Clarity, Warmth, Positivism	McDonalds, Best Buy, Subway, Hertz, IKEA, Denny's

Source: Lasquite, M. (2015, August 5). Color Psychology in Marketing and Brand Identity: Part 2. Retrieved from http://blog.visme.co/color-psychology-in-marketing-and-brand-identity-part-2/

particular attention to how their brand is represented. When swimmer Ryan Lochte lied about being robbed in a gas station during the 2016 Olympics in Rio de Janeiro, he quickly lost his four major sponsors: Speedo, Ralph Lauren, Airweave, and Gentle Hair Removal. Why? Because his actions were not in line with the brand image of the companies he represented. In a statement released by Speedo, the company said,

> While we have enjoyed a winning relationship with Ryan for over a decade and he has been an important member of the Speedo team, we cannot condone behavior that is counter to the values this brand has long stood for.[11]

In an effort to repair their brand image, Speedo donated $50,000 of Lochte's sponsorship fee to the Save the Children charity, which directed the money toward youth in Brazil.

Branding Basics: Brand Positioning

Positioning is a concept developed by Al Ries and Jack Trout, first coined in 1969 and then expanded upon in their groundbreaking book, *Positioning: The Battle for Your Mind*. Ries and Trout defined *positioning* as the differentiated perceptions among different brands that happens in the minds of consumers.[12,13] Positioning incorporates the four dimensions that affect sales: price, product, promotion, and place. Positioning ensures that all brand activity is focused, united, guided, and directed. For example, the positioning of the outerwear brand The North Face has long promoted an active, athletic lifestyle filled with challenges and adventures.

Branding Basics: Brand Personality

Brand personality is a set of human characteristics that are ascribed to a brand and to which a consumer can relate.[14] Effective brand personas increase a company's brand equity by having a consistent set of traits that a specific consumer segment experiences.[15] Every element of the brand identity, including the color of the logo and the typography on the brand name, adds to the personality. Is a brand energetic or calming? Cutting edge or traditional? Exclusive or welcoming? Warm or detached? Such traits should be reinforced through a variety of design decisions, language choices, brand strategy, and organizational actions.

---

[11] Bonesteel, M. (2016, August 22). Ryan Lochte loses all four commercial sponsors after Rio Olympics incident. *Washington Post.* Retrieved August 23, 2016, from https://www.washingtonpost.com/news/early-lead/wp/2016/08/22/speedo-drops-ryan-lochte-after-rio-olympics-incident/

[12] Trout, J. (1969, June). Positioning is a game people play in today's me-too market place. *Industrial Marketing.*

[13] Ries, A., & Trout, J. (1981). *Positioning: The battle for your mind.* New York, NY: Warner Books.

[14] Gurnani, S. (2016). How to establish a unique brand personality. *Yourstory.* https://yourstory.com/2016/08/establish-unique-brand-personality/

[15] Staplehurst, G., & Charoenwongse, S. (2012). *Why brand personality matters: Aligning your brand to cultural drivers of success.* New York, NY: Millward Brown.

Branding Basics: Brand Experience

Brand experience is everything that a customer feels when purchasing, using, and interacting with a brand. Every touch point with a customer is an opportunity to enhance the emotional connection. Good experiences produce positive feelings, while bad experiences become missed opportunities and could end up hurting the brand. Look at most Honda dealerships today. While getting an oil change, a customer can sip a fresh hot latte, munch on a breakfast sandwich, and sit in a comfy leather chair as they peruse the Internet on free Wi-Fi. Honda's approach to customer service is to take the mundane, sometimes frustrating experience of car repair and make it unexpectedly enjoyable for their customers

> by providing a level of value that not only satisfies the expectations that customers have when they receive services based on their past experiences and information, but also exceeds them. The experience of excitement through these services forges an emotional connection between customers and Honda, ensuring that the company remains a mobility manufacturer that customers choose based on their high expectations.[16]

Every interaction should be considered, and leading brands find ways to improve even seemingly inconsequential touch points to elevate the overall experience.

Branding Basics: Brand Voice

Brand voice is the language used in combination with brand messages. The visual tone works alongside with clarity and personality to engage customers when they are listening, scanning, or reading.[17] Brand voice must be memorable, unique, and customer centric. Each integration with the target audience, whether online or in person, offers an opportunity for a brand to inform, stimulate, and promote word-of-mouth. Because brands communicate through a variety of platforms, consistency is critically important. Memorable brands use one distinctive voice any time their brand is promoted. Whether their message is shared on the web or in a tweet, is happening in conversations between employees and consumers, or is communicated in a presentation, the company must find an appropriate and consistent voice.[18] That said, different brands may have varying degrees of flexibility, depending on their audiences. A key aspect of executing brand voice

---

[16] Customers: Honda's approach to customer satisfaction. (2012). Retrieved November 6, 2017, from http://world.honda.com/sustainability/report/pdf/2012/report_2012-08.pdf

[17] Neumeier, M. (2016). *The brand flip: Why customers now run companies—and how to profit from it.* Berkeley, CA: New Riders.

[18] Rowles, D. (2015). *Digital branding: A complete step-by-step guide to strategy, tactics and measurement.* London, England: Kogan Page.

is determining whether a brand has a particularly rigid voice and tone (such as well-developed global behemoths like Apple and Nike) or a bit more flexibility (such as business-to-business companies, like a law firm that focuses more on the qualifications of employees). Moosejaw, a company that sells outdoor clothing and accessories, has a casual, almost irreverent brand voice. Through funny, quippy, and downright sarcastic messaging, they have connected with their audience in a way that most organizations would stay away from. Here is an example from their "About Us" page:

> 2012—Someone brought finger darts in and I've been hit in the face 4 times and once in the eye. We also opened 3 1/2 new shops in Natick, MA; Boulder, CO; Kansas City, MO; and a pop-up shop on Woodward Ave. We're counting the pop-up as the 1/2. In case you didn't pick up on that.[19]

Building, Managing, and Sustaining Brands

Brands are never static. They will transform over time and, and depending on a company's brand strategy, they become stronger or diminish and fade. Even if organizations do not change their construction of a brand, its perception by the public will constantly shift based on competition, current events, and customer experiences. The responsibilities and expectations increase as brands develop and mature. Branding strategist, Annetta Powell suggests that a good business practice is to take time each year to review branding activities and evaluate both successes and failures through metrics such as levels of brand awareness and levels of engagements.[20]

Branding of Dracula[21]

Reprinted with permission from Michael DiFrisco; this article first appeared in Marketing Profs.

Tod Browning's production of Bram Stoker's *Dracula*, from 1931, is a favorite of the Universal horror collection. Bela Lugosi's portrayal of the creepy count from Transylvania continues to inspire moviegoers and enthusiasts as well as inform all other depictions of vampires on stage, screen, and in books. Because of that consistency and memorability, Dracula can actually teach important lessons about branding for small businesses, associations, or entrepreneurs.

[19] Mooosejaw. (n.d.). *About Moosejaw.* Retrieved December 17, 2017, from https://www.moosejaw.com/moosejaw/shop/madness_about____

[20] Powell, A. (2017). 5 effective brand building strategies to attract customers. *Cox BLUE.* Retrieved December 17, 2017, from https://www.coxblue.com/5-effective-brand-building-strategies-to-attract-customers-2/

[21] DiFrisco, M. (2000). *Brand Dracula: Four branding lessons from the undead.* Retrieved October 25, 2013, from http://www.marketingprofs.com/articles/2013/11927/brand-dracula-four-branding-lessons-from-the-undead

Lesson 1: Positioning Dracula

Brand positioning should always be done *relative to* the competition. In Dracula's case, he is positioned *against* other classic monsters of the day: Frankenstein's monster, the Wolfman, the Mummy, the Gill Man from Creature of the Black Lagoon, and many others. Effective positioning defines what makes you unique. The famous vampire is differentiated by his aristocratic alter ego—Count Dracula—and by his ability to morph into a bat on demand. While other movie monsters terrified their victims simply by their presence, Dracula first hypnotized with his gaze, and then sucked their blood for a protein-rich midnight snack. Dracula was different—not the same old robot, alien, or zombie. So he has a clear and consistent position in our minds.

Lesson 2: Defining Brand Dracula

Developing the Dracula brand is pulling together various attributes like personality, image, and core competencies. What did Dracula stand for? Dracula was good at mixing with high society. His personality was sophisticated, and—in later movie evolutions of the character—he's quite the ladies' man. He was mysterious, shrouded in intrigue, and he was repelled by wolfsbane, garlic, and a cross. A mirror could not hold his undead reflection. Those, and other characteristics, are what make up the memorable and unique brand. That's how he got noticed, got publicity, got word-of-mouth buzz—and, ultimately, got new customers (or victims!).

Lesson 3: Developing Dracula's Identity

This is the fun part. In business, it includes a name, logo, tagline, colors, and other elements that make up your **trade dress**. For the Count,

it's his signature cape (Lugosi was actually buried in his Dracula cape; it was that important a part of his personal brand). It's also his widow's peak hairdo, eastern European accent, hypnotic eyes, nocturnal feeding habits, and his propensity to shape-shift into a bat. It's important that all *your* identity elements are in place before spending a penny on marketing, communications, or advertising. Dracula with a British accent or a blond crew cut would strike us as wrong or even humorous: These features would be decidedly *off brand*.

Lesson 4: Going Public With Dracula

Dracula enlisted the assistance of Renfield, the real estate broker who unwittingly helped the Count secure a derelict abbey near London from which to "run his business." This was Dracula's "brand launch." That launch started *inside* Dracula's castle, as Lugosi prepared his undead minions and his daytime hangout—his casket—for the public launch. That's because he realized that his staff was critical to building a strong brand. Employees and front-liners are an organization's best advocates, most loyal evangelists, and best brand ambassadors. Like Dracula, your job is to make sure staff is engaged, involved, and communicated with continuously in the branding or re-branding process. Only when safely in Carfax Abbey with his staff—which now included the hapless Renfield—did Dracula make his grand entrance into London society, his "target audience."

Here's how you can be sure that—like the Count—you'll effectively stand out in a crowded marketplace:

- **Position your business and stand apart.** Positioning is the process by which your business creates an image or identity in the minds of your core market, giving them a

(Continued)

reason to choose your offerings. Positioning is always done relative to your competition. Consider what makes your business really unique. Why should people support Brand You and not Brand B?

- **Specialize and focus.** The aristocratic vampire drank blood from his victims' necks to stay alive. Like Dracula, specialization lets you build your brand around your strengths. And this focus allows you to differentiate your business, offers you presumed expertise and perceived value, and makes it easier for prospects and customers to understand your business. Focus allows you to first *simplify* and then *amplify* your message. Because the less information we're given, the more likely we are to remember it.

- **Your business's identity is made up of "outer layers"**—attributes that prospects and customers see and experience. Make sure you're clear on what makes your offerings unique, and align that difference with your name, logo, tagline, messaging,

and other visual and verbal cues that will allow your target market to "get" what you're all about. Like the Count's cape, your visual identity can be a memorable branding tool.

- **It's critical to engage staff and other stakeholders** in embracing what you stand for. In fact, 86% of employees say being engaged in the brand would make them more likely to speak positively about the company they work for with those outside the organization. Customers' notions of your brand are formed from their experiences with your business or services. Every interaction is a chance to enrich your brand. Your staff should be able to answer this question every day: "How am I helping to deliver on the company's brand promise today?"

Sure, Dracula eventually had a stake pounded through his heart. But don't let his demise distract you from building a strong brand to help increase your business's awareness, differentiate you from the competition, and drive revenues.

Reflect and Discuss

1. What are the main objectives of branding?

2. What steps should a company take to connect with its audience?

3. Can a person be a brand? If yes, how? If no, why not?

4. Is a brand something tangible and, at the same time, intangible? Support your response with examples.

5. A brand is more than what a product does or what a company communicates. What attributes contribute to a successful brand?

Michael DiFrisco

Michael (Mike) DiFrisco, certified association executive and founder of BrandXcellence, has developed marketing programs for business-to-business (B2B) and business-to-consumer (B2C) companies for most of his professional career. He has more than 25 years of experience helping businesses effectively connect with their target audiences. A leader of numerous organizational and brand assessments to achieve strategic-level mission relevance, Mike specializes in brand oversight, consistency, coordination, and efficiency in marketing communications. Mike has published two books, including *How to Craft a R.A.D.I.C.A.L. Brand for Your Business or Organization* and *Shadowcasting: How to Grow Your Business by Growing Your Reputation*.

What does BrandXcellence do?

After spending most of my career working in associations, I noticed that leadership often looks at brand strategy as separate from business strategy. They treat the two separately. Everything that makes up the company *is* the brand. What makes it unique, what makes it relevant, is a company's strategy. I think that's what caused me to dive into branding: the act of branding a business or association. This realization led to launching BrandXcellence.

What is the difference between a brand and branding?

There seems to be confusion on the part of businesses. Branding is a verb. It is something that we do; it is an active, dynamic process to understand what the brand (the noun) really is. What I try to develop through Brand-Xcellence is to draw people through the act of branding.

What are some branding basics every professional should keep in mind?

Over the years of talking with people, I've developed seven steps to branding. I call this the R.A.D.I.C.A.L. approach:

1. Relevant: Make sure your business is relevant—that people care, that it's something they want, and that they find compelling.

2. Authentic: Don't try to be a "me too" or copycat business. Be real and authentic.

3. Differentiation: I don't believe in being just a little different; my philosophy is to be radically different—to be so different that buzz starts to be created around your business.

4. Iconic: All businesses should have images and symbols that resonate with their target audience to have a visual persona that is unique and memorable.

5. Character/Conduct/Conversation: I believe a business should know who they are and what makes up their character. Then, they need to conduct

(Continued)

(Continued)

themselves in the likeness of their character. Finally, their messages into the marketplace, social spaces, advertising should all line up with their character and conduct.

6. Audience: Always have a specific target audience in mind.

7. Live the brand: All the people that represent your brand—staff, front-liners, customer-facing people, leadership—need to live the brand. They need to embody the brand and know the recipe for success.

What mistakes do most companies make when trying to build and/or sustain their brand?

It's tough for businesses to see what makes them different. Recently, I was working with an iced tea company, and they had some unique aspects within the packaged beverage market. The product was developed by a dentist and he used a sweetener called xylitol, which is good for your teeth. So, I had them reflect and ask themselves, "What is it that is a non-parody component to this iced tea?" There are already iced teas on the shelf that claim they are healthy and use natural ingredients, so I needed them to articulate what made this product different. We essentially built the brand by taking a deep look at the audience and understanding their motives for purchasing this product over other similar products. In the end, the success was in how the product was made and who it was made by—a dentist.

What advice would you give a client looking to break through the clutter in a saturated marketplace?

The simplest way is to use the inside-out method. First, look inside at your company's character, conduct, uniqueness, and relevance. Then communicate those attributes to those outside. A business's inside reality must match its outside perceptions. There must be one voice/tone with consistent images on all platforms—web, social, print, advertising, and other channels. Marketing is a process, not an event.

Why is the logo often seen as the gateway to the brand?

What often confuses businesses is that they see the logo *as* the brand. It's not. It's a symbol that represents the brand. But, if it's unique, if it's done well, and if it has iconography that sticks with the target audience, the logo can make a big splash. The example I often use is Susan G. Komen for the Cure. Their logo of the ribbon is recognized by almost everyone, and their organization has been around for more than 35 years. Then, compare the pink ribbon with the logo for the American Cancer Society, which has been around for more than 100 years. When you talk with people about the American Cancer Society's logo, it is difficult for them to articulate what the symbol is. It's not an image that is easy to describe or say or remember. The truth is that, although the American Cancer Society has been around for a century and does great work, Susan G. Komen for the Cure has an icon and brand purpose that is more memorable.

Top 5 Characteristics Every PR Professional Should Have

1. **Make data-driven decisions:** I think, whenever possible, use qualitative or quantitative data to drive your choices. Get used to finding data, asking for data, and analyzing any available data to make decisions.

2. **Listen:** A lot of people like to talk, but if you listen more than you talk—listen to what the client wants, listen to what the marketplace is saying, and analyze what you've heard—then you're better able to understand what you need to do.

3. **Understand why people really buy:** I call this *the benefit of the benefit.* Don't tell me about your product, rather tell me what your product will do for me. Customers are looking for results.

4. **Have a genuine desire to learn and grow:** The field of media is constantly changing, and we need to stay current. The tendency is to stop learning as you move up the organizational chart.

5. **Write. Speak. Get published. Start a blog. Get active on social media.** The skill of observing something, learning how to articulate it, and then sharing your knowledge is going to be beneficial, regardless of career path. Writing, speaking, and publishing will give you authority, credibility, and recognition.

Top Must-Haves

- **Must-download app:** Evernote. Not only does Evernote store my thoughts, but it also saves them to the cloud, so I have access anywhere.

- **Must-read book/blog/news outlet:** I read these three outlets every day and I would be lost without them:

  - *MediaPost*'s Marketing Daily

  - Brand New from *UnderConsideration*

  - *Adweek.*

- **Must-use tool:** HARO (Help a Reporter Out). I like HARO because it helps me understand what topics editors and writers want. It keeps me up to date to on what's hot, but it also helps me find authors and editors looking for subject matter experts.

CHAPTER

9

Internal Communication

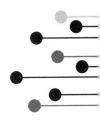

Cultura Creative (RF) / Alamy Stock Photo

Objectives

- Decipher how internal communication is a part of public relations.

- Identify how agencies support and improve internal communication efforts.

- Understand the role internal communication plays in organizational change.

- Demystify the obstacles and barriers to excellent internal communication.

Imagine that a local nonprofit launches a new community outreach project. Two scenarios are presented: one where the organization makes a concerted, strategic effort to educate its entire staff about the launch, while the other focuses on diverting all of its resources toward external communication. In the first situation, each staff member is provided a full presentation by agency partners as to the importance of the new venture, his or her individual roles, the potential growth of the organization, personal and professional opportunities, and any other benefits to the community. In the second scenario, each staff member is instructed on what his or her responsibilities are to support the campaign. If you were a newly hired media relations specialist at the agency working with this organization, consider the difference that the first scenario would make in empowering you to execute your job better. All of your client contacts would have an improved strategic perspective when making day-to-day decisions and a heightened sense of motivation based on the larger purpose. Imagine the implications if your collaborators clearly understood the value and potential impact of the project, contrasted with a world where they do not.

The practice of internal communication carries significant responsibility. According to Broom and Sha, the goal of internal communication within a public relations framework should be to "establish and maintain mutually beneficial relationships between an organization and the employees on whom its success or failure depends."[1] From this perspective, employees are **internal publics**, which can represent a variety of subgroups, such as executive leadership, management, and front-line staff. It is not always clear who fits into each category, and they are often not wholly distinct.[2] For example, a nonprofit's employees are clearly an internal public or publics, while members or donors may be considered internal or external, depending on the circumstances. Many organizations communicate with such groups directly through e-newsletters, internal magazines, and other programs that reflect an internal communication mindset.

Additionally, internal communication often receives less than its fair share of attention and resources within organizations. Its work is often fragmented, split between communication, PR, human resources, executive leadership, and other departments. This creates difficulties for strategic and holistic implementation of internal communication, both for basic organizational function as well as support of external communication efforts. Small businesses and local nonprofit organizations generally face the largest obstacles, as they lack the size to allow staff specialization and dedication to execute programs effectively. Larger organizations are more likely to have the expertise and resources, but the challenges of fragmentation and lack of prioritization still exist.

PR agencies frequently begin working with organizations to help solve issues that clients perceive as external. However, upon further investigation, obstacles often reside within internal communication efforts. Some agency professionals may shy away from tackling these issues for fear of invading their clients' turf. They may feel that solving this specific problem lays outside their realm of expertise or influence or that their clients will not view such efforts with the same level of importance or value as external communication efforts. But seasoned practitioners know that making incremental and systemic changes to internal communication programs can be critical to the overall success of communication programs. Allocating the appropriate resources can lead to tangible benefits for the organization and, often, improve the efficiency and value of an agency's external efforts.

---

[1] Broom, G., & Sha, B-L. (2013). *Cutlip & Center's effective public relations*. Boston, MA: Pearson, p. 190.

[2] Whitworth, B. (2006). Internal communication. In T. L. Gilles (Ed.) *The IABC handbook of organizational communication: A guide to internal communication, public relations, marketing, and leadership*. San Francisco, CA: Jossey-Bass, pp. 205–214.

What Can Agencies Add to Internal Communication?

FitzPatrick and Valskov's *Internal Communications: A Manual for Practitioners* outlines four benefits of building or strengthening internal communication. Such programs help organizations to "(1) retain good people, (2) help people work harder and better, (3) help people say the right things about you, and (4) support major change."[3] Many of these goals are strengthened by an outside perspective and specific communication expertise. Employee retention—a significant challenge for a variety of organizations—encompasses many facets: Are employees compensated well? Do they enjoy their job duties? Do they have functional, productive relationships with their managers and coworkers? Effective two-way communication between leadership and other levels of the organization can identify and assist in solving such challenges. Improving the flow of information shared with employees does not necessarily mean providing more information; it should be driven by selecting the right information in the best possible format for employees to receive it appropriately. It also means that one size does not fit all: The same message should be shared with distinct employee groups using different channels. Agency practitioners often are in a unique position to provide unbiased perspective and expert guidance on many delicate decisions.

The Value of Strong Employee Communication

Strategic internal communication can strengthen project teams, increase morale, and make work more enjoyable.[4] In order to perform at their best, team members should understand where their role fits into delivering on the organization's goals and objectives. Organizational leaders have a responsibility to provide this information to "help people feel that there is a purpose in their work."[5] In the landmark "Excellence in Public Relations and Communication Management" study, executed by James and Larissa Grunig and Fred Repper, "excellent" organizational communication was shown to be enabled by "a participative rather than an authoritarian" culture, "symmetrical" two-way internal communication, and equal opportunities for "men and women and minorities" to hold leadership roles.[6] Taken together, these factors contribute to an **organic/participative organizational structure** rather than one imposed by leadership.

---

[3] FitzPatrick, L., & Valskov, K. (2014). *Internal communications: A manual for practitioners.* London, UK: Kogan Page, p. 11.

[4] Grunig, J. E., & Grunig, L. A. (2006). Characteristics of excellent communication. In T. L. Gilles (Ed.) *The IABC handbook of organizational communication: A guide to internal communication, public relations, marketing, and leadership.* San Francisco, CA: Jossey-Bass, pp. 3–18.

[5] FitzPatrick, L., & Valskov, K. (2014). *Internal communications: A manual for practitioners.* London, UK: Kogan Page, p. 13.

[6] Grunig, J. E., & Grunig, L. A. (2006). Characteristics of excellent communication. In T. L. Gilles (Ed.) *The IABC handbook of organizational communication: A guide to internal communication, public relations, marketing, and leadership.* San Francisco, CA: Jossey-Bass, p. 14.

Important organizational language, such as mission statements, should include input from a variety of team members. Agency practitioners can play an important role in gathering ideas.

An emphasis on organic approaches can ultimately begin during the onboarding and **acculturation** processes, wherein new hires learn about the company as a whole as well as their specific position/department through formal and informal interactions. Onboarding—generally managed by the human resources team—includes the official orientation to the organization and its policies.

While some argue that the concept of company culture is more mythology than reality,[7] many leading practitioners and scholars have investigated the impact of factors such as the centralization of decision-making power or the degree of participation that employees perceive.[8] New employees interpret each early step they take into the company as part of their broader acculturation—indicating whether they are working for an organization that values their new ideas and appreciates challenges to executive authority or one that rewards embracing existing mission, goals, and strategies. Neither approach is inherently superior, but organizations may or may not be approaching their employees with the best method based on their industry and business model. Agency counsel can support the identification and creation of values, language, and actions that help organizations accurately match their internal brand. Reviewing and revising onboarding materials and the onboarding process can be a valuable place to begin.

Focusing the Organizational Mission

In addition to onboarding, agencies can also help drive the development or refinement of **mission statements** and **vision statements**, policy documents relating to external behavior (such as a **media policy** or **social media policy**), training materials, and communication channels (such as internal newsletters, blogs, or intranets). Each of these elements reflects the organizational brand, and agency insights can ensure that the objectives, language, and user experience for employees mirror the organization.

Building Bridges

Internal communication succeeds when organizations break down silos and empower different departments within an organization to communicate more effectively with each other. While many corporate leaders see the benefit of internal communication programs as helping to develop **corporate culture**—a set of

[7] Cowan, D. (2014). *Strategic internal communication: How to build employee engagement and performance.* London, UK: Kogan Page.

[8] Broom, G., & Sha, B-L. (2013). *Cutlip & Center's effective public relations.* Boston, MA: Pearson, pp. 192–193.

Best Practices
Internal Communication & Mission Statements

Organizations and their communication can, and should, be distinctive. A mission statement is one place to clearly and concisely find such a niche. Statements differ greatly from one organization to another, reflecting different organizational strengths, cultures, and aspirations. Agency practitioners are well equipped to use their external perspective to help organizations craft such language. The following are examples of several best practices for mission statements and other internal language.

- **Reflective:** Internal communication must be grounded in the actual organization and responsive to changes in day-to-day work. Employees should be able to easily recognize it as such.

- **Clear:** Internal communicators must strive to avoid jargon and construct information that is easily digestible for employees. This may require multiple versions or formats, as different team members have distinct interests, perspectives, and vocabularies.

- **Unique:** An organization's internal communication should be distinctly

different from all others. It should reflect unique organizational values, original ideas, and a distinctive brand voice.

- **Concise:** Making all internal communication as succinct and targeted as possible demonstrates to employees that organizational leadership values their time. Often, this is best achieved through segmentation of content, messages, and mediums.

- **Inclusive:** Employees at all levels should feel empowered and engaged by such communication, rather than excluded or isolated.

- **Aspirational:** Internal communication should highlight what an organization aspires to be, while being honest about where it currently falls short of such achievements.

- **Narrative:** As consultant Keith Burton notes, "corporate cultures are woven with stories."[9] Facts, data, and logic alone cannot make the case for employees to get excited and engaged in an organization. It takes a more holistic narrative approach to paint pictures of the motivation, effort, and impact integral to successful organizations.

shared organizational behaviors and values—author, scholar, and PR consultant David Cowan lays out the case for a different approach in his book, *Strategic Internal Communication*. Cowan argues against the assumption of a definable corporate culture, as it "does not get to the heart of organizational life."[10] For him,

---

[9] Burton, K. (2012). Listen up: Why employees are your key. In C. L. Caywood (Ed.), *The handbook of strategic public relations and integrated marketing communications* (2nd ed.). New York, NY: McGraw-Hill Education, p. 134.

[10] Cowan, D. (2014). *Strategic internal communication: How to build employee engagement and performance.* London, UK: Kogan Page, p. 31.

investigating and improving the interrelationships among individuals and departments within an organization should be the goal.

Cowan emphasizes the importance of productive dialogue among groups within organizations to allow for feedback and listening as a critical part of the communication process: "understanding the people in the organization as people."[11] Information does not merely flow from the top of an organization down to employees but moves vertically and horizontally in all directions. Harnessing this approach, organizations should more clearly understand the reality facing its employees. How can organizations encourage two-way internal communication? Cowan recommends participatory decision-making processes, action to back up language, and a clearly articulated openness to feedback.[12]

Ethical and Legal Considerations

While effective internal communication conveys information useful for employees, it is often also designed to be persuasive. Employers actively attempt to get employees to participate in activities, gather buy-in for initiatives, or take specific actions or join particular programs. Many of these, such as wellness initiatives, are squarely designed in the employee's best interests. Particularly because of this structure, ethics are a critical component of effective communication efforts. Communicating in an ethical manner builds trust and strengthens the relationships among staff members.

However, ethical communication must go both ways: It is difficult to communicate both ethically or effectively without actively listening. This skill involves formal processes (open staff meetings, processes for making anonymous suggestions, a two-way annual review structure, and watching key statistical indicators, such as employee retention rates) as well as informal observations (awareness of employee tone and response at organizational events) and—as Cowan describes—an articulated willingness to take and implement feedback. Organizations willing to invest both the time and effort to listen and to make changes based on employee insights and concerns have a significant leg up in building trust over the long term.

Just as addressing difficult issues can build trust, the practice of only sharing positive news with staff inherently creates challenges and breeds mistrust. Leadership must become comfortable communicating realistic messages to employees, both positive and negative. For effectiveness and trust, organizations must demonstrate a candid and open approach to communication. Broom and Sha refer to "honest, candid information flowing freely up, down, and sideways in the organization."[13]

Another key differentiator of internal communication is the legal component: Organizations have an obligation to communicate particular information to their

---

[11] Ibid., p. 36.

[12] Ibid., see pp. 43–44.

[13] Broom, G., & Sha, B-L. (2013). *Cutlip & Center's effective public relations.* Boston, MA: Pearson, p. 190.

staff, including benefits, workplace safety, sexual harassment, and a variety of other topics. Required information is often presented poorly, but it doesn't have to be. An agency professional, while not a legal expert, often will be able to provide strategic and tactical counsel for the communication of such materials.

Communicating Change

The topic of organizational change demands communication support. Change generally equates to increased uncertainty, and effective communication can help reduce some potential insecurities. In times of change, organizations are often afraid to communicate, creating a vacuum or "gaps and disconnects" that are filled by rumors, speculation, and assumptions.[14] This understandably creates a climate conducive to fear. It is the responsibility of an employer to alert staff about when and why change is coming, how it will impact them, and what they can do about it.[15] Such communication, when combined with constructive dialogue, empowers employees to communicate with leadership to ensure that concerns are addressed and messages are clear. It also assists in identifying and breaking down barriers and silos within the organization that may have been the root of the issues at hand.[16] Grey and Castles refer to the first step as "information sufficiency," or providing enough information so that employees see the organization as a reputable and useful source.[17] Dialogue can take the form of "upward communication" or executive listening as well as more formal methods for collecting diverse employee input and insights about potential change and how it may affect them.[18]

Despite the best intentions, many organizations that attempt to communicate change logically to internal publics find that, as Grey and Castles state, such "rationality falls short of wisdom."[19] The approaches and messages that may seem clear and reasonable to executive leaders do not always resonate with employees, particularly in the stressful environment of organizational change. This is why internal communicators, and agency practitioners managing employee-focused programs, must attempt to put themselves in the shoes of their audience, provide avenues for meaningful feedback throughout the process, and be flexible enough to act on what they hear.

[14] Cowan, D. (2014). *Strategic internal communication: How to build employee engagement and performance.* London, UK: Kogan Page, p. 50.

[15] FitzPatrick, L., & Valskov, K. (2014). *Internal communications: A manual for practitioners.* London, UK: Kogan Page, p. 14.

[16] Cowan, D. (2014). *Strategic internal communication: How to build employee engagement and performance.* London, UK: Kogan Page, p. 34.

[17] Gray, R., & Castles, G. (2006). Communicating major change within the organization. In T. L. Gilles (Ed.) *The IABC handbook of organizational communication: A guide to internal communication, public relations, marketing, and leadership.* San Francisco, CA: Jossey-Bass, p. 242.

[18] Ibid., p. 243.

[19] Ibid., p. 55.

Challenges to Successful Internal Communication Programs

- **Internal resistance**: There may be very real pushback from client communication teams.
  - Solution: Clarify reporting and decision-making structures at the beginning of the agency relationship. Be clear on both the depth of change needed and the reasoning behind it. Emphasize the benefits of improved employee communication for the communication team: improved employee response to company messages, a more positive working environment, and (hopefully) more value placed on communication and listening by leadership.

- **Perception as less valuable**: Many organizations see internal communication as less valuable, and less worthy of the time of an outside agency, than other tasks, such as media relations. For example, securing an interview for a company's chief executive officer (CEO) with a reporter from *Wired* magazine or the *Wall Street Journal* has a certain appeal—a sense of accomplishment and recognition for the organization by outside influencers. While these outcomes may be important, improving the clarity with which staff perceives an organization's mission is equally critical.
  - Solution: Even small improvements can make an outsized difference in commitment, quality, or work and the way they share a company's messages and perspective with the outside world. Define clear metrics to demonstrate tangible improvement.

- **Need for systemic solutions**: Internal communication solutions often involve a mix of structural and communicative changes.
  - Solution: Approaches should be holistic. Agency professionals should understand what is needed to make an internal communication program successful and stand their ground or adjust expectations when a client attempts to undermine or change necessary strategies, channels, or tactics.

Internal Communication for External Results

Employees as Message "Channels"

Much has been made of the term **brand ambassador** as a catch-all for encouraging both internal and external publics to be supportive of an organization or its mission. Often, the term describes ambassadors arising organically. Consistent, clear, and valuable internal communication is one way to encourage identification and participation with an organization's brand as well as to arm potential ambassadors with language. Regularly overlooked is the importance of cultivating employees to serve the same purpose: Informed employees are often valuable brand ambassadors.

Successful employee communication programs are as strategic as external campaigns, and brand-specific language should never be the only content shared. Employees should have an understanding of their organizational brand reflective of their positive relationship with their employer. The approach must be comprehensive and honest, reflecting the brand inside and out. This is easier said than done, and it gets increasingly difficult for large organizations. However, leaders at small companies tend to have more direct impact on employee experiences and, even with limited resources, can take steps to make employees feel valued. Including them in strategic decision making and communication is one approach that supports both of these objectives.

©iStockphoto.com/YinYang

Front-line staff play a critical role in interacting with organizations' customers, members, and communities. Agencies often undervalue the importance of regular and relevant communication to these important publics.

Front-Line Staff

Communicating effectively to the various functional areas of an organization requires distinct internal communication approaches. Many businesses have an employee layer that spends significant time connecting directly with customers, members, and other important organizational publics and stakeholders. This may include sales team members, customer or member service representatives, retail associates, fundraising staff, and those in similar roles. These employees are often large in number and may have high turnover relative to the rest of the organization. Regular training, guidance, and reinforcement are critical, and exposure to internal branding efforts should also become part of the onboarding process with newly hired staff. The more information and engagement an internal communication program can have with this group, the more supportive they can be. Additionally, listening, understanding, and addressing the needs of front-line staff can go a long way toward improving their work environment and providing value and perspective as agency professionals.

An important decision that organizations need to weigh is the degree to which their brand and brand language should be flexible. This has implications for internal communication with front-line staff: more flexibility for employees can be perceived as more empowering, but it does give up some degree of control. Depending on the brand and the industry, increased or decreased message control may be required. For example, highly regulated industries such as finance and health care may need to restrict flexibility in order to ensure everyone is following the requirements. On the other hand, business-to-business (B2B) companies in service or consulting industries often benefit from more flexible brand language that allows individual members of sales, client management, or service teams to customize messages for specific clients. One critical variable is the size of the client. Larger organizations often require following strict brand guidelines based on the sheer size and complexity of engaging with hundreds or thousands of staff members, while smaller organizations have more options and opportunities to be flexible.

Managers and Executives

Both middle managers and executive leaders are valuable internal audiences that—under the right circumstances—support internal communication by giving it an authoritative voice. Ideally, as conduits and messengers to other employees, they can provide informed customization of information for different departments, geographic locations, and employee identities. It is possible to execute successful corporate communication without the explicit backing of the management team, but programs that provide long-term value for organizations most often cultivate a deep connection between executive values and the approach for internal outreach.

Burton describes managers as "corporate communicators' best friends" because they are the most trustworthy source in providing information to their teams.[20] Having the advantage of closer interpersonal relationships, managers are more often able to deliver messages directly, personally, and colloquially to their team members.

With that in mind, there is also an expectation from employees that managers should provide relevant information about the organization, creating both advantages and disadvantages for those overseeing internal communication.[21] For example, while long-tenured managers may have internalized company messages and procedures, they may have difficulty explaining them to those with less experience. The specialized language of industries, organizations, and even departments can all serve as barriers for interactions among teams that may have different education levels and experiences. Agency practitioners can identify obstacles managers might face (language, tone, attitude, goals, etc.) and help them better understand their audiences (internal constituencies).

---

[20] Burton, K. (2012). Listen up: Why employees are your key. In C. L. Caywood (Ed.), *The handbook of strategic public relations and integrated marketing communications* (2nd ed.). New York, NY: McGraw-Hill Education, p. 135.

[21] Whitworth, B. (2006). Internal communication. In T. L. Gilles (Ed.) *The IABC handbook of organizational communication: A guide to internal communication, public relations, marketing, and leadership*. San Francisco, CA: Jossey-Bass, p. 206.

As mentioned above, an additional wrinkle must be considered when practicing internal communication with managers and executive leaders: These individuals should be considered a direct audience as well as a conduit (and often the primary channel) for delivering information to front-line staff. Many organizations filter information down through several layers of management before it reaches the full staff. In this framework, the majority of communication about a specific announcement may come directly from middle managers rather than from a centralized source. While the intimacy and flexibility of this approach can be beneficial, its effectiveness depends of the ability of managers to understand a message, modify it appropriately for their specific audience, and deliver it effectively. This is not a small or easy task.

On the executive level, there is often the responsibility of shouldering both internal and external speaking obligations that require a deep understanding of organizational values and messages. They are frequently asked questions requiring a connection of information to the broader mission or vision of the organization. In this role, these individuals may require additional support to adapt such messages to a variety of audiences. The adjustments in vocabulary, depth of content, and tone that may be crystal clear to professional communicators are likely less obvious to those in other departments. A communication consultant's time can be valuable in the development of content (such as internal fact sheets) or talking points that are either flexible or distinct for specific audiences. These experts may also spend their time training executives to think as communicators, analyzing each audience and learning to apply an audience-focused approach. In short, the tools of media relations and external communication can also be used effectively to help organizations better communicate to their own internal teams.

Reflect and Discuss

1. What advantages do consultants (external) have over internal team members in executing employee communication programs?

2. What challenges face agency communicators when working on internal communication projects for their clients?

3. Why do different employees need potentially distinct styles, channels, and messages for internal communication?

4. How can integration of internal and external communicators improve idea generation?

5. How can consultants identify the right communication approach for a specific internal audience?

VicRoads is the registered business name of the Roads Corporation, a statutory Corporation within the Victorian Government infrastructure portfolio in Melbourne, Australia. Its purpose is to deliver social, economic, and environmental benefits to communities throughout Victoria by managing the Victorian arterial road network and its use as an integral part of the overall transport system.

Nadine is a PR and internal communications professional with VicRoads. In an interview, she revealed what it is like being part of an internal communications team.

Tell us a little about yourself and what you do. If someone were to apply for a position titled internal communications specialist, what would their job entail?

I'm naturally curious and love to hear people's stories, what shapes and motivates them, and what part they are playing in the world. Everyone has a unique background and story to tell and that's where I step in. Helping others share their experiences and pockets of their life is a large part of why I'm in communications.

Internal communications require a special type of communicator and personality. It's an area that involves numerous skills that are transferrable. My background is largely in public relations, dealing with external audiences and understanding the media landscape. I've recently moved into internal communications to learn about the other side of communications and what it means to work with an internal audience.

My writing skills and understanding of content engagement, along with always thinking "Why does the audience need to know this?" while developing communications, has helped me succeed in my current role. Internal communications requires being a strong writer as well as being able to manage different personality types and having a whole lot of patience! An internal audience is so much more invested in the communications that go out and will have the tools to voice their opinions about it.

Is there crossover between internal communications work and those practicing external communication, such as media relations, marketing, or advertising at the same organization?

Absolutely. We call it the *Herald Sun* test at my current work. This essentially means that if the local newspaper got hold of a communications piece we were sending out internally, would it matter if it ended up on the front page? Internal messages need to be aligned with external messages and vice versa. While employees form an internal audience, they are also part of the public.

How do internal and external communications teams work best together?

Naturally, regular communication and collaboration ensures a successful working relationship between the two groups. Having constant two-way communication means consistent messages and allows an internal audience to hear news at the same time an external audience does.

What advice do you have for someone looking to work in this field?

A large portion of internal communication skills, including writing, event organization, and understanding the benefits of various internal communication tools, can be learned at university. What really sets you apart from others is being able to work with different personality types: essentially, people management. Having the patience, as well as the persuasive and strategic communication skills to communicate with others, is critical to success in this field.

What do you feel is important for readers to learn?

Thoughtful strategic internal communications make up the backbone of a successful organization. Internal communication offers transparency, which I believe is needed for a strong and positive culture in organizations. Internal communications works very closely with various teams, including human resources and corporate affairs, as well as being a trusted advisor for the leadership team and CEO. Always think strategically about the communications that go out within an organization. Check to see whether they support the corporate values, and always think about the best channels to use when distributing these communications to your audience. Write for your audience and constantly think about what they want to know and how will they benefit.

Top 5 Characteristics Every PR Professional Should Have

1. Strong people management skills

2. Writing skills for multiple channels

3. Understanding of the media landscape

4. Persuasive communication skills

5. Creative thinking

Top Must-Haves

- **Must-download app:** Instagram. In a time-poor society, it's very easy to scroll through thousands of photos while getting an update on what's going on in your friends' lives. Instagram is a creative outlet and allows anyone to really see the world differently. I love looking at how a photo is framed and the pops of color that fill my feed. It's a highly influenceable tool. I often get inspired to travel, to think differently, or to visit numerous cafes and restaurants just by seeing the photos my friends take.

- **Must read book/blog/ news outlet:** Australian Broadcasting Corporation (ABC) news online. It's an Australian news source that reports

(Continued)

(Continued)

relevant and timely news from around the world. With an increase in tabloid journalism, it's refreshing to read news that increases your understanding of current affairs, opens you up to seeing things differently, and really helps you keep your mind active. Any media outlet that does this should be read daily to keep you informed about what's happening around you.

- **Must-use tool:** My voice. Face-to-face communication is the most important and crucial when you are trying to persuade and communicate effectively.

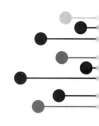

CHAPTER
10
Creative Production

"This logo just doesn't quite get there. Could you take another pass and try to jazz it up? What if we used more green . . . and an edgier font?"

This is every designer's worst nightmare. An otherwise intelligent, knowledgeable, good-natured agency public relations practitioner reviews a designer's work on a project and provides feedback that is of relative little value: *What* about the design does not reflect the brand, product, or event at hand? *What* could "jazz it up" possibly mean? *Why* would green be a more effective color choice? *What* does "edgy" actually describe? PR practitioners do not need to know all of the answers, but agency team members should be able to, at minimum, ask intelligent questions and provide useful feedback to the designers. Just as PR content should be justified and logically supported at every turn, practitioners should expect professional designers to be able to make similar visual or user-experience choices.

At some point in their careers, all PR professionals will be asked to take on or oversee design work. Many will

Objectives

- Decipher how agency practitioners can best manage projects between clients and designers.

- Know the difference between design considerations for print and digital media.

- Recognize the potential challenges and obstacles during the design and production processes.

- Understand how social media content needs impact video and audio production demands for public relations practitioners.

Hero Images Inc./Alamy Stock Photo

make layout and design a significant part of their daily practice, while the balance will interact with designers who are completing this work. PR practitioners should take responsibility for understanding the basic elements, processes, and languages of visual design, print production, video production, and web design. Such projects could range from relatively basic document design to full-scale website or video production. In many cases, expert design professionals will be contracted to handle most of the heavy lifting. These interactions should be collaborative and make the best use of the insights, knowledge, and expertise of the designer as well as the PR team. Too often, organizational silos separate these areas to the point that they can no longer work together effectively. The distances, language barriers, and differing perspective can cause tension, leading to disagreement and mediocre results.

This chapter reviews basic tenants of effective creative production in a variety of formats, serving as an introduction to both the language and the processes that agency professionals must often oversee. It should not be considered in any way a comprehensive approach or guide to design, but a starting point for working *with* designers. More importantly, PR practitioners should leverage the knowledge and talent of designers in the same light that we expect clients and journalists to respect our expertise. Knowing how to use Adobe Photoshop does not magically transform an individual into a designer any more than taking pictures with a smartphone makes us professional photographers. We should learn about the craft of design so that we can gain more respect for the professionals who do this work and so that, when we do have to make design decisions ourselves, we are aware of our own limits.

Basic Visual Design Principles

Every creative discipline has its own accepted genres supported by specific standards. Those creating and overseeing the creation of content in each of these areas should be aware of the practices that exist. As video expert Steve Stockman points out, such standards "help you understand what the audience expects."[1] PR practitioners know what a press release is supposed to look like, how it should read, and what type of information to include. They are keenly aware of the rules. If they break them, they do it consciously. Such rules also apply to print production, video production, and web design.

Every piece of content that we create should have a singular, clear message. As agency practitioners, we must play a careful balancing act between including and integrating people and ideas while driving the creation of creative content to its best possible end. This often involves advocating for certain perspectives on behalf of our designers as well as acting as the guardians of a project's client-driven message and ultimate purpose.

---

[1] Stockman, S. (2011). *How to shoot video that doesn't suck.* New York, NY: Workman, p. 60.

Communicators should see design as the process of envisioning information, as eminent designer Edward Tufte titled his book.[2] Before discovering the best way to present content, practitioners must understand its purpose, its challenges, and its opportunities. PR practitioners write keeping in mind the best format to present information, and visual design must follow the same principles. Rather than starting with a bar graph, pie chart, or table in mind, Tufte encourages his readers to let the content drive the most appropriate format for representing that information to an audience:[3]

- What are the most important elements represented by the visual?

- What is the best way to convey this information?

- How will different formats highlight these elements and make them easily understood?

This approach supports a goal of increasing the amount of information an audience can quickly understand. The best methods remove unnecessary information and increase the density of content a reader can grasp at a glance.[4]

Design decisions should bring out relevant information. Simple uses of color, spatial separation, white space, and layering of data go a long way toward making elegant and effective designs. For example, Tufte recommends avoiding bold, overbearing colors next to each other; while visibly clear, they often distract from the information being presented.[5] Additionally, different textures (color shades or patterns) can be used to indicate the degrees of certain elements while keeping them separated. This approach layers detail without sacrificing clarity.

Design for organizations should also reflect the overall visual brand. Each piece should not live in its own world but must reflect the design language portrayed in the organization's digital and physical footprint. To this end, many organizations have brand guidelines that further define the usage procedures for key

Edward Tufte is a leading voice in the world of information design, challenging communicators to create graphics that increase the depth of content conveyed by making meaningful design choices.

---

[2] Tufte, E. (1990). *Envisioning information*. Chester, CT: Graphics Press.

[3] Ibid.

[4] Ibid., p. 13.

[5] Ibid., see pp. 84–90.

elements such as logos or other materials. While PR practitioners do not necessarily need to memorize every detail of these design-centered documents, it is often useful to review them with designers to avoid potential pitfalls (such as using the incorrect form of the logo on a press release) and to better understand their impact on collaborative projects. Even agency professionals without significant design training should be able to understand why a visual brand looks the way that it does and how it relates visually to associated brand language.

Key Elements From *Universal Principles of Design*

Lidwell, Holden, and Butler provide valuable insights in their book, *Universal Principles of Design*, and present 100 concepts to drive more effective creative work. Several highly relevant principles related to working with creative and design professionals are included:

- *Aesthetic-usability effect*: People perceive well-designed objects, products, and systems as easier to use.[6]

- *Alignment*: Lining up elements creates a sense of unity and cohesion.[7]

- *Chunking*: Breaking information into smaller elements makes it easier to digest.[8]

- *Control*: The amount of control given to a user should be dependent on their "proficiency and experience."[9]

- *Five hat racks*: Information can be organized by "category, time, location, alphabet, and continuum."[10]

- *Ockham's Razor*: When multiple approaches to solving the same design challenge are presented, the simplest approach is often the most effective.[11]

- *Proximity*: The nearer two objects or elements, the more they are perceived as being related.[12]

Working With Designers

While some PR practitioners have the opportunity to develop their personal design skills on the job, many more do not. At a minimum, it is important to

---

[6] Lidwell, W., Holden, K., & Butler, J. (2003). *Universal principles of design*. Gloucester, MA: Rockport, p. 18.

[7] Ibid., p. 22.

[8] Ibid., p. 30.

[9] Ibid., p. 52.

[10] Ibid., p. 84.

[11] Ibid., p. 142.

[12] Ibid., p. 160.

understand how best to work with the design professionals that will be supporting your desired content. This can involve educating the designer on the elements that are most important to a particular project and helping them to evaluate whether their creative elements have accomplished those objectives. In doing this, we must put ourselves in the shoes of the intended audiences. What information will they have? What relevant language, concepts, and design elements will be familiar or foreign? What is the single most important takeaway? Answers to these questions may help drive practitioners (and, by proxy, designers) to move toward a more effective design.

When providing feedback, it is important to explain potential challenges or concerns from the perspective of the audience. Clarity, readability, and impact are valuable factors to evaluate. Always be specific and prioritize challenges. Take time to explain any concern and discuss how they would recommend solving it, particularly in a project's early stages. In the same manner that agency practitioners do not enjoy a client rewriting press releases (often with more mistakes than corrections), a conversation can be effective to convey challenges and realign expectations. However, these discussions do not only need to occur among a designer, agency practitioner, and a client. Audience testing—even informally—can identify potential improvements or uncover unforeseen problems at various stages of design.

Overseeing the Creative Process

In order to get the most from the creative production process, it is often necessary for practitioners to act as both the project manager *and* as an inspirational, enthusiastic coach. Veteran agency practitioners understand the importance of enthusiasm and energy when communicating both to designers and to clients. Passionate practitioners motivate team members by clarifying expectations while also being respectful of their expertise. They hold each individual (including client staff) accountable to deadlines and quality standards in order to keep projects moving forward while also providing useful, constructive feedback. Like a coach, the agency leader for creative projects must devise a game plan and take responsibility for the final product. Within that framework, the best managers empower individual team members—particularly designers—to push their own creativity.

Creative projects can turn into large, difficult-to-wrangle animals that require constant care and feeding. Even the best-laid plans may not work when the rain starts falling on an outdoor photoshoot or when a competitor's website launches first with a similar design. Within this framework, both planning and flexibility become critical for success.

Planning

Each discipline within the creative production process has a different time line for design, development, execution, and production. Consulting with an experienced creative team member can provide more reasonable estimates of the time needed for each step. Agency practitioners should work backward from the deadline to create a project time line that reflects design, development, and production as well as approvals at multiple stages in the process. In addition to timing, practitioners should ask themselves:

- What decisions need to be made before this step can move forward?

- Who needs to approve this design, language, or interface?

- How can we—given the available resources—test our approach on real or simulated users?

The audience should be considered and, if possible, included in multiple stages within the development of major organizational projects. Such work may also draw from prior research done for PR campaigns, sales initiatives, or member/customer surveys.

As with any strategic PR project, practitioners must also ask, "What does success look like?" What would make a new website valuable for an organization? How can we measure it? Organizational leadership, communication team members, and designers should all agree on the measurable objectives for such projects before they begin. Shared understanding allows each group to make the best possible contribution toward the project's success.

One key step to help define these elements is the *creative brief* used in many agency settings as a way to ensure that those in charge of language, visuals, and purpose (as well as those from the client and agency sides) are on the same page. In *How to Write an Inspired Creative Brief*, Howard Ibach underscores the need for a singular, focused message—agreed upon by all parties—as a starting point for successful projects.[13] An effective brief should answer some specific questions: What is the problem? What are we trying to say and how should we say it (tone)? What action do we want our audience or publics to take? What's nonnegotiable (from a design perspective)?[14] Despite their importance in the planning process, briefs should also not be set in stone: The best practitioners adjust briefs to changing circumstances as projects progress. This comes, of course, with the input and approval of all teams involved in the project.

Flexibility

Even the most successful creative projects often deviate from their initial plans. The best teams embrace flexibility—in this case, learning and applying new information to overcome challenges throughout the project. For example, user experience testing of a new website may demonstrate that potential customers want to complete a task in a different way than the team initially envisioned. The team of writers, designers, and developers must be open to such potential changes to have a significant positive impact on achieving the project's goals and objectives.

---

[13] Ibach, H. (2015). *How to write an inspired creative brief* (2nd ed.). Los Angeles, CA: Ibach Media Group LLC.

[14] Oetting, J. (2016, April). 13 questions to help you write a compelling creative brief in 2017. *Hubspot.* Retrieved August 19, 2017, from https://blog.hubspot.com/agency/create-compelling-creative-brief

Practitioners must also be aware of every step in the project time line in order to make adjustments to plans with minimum impact on hard deadlines. Additionally, they must know their team members' skill sets and overall workloads to understand the impact of changes to their assignments. Generally, every team member—not just PR staff—are managing a variety of projects simultaneously. Balancing all of these elements allows for decisions to be made that best reflect the changing environment as a project progresses.

As project coordinators, part of embracing flexibility is empowering every member of the team to contribute their ideas at multiple steps in the process. If designers and PR practitioners are open to each other's insights about ideal results, process improvements, and tactics for a project, the end result has the potential to capture the best of both perspectives. For example, a designer may recommend that a digital display ad is a valuable way to reinforce a company's new visual brand, the PR team can add expertise in publics to identify potential channels for placing the ad, and leadership can provide insights on how to differentiate the approach from competitors in the field. That said, if, during the process, designers identify technical limitations with the selected channels and communicate them appropriately, PR team members may be able to change course on the channels or refine the purpose/approach to ensure that the outreach adds value for the organization.

Learning the Language of Design

Just as public relations and journalism have their own distinct vocabularies, each subdiscipline within the design team has its own terminology as well. Agency professionals, particularly if they work with outside design vendors, should aim to understand as much of this language as possible: Fluency is not expected, but one should know the essential elements. Often, exposure and understanding happens in the midst of projects themselves, particularly the first time a practitioner works on a new type of creative assignment. What follows is an introduction to several key elements of the language of visual design.

Color

For many non-designers, color choices and pairings may seem somewhat arbitrary, but creative professionals understand the deeper meaning, societal context, and framing that color use activates. According to Eiseman, "Color informs, bringing instant comprehension, calling attention, delivering information, creating an identity and explaining the characteristics of a product (or service)."[15] Color combinations work together to create specific moods for the audience. They may

---

[15] Eiseman, L. (2006). *Color: Messages and meanings.* Gloucester, MA: Hand Press Books, p. 66.

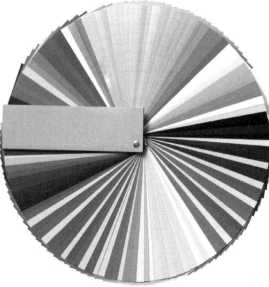

influence individuals in varied ways, including emotion, energy, and appetite. A person's color preferences are often learned within their environments and can be indicative of their cultural, geographic, and socioeconomic roots.[16]

Color use may also be driven by national and global design trends. When working with brands, PR practitioners and designers must decide whether to follow, buck, or avoid such trends. An event-specific logo or product launch may benefit from trendiness, but a company's brand—built for the long-term—may look dated quickly if trendy colors are used. As with many such decisions, it can be valuable to talk them through with a designer to understand why the practitioner or client is interested in a specific approach, as well as to avoid potential obstacles.

Color guides, such as Pantone's, set the standard for color matching in print production.

Printing With Color

According to Johansson, Lundberg, and Ryberg's *A Guide to Graphic Print Production*, there are two color approaches used by designers. This first is called **additive color**, known as **RGB**, and the second is subtractive color, or **CMYK**.[17] Additive color works by contributing some amount of red, green, and blue light (hence, RGB) to create a variety of colors. Using all of the colors at full intensity produces white, and using none of the colors produces black. RGB is used in systems where light creates color, such as television and computer monitors and digital cameras. In a monitor, each **pixel** (the smallest dot on a screen) can produce any color based on RGB. By contrast, **subtractive color** mixing is used for print work, where no addition equals white, and the addition of all colors equals black. CMYK stands for *cyan, magenta,* and *yellow* for *CMY* and *black* for *K*. Printing in full color is known as *four-color*, which entails the use of all four of these inks to produce any color. When only printing one or two specific colors, a more cost-effective option is to use *spot color*, where the printer mixes a specific color of ink for the project at hand. These ink-based printing methods are referred to as **offset printing**, and professional printers often offer either offset or digital printing options (the pros and cons of digital and offset printing are described in more detail on page 157).

[16] Bleicher, S. (2012). *Contemporary color: Theory and use.* Boston, MA: Cengage Learning, pp. 48–52.

[17] Johansson, K., Lundberg, P., & Ryberg, R. (2012). *A guide to graphic print production.* Hoboken, NJ: John Wiley & Sons, p. 71.

A **color system** is a structure for organizing and categorizing specific colors. RGB and CMYK are examples of such systems, as is the internationally recognized Pantone color management system.[18] Designers often refer to a color by its Pantone code. Its famous catalogue comes in fanlike books often seen at agencies and nearly always within reach for professional designers.[19] Matching colors between these systems or from existing materials is extremely difficult. Different printers and techniques, equipment, and materials (both paper and ink) all contribute to such differences.[20] For agency practitioners, this can cause a significant challenge when a client needs to print new stationary or business cards and a printer struggles to match the color in a logo based on existing materials. In this situation, the best scenario is to work with the same printer, who will often keep archives of past jobs and maintain the same or similar equipment and materials. Digital printing will never be able to match color as well as offset printing, because there is a lack of control of the color as part of the process. Therefore, organizations looking to match colors should attempt to use the same printer, the same materials, and an offset production process as often as possible.

Fonts

As communicators, we often ignore or downplay the functional importance of font choices. Font selection and innovation makes highway signs more readable and reduces accidents. Fonts such as **Trebuchet** and the much-derided **Comic Sans** have been shown to improve readability for those with dyslexia. Agency practitioners should not underestimate the importance and value of informed font choices in design work.

An understanding begins with differentiating *serif* and *sans serif* typefaces. Serif fonts include a "finishing stroke" at the base or tip of the font, as seen in **Times New Roman**, Garamond, or `Courier`. Serif fonts—often stereotyped as more formal and traditional—represented the earliest typefaces from Gutenberg's printing press and were nearly universal until well into the 19th century. The now-ubiquitous sans serifs such as **Calibri**, **Gill Sans**, and **Helvetica** rose to prominence in large part because of their clean, modern sensibility.

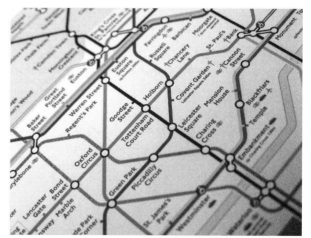

Panther Media GmbH/Alamy Stock Photo

Typefaces, such as the Underground font designed for the London subway, are often indispensible parts of a brand's visual identity.

---

[18] Ibid., p. 74.

[19] Finlay, V. (2002). *Color: A natural history of the palette.* New York, NY: Ballentine Books, p. 394.

[20] Johansson, K., Lundberg, P., & Ryberg, R. (2012). *A guide to graphic print production.* Hoboken, NJ: John Wiley & Sons, p. 77.

Fonts have value both in function and design. In *Just My Type*, Simon Garfield articulates the difference between legibility and readability by explaining that "some type is meant to be seen rather than read."[21] For the PR professional, it is imperative to consider the implications for a brand. Classic typography—such as the Underground font designed for the London subway—is a core part of the institution's brand identity. Practitioners must balance these elements and work closely with designers to ensure that organizational brands are distinctly represented and that font choices reflect the function of each piece and each project.

In web design, font availability creates another potential wrinkle: Not all fonts are available on all computers. For example, there are often significant differences between fonts available on Mac and PC-based systems. Certain widely used fonts have been designated as *web safe*, meaning that they are available to all web users and will display correctly on the vast majority of machines.

Useful Font Terminology

- *Tracking*: The relative spacing between letters in a font.

- *Kerning*: The differentiated spacing between individual letters in a font. For example, in the word *font*, the *f* and *o* are closer together than the *o* and the *n*.

- *H-height*: The standard height of a capital letter in a specific font, based on the letter *H*.

- *Typefaces*: What is colloquially known as a *font* or *font family*, such as Times New Roman or Calibri, including all variations of that font.

- *Stylistic variants*: Within a font family, the variations such as regular, italic, bold, and small caps. Professional designers always prefer the official variant rather than a computer program's calibration of a bold, italic, or small caps version.

Image Use

Working with digital images requires a basic knowledge of file types, size, and resolution. The most common formats practitioners encounter are **JPEG**, GIF, and **TIFF**. JPEG images are compressed using a method generally supportive to preserving the quality of a full-color photograph for web use. GIF compression does not preserve image quality as effectively, although the format provides more functionality—such as animation. TIFF images generate much larger file sizes, which can provide higher quality and resolution. This is valuable for design and printing purposes, but less useful for web-driven projects, where smaller images (and faster download speeds) are the main challenge. Generally, the larger the

---

[21] Garfield, S. (2011). *Just my type: A book about fonts*. New York, NY: Gotham Books, p. 50.

image size and the larger the file size within each of these formats, the higher the resolution, meaning a higher-quality image for print purposes. All compression removes data from the image, reducing its quality. Printers will often use the standard of 300 PPI as a minimum image quality for printing. *PPI* stands for pixels-per-inch, which is the image's resolution (300 *dots-per-inch* or *DPI* is the older print-centric term, which is still used as well). With image editing software such as Adobe Photoshop, designers can reset an image's size based on the resolution available. Digital images can never have their resolution increased, so it is important that practitioners save and archive original, high-resolution images for future use.

Learning the Language of Print Production

High-quality printing may seem like a dying art in an environment where so much of marketing is moving to digital distribution. It is for exactly this reason, because it is less ubiquitous, that print is still powerful. Less often today are businesses bombarded with mailers, carefully designed brochures, and glossy magazines or newsletters. As many organizations have eliminated these items due to production costs, it opens up opportunities for others to create memorable content and deliver it using a medium that gets users away from their computer, tablet, or smartphone screens. It can be both effective and refreshing.

Another barrier is that print production has its own distinct language and process expectations that may seem very foreign to PR practitioners when they encounter them for the first time. As fewer and fewer practitioners learn these skills, they actually become increasingly valuable to organizations.

Professional printing is divided between **digital printing** and offset printing. In general, digital printing is faster and cheaper for smaller volumes, as the setup costs are very low. Depending on the type of project, the quality may be comparable to offset printing when done by a professional print shop. It also allows for differentiation, such as printing a thousand letters with a personalized greeting based on the recipient. Offset or traditional ink printing takes longer to set up and execute but is generally higher quality and more cost-effective for large volumes. It also provides more flexibility for printing on different surfaces and paper types.

Paper is another important printing consideration. To inform selection, practitioners should ask themselves what tone or feel they want to get across through a particular product.[22] It is important to note that paper can be light or heavy, glossy or matte, depending on the objectives of the project. These choices can reinforce formality/informality, expensive/efficient, or light/sturdy, depending on the organizational brand and needs of the specific project. All of these components affect the tone conveyed by the piece as well as its cost, the quality of images or text (often as a trade-off), and restrictions on distribution (such as mailing).

---

[22] Johansson, K., Lundberg, P., & Ryberg, R. (2012). *A guide to graphic print production*. Hoboken, NJ: John Wiley & Sons, p. 308.

When laying out text, readability and visual hierarchy should be the primary concern. Practitioners can point designers toward the message elements of highest importance and be an initial judge of the audience's ability to interpret these choices. It is valuable to understand the page layout language used by designers. On a page of text, the white space above the main content is referred to as the **head**, the corresponding area below is known as the **tail**. In a bound product such as a book, areas to the right and left of the text are known as the **margins**, and the space in between two pages of bound text is called the **gutter**.[23]

Once the layout process is complete, a printer will move to prepress, ensuring that all files are correctly put together and that the content is set up correctly for the printing, cutting, folding, mailing, or other processes that may be involved, as well as providing a final proof for agency or client sign-off. The final steps are the physical printing process and the finishing and binding stage, where the raw printed material is turned into the completed product.

The Stages of Print Production

Johansson, Lundberg, and Ryberg break down the print production process into four main steps: [24]

1. Layout: Organizing the images, illustrations, and text using software such as Adobe InDesign

2. Prepress: Creating print-ready files and generating final printed proofs

3. Printing: Through a printer (digital) or a press (offset)

4. Finishing and binding: Cropping, folding, and binding to final specifications

---

Cost

Estimating the cost of specific projects is often a challenge. According to Johansson, Lundberg, and Ryberg, "pricing in graphic print production is far from standardized and can vary greatly from service provider to service provider."[25] As printing equipment and expertise differ widely, practitioners should seek a printer who is accomplished and accustomed to doing the type of work (size, complexity, quality, volume, and turnaround time) that the project needs. It is always good practice to gather multiple bids and discuss the expertise of each vendor prior to selecting partners for a particular project.

---

[23] Ibid., p. 381.

[24] Ibid., pp. 13–15.

[25] Ibid., p. 21.

Factors that affect the overall cost include startup/setup pricing, the size and format of the final product, the number of colors needed, paper selection, and finishing and binding decisions (such as collating, folding, perforating, scoring, stapling, and trimming) as well as packaging and distribution. And this assumes that all design work will be fully final before submitting content to the printer. A higher-volume project means higher costs, but the costs are not always incremental. Because of paper sizes and sheets needed for offset printing, the breaks in price are determined differently for different projects.

ton koene/Alamy Stock Photo

Printing technology provides a wide variety of options for speed, quality, materials, processes, and pricing. Agency practitioners can help their clients successfully and strategically navigate these possibilities.

Choosing a Printer

Finding the best printer to begin a specific project, to meet the needs of a demanding client, or to build a long-term agency partnership is never easy. Johansson, Lundberg, and Ryberg offer the following factors to consider when choosing a printer.[26]

- **Competence and reputation:** Does the printer have a strong reputation within your industry? Do they regularly execute work similar to what your project needs?

- **Delivery timing:** Printers should have clear guarantees about timing and expectations for each step of the process.

- **Capacity:** Do they have enough time in their schedule to fit your project into their workflow? Does their equipment allow for efficient production of needed materials?

- **Organization and personal interaction:** Are they able to assist and guide those outside their industry to better understand the processes, structure, and cost of complex projects? Do they communicate clearly and in a timely fashion?

- **Proximity:** Geographic considerations can play a significant role if you need to check proofs in a timely fashion and deliver final products.

- **Business outlook:** If you'll be doing similar work in the future, it is always preferable to build an ongoing relationship with the printer. The better their business, the more stable they will be.

---

[26] Ibid., p. 28.

Learning the Language of Video Production

In digital communication, video production is becoming more of a requirement for many organizations, as technology has made the tools of shooting, editing, and distribution available at very low cost. Videos that cost thousands or tens of thousands of dollars to produce in 2005 can now be shot with most smartphones, edited on laptops, and shared easily via YouTube and other social media channels. Organizations that have compelling visual content can and should have very few barriers to getting started. That being said, having the tools to create video is separate from having the skills to produce valuable content. Effective video must utilize best practices of messaging and design. From a technical perspective, aspects such as lighting and sound quality are difficult for most amateur videographers to master.

The video production process can be broken down into three stages: (1) planning and preparation, (2) **production**, and (3) **post-production**.[27] Production includes the act of shooting the video, while post-production involves the editing and creation of the final deliverables.

Audio Recording and Editing

Whether it's to accompany video production or to create a podcast, audio recording and editing can be challenging (and, thus, valuable) skills for practitioners to understand at a basic level. Jay Rose's excellent guide, *Producing Great Sound for Film and Video*, emphasizes that, with some basic tips and planning, we can greatly improve the quality of sound in our creative work.[28] Agency practitioners may need to handle some of this work themselves (for example, in creating quick, low-budget social media content) or collaborate with other team members and vendors as part of project teams.

- **Audio Terminology:**
  - *Clipping*: When the volume level is louder than the microphones can handle, creating distortion. Adjust your levels so that this doesn't occur.
  - *Directional*: Microphones that pick up sound better from one direction
  - *Lav*: Short for *lavaliere microphone*, lavs are small microphones usually clipped to the body (often near the subject's mouth) for improved speech pickup.[29]

---

[27] Millerson, G. & Owens, J. (2008) *Video Production Handbook*. Burlington, MA: Focal Press, p. 37.

[28] Rose, J. (2014). *Producing great sound for film and video: Expert tips from preproduction to final mix*. New York, NY: Taylor and Francis.

[29] Ibid., p. 174.

- *Mono*: Sound recorded with a single track
- *MP3*: A compressed audio format that saves space but can sacrifice quality if not handled carefully
- *Omni*: Short for *omnidirectional*, this refers to microphones that pick up sound equally well from all directions
- *Stereo*: Sound recording with a separate left and right channel
- *Tracks*: Separate layers of recorded audio that are mixed together to create the final audio
- *WAV*: A digital sound format that retains more information than MP3, resulting in a larger file size

- **Preproduction: Planning Sound Recording**
  - Ask yourself: How will sound help to tell the story?[30] Is clarity of the dialogue or main speaker the most important? Will background noise distract or help to set the scene? Will music and other effects be added later?
  - Plan the sound for each piece of your storyboard—it's not just for the visual elements.[31]
  - Check locations and equipment ahead of time to ensure that they are able to meet your expectations for sound.[32]

- **Production: Recording Sound**
  - Know your equipment's capabilities, strengths, and weaknesses.
  - Watch your levels: Carefully set and regularly check that your recording volume is set at a reasonable mid- to high level.
  - Be conscious of potentially distracting noises as you shoot, including weather, traffic, building heat and air conditioning, and even noisy refrigerators and fish tanks![33]
  - Be flexible: Try different angles, positions, and placements for sound equipment when you're shooting in a particular space to find the best positioning.

(Continued)

---

[30] Ibid., p. 83.

[31] Ibid., p. 84.

[32] Ibid., p. 88.

[33] Ibid., p. 136.

(Continued)

- **Post-production: Editing Sound**

  ○ Dialogue and narration (voiceover) should sound different, which should factor into both their recording and post-production.

  ○ Audio editing can be performed within nonlinear video editing software (such as Adobe Premiere) or in audio-only programs such as WaveLab, GarageBand, or Audacity.

  ○ Editing is a creative process—a lack of knowledge about the software and technology tools involved limits our ability to create.[34]

  ○ Volume levels should be adjusted throughout so that the listener does not need to change their settings in the middle of the piece.

Planning and Preparation

Video projects should begin with goals and objectives—like any other strategic effort. Working with an experienced producer can help PR practitioners plan a project appropriately and provide the best opportunity for success. Often, before a budget can be finalized, the producer will need to create a **storyboard** to ensure that all parties agree on the specific direction of the production and understand what types of shots need to be captured. Although they can take many forms, a storyboard is simply a series of rough sketches to arrange and organize the most important visual moments. Once a storyboard is set, the producer will work with their team to create a **shot sheet** or **shot card** to ensure that all of the necessary footage is captured for specific scenes. Working from these outlines, the producers, writers, and agency team members can assemble the **full script**—the document housing the language used in the production as well as the necessary stage and camera directions. One key element in a video production is **continuity**, the logical progression of action from shot to shot. For example, actors shooting multiple scenes over multiple days often must wear the same clothes in order to convey a sense of unity to the overall project. Some of this context can be dealt with in the full script and shot card, ensuring that all parts of a sequence are represented, but it must also be followed during the editing process in post-production.

Budgets are determined from one of two perspectives: a hard dollar amount, where producers are asked to create the best-possible product given those constraints, or a line-item budget built based on the size, scope, timing, and complexity of the project. Both require a detailed understanding of the final product and what will be executed in production and post-production to achieve it.

---

[34] Ibid., p. 253.

Production and Post-Production

Editing the footage to select the right shots and takes, maintain continuity, and focus the content on the most important messages is never an easy job. Even for short clips, editing can be a long and challenging process. Practitioners should consider the use of additional elements such as still images and *b-roll* (footage without dialogue, often of a process, background, or environmental setting) to intersperse with the main footage during editing to maintain viewer interest.

mark phillips/Alamy Stock Photo

Video professionals and PR practitioners alike rely on nonlinear video editing software, such as Final Cut Pro and Adobe Premiere.

Post-production often includes the options for adding effects, graphics, and other on-screen features. The general rule of thumb is to keep such extras to a minimum, only using them when they enhance understanding and impact of the overall message. Graphics and titles, from the simple titles to complex animation, can add professionalism, context, and valuable information density to many video productions. Most editing software facilitates the creation of useable graphics, but those with a knowledge of Photoshop and other graphic design programs can utilize these vastly more focused tools to customize exactly what graphics are needed. Subtitles (also known as *closed captioning*) are another use of on-screen graphics, which has grown in popularity for digital video. As many social media users scroll down their

---

Additional Video Terminology:[35]

- *Clip*: A segment of video

- *Dissolve*: An editing effect fading directly from one image into another

- *Fade*: A gradual dissolve to or from an image and a black screen

- *Nonlinear editing*: Digital editing processes wherein the editor can continuously rearrange the order of footage, add effects, and adjust audio and graphics

- *Running order*: The final order of the scenes and shots in a video, often very different from the order in which they are shot

- *Shooting order*: The order in which shots are gathered, generally based on convenience and location needs

---

[35] Millerson, G. & Owens, J. (2008) *Video Production Handbook*. Burlington, MA: Focal Press, pp. 295–297.

feeds, most videos do not play sound automatically, and many users also have their device's sound turned down or off. With these end-user realities, content creators benefit from including subtitles so that everyone can get a clear picture of the message and content of a shared video, no matter where or how they encounter it.

Reflect and Discuss

1. What do agency professionals need to know before starting a project with a professional designer?

2. What are some common mistakes made by inexperienced agency professionals working with designers?

3. Why do designers use multiple systems to organize color?

4. Why do video producers need a nearly finalized script to provide an accurate quote for the project?

Stephanie Baumer

Stephanie Baumer is a print, web, and branding designer. She has worked at a handful of different design studios and currently works at Taylor Design as an art director. Stephanie likes to work with a variety of clients, from large corporations and universities to the smallest local cafes and businesses. She dabbles in illustration as well. Since 1992, Taylor Design has helped shape brand destinies through deep strategic understanding and an innovative mind-set. Based out of Stamford, Connecticut, they help clients reposition, communicate, promote, train, and entertain through a strategic mix of communications tools.

Stephanie shared with us a few secrets for PR professionals to take into consideration the next time they work with graphic designers.

Explain what an initial brainstorming session with a PR professional may entail for a creative piece.

Typically, this process begins with a creative brief describing the goals and intentions of the piece, including how the piece will be used, where and how it will be distributed, who the audience is, and the strategic goal. The client may have firm answers to some of these questions, but on others, they may ask for your recommendation. We also need to consider if the piece will introduce a new brand/product/person or if the piece will be part of an established brand, as that will influence the messaging. These elements will start to mold the appropriate overall look and feel (formal or casual, understated or energetic, intricate or clean, etc.) as well as what structure would be appropriate. To use an invitation suite as an example: If the end goal is a relaxed happy hour that the client has set up with the strategic goal of strengthening their community, an email invitation with fun and casual messaging would be appropriate. If the client sets up a black-tie event with an end goal of raising $5 million for a campaign, a print piece with a hand-lettered address and formal messaging may set the most appropriate tone.

To match the messaging that you establish, the designer will come up with options for color palettes, typefaces, photography or illustration style or other graphic elements, paper, and physical structure as well as printing techniques or digital development requirements. While you may not have the exact costs for all the options, it is a good idea to keep the budget in mind in this early stage. Clients often give a range of funds and may or may not be able to get additional money to pay for a more expensive option.

Most PR professionals are not graphic designers; however, the two work together often. With this in mind, what common terminology should every practitioner know when communicating with a graphic designer?

It's important to familiarize yourself with different styles of typefaces, especially the difference between the two largest groups: san serif and serif typefaces. Sans serifs are more common and easier to read in digital formats; serifs are easier to read in print and can look more traditional. There are also scripts, slab serifs, blackletter, decorative fonts, and a whole slew of other categories.

If you are working on a print piece, there are many technical terms, but familiarizing yourself with some common high-end print techniques, such as emboss, deboss, engraving, and foil stamping, will give you a head start in knowing what possibilities are out there.

Terms involving color are also important. RGB (red, green, blue) or Hex numbers are digital color modes. CMYK (cyan, magenta, yellow, and black) is a print color mode. Pantone colors or PMS (Pantone matching system) are a set of pre-mixed colors that you can use as a brand color to create consistency in materials across print, web, plastics, fabrics, and many other applications.

What do you love about working with other communication professionals such as PR professionals, marketing mavens, or social media experts?

I think the best work comes out of a team of people who are all good at what they do. It is refreshing to work with others who approach a project slightly differently than you would and who have points that can change and enhance the work that you are contributing to. When a piece has the messaging and copywriting, design, photography, marketing, and so on all working in sync, you can get some inspiring work.

What is your biggest pet peeve when working with someone who does not have intimate graphic design knowledge?

My biggest pet peeve is working with clients who have too many decision makers. "Design by committee," as designers often say, can completely ruin even the best projects. When the project has been tweaked to 12 different

(Continued)

(Continued)

peoples' preferences (which are often at odds), the project will undoubtedly end up a meek version of where it began. And, more often than not, the client is not even happy with the final product—most of the time, the only thing a large group of people can agree on is the most expected, ordinary ideas (and I have never had a client ask for that!)

If the situation arises where you're working with a large group of stakeholders (for instance, if the piece must be approved by a board of directors), I would recommend assigning one person on the client side the task of gathering—and more importantly, culling down—feedback. That way, the designer has one set of comments to work with. Remember: Too many chefs spoil the soup!

What is the best strategy for successfully working with a graphic designer?

The best way to approach working with a graphic designer is to explain the problem and not dictate the solution. If you receive a design that you think misses the mark, don't be prescriptive in your feedback by asking the designer to "make the bright red box gray." Instead, let them know that you think the colors set the wrong tone and ask how they might address it, perhaps by saying, "I think the boxes are giving the piece a youthful look and feel that doesn't relate to this audience—is there another color palette or other solution that may work better for this audience?" When you leave the problem open-ended, the designer will use their expertise to give you the best design solutions. Instead of simply changing the box to gray, the designer may come up with something that better achieves your goal. For instance, they may reply, "I would suggest keeping the bright red on this page because it works so nicely with the photograph; however, I changed the box from a solid red fill to a thin red outline, which is much more elegant and not as loud."

Anything else that you feel is important for readers to learn?

One other important note in working with graphic designers, or any creative team, is to keep your personal preferences out of the decision making. Every decision should work toward the goals of the project. When you are reviewing a piece, do not ask, "Do I like this typeface?" but instead ask, "Is this typeface appropriate for the project?"

Top 5 Characteristics Every PR Professional Should Have

1. **Interest in problem solving:** Really, what any creative professional does is problem solve—whether it is with words, visually, and so on. The desire to get to the heart of the project and find the best solution is what creates passion in your work.

2. **Flexibility:** Any work that is client based requires great patience and flexibility. Budgets, project goals, and any other decisions can all change mid-project. It can be frustrating, but to create the best project within the (changing) constraints, you must be able to roll with the punches.

3. **Organization:** I think that organization is very helpful to anyone working in large teams. Keeping track of versions, edits, comments, where you are in the schedule, where you are in the budget, and so on are all crucial parts of a successful project.

4. **Trust:** It is important to trust that the professionals you are working with are experts in their field. You are the expert in PR, the designer is the expert in design, and the client knows their business best.

5. **Reflection:** With all the small pieces of feedback, compressed schedules, and changing parameters, it is easy to get caught up in the details of a project and forget to take a step back to evaluate whether the project is still on course. It's important to consider the end goals and larger picture at each turning point.

Top Must-Haves

- **Must-download app:** Because I am a visual learner, Pinterest is my favorite app. I can save illustrators, photographers, copywriters I want to work with, and typefaces I'd like to use. I can create mood boards for clients or pin inspiration for an upcoming project to share with my team.

- **Must-read book/ blog/news outlet:** My favorite design blog at the moment is "It's Nice That"—a great, curated mix of all sorts of art and design.

- **Must-use tool:** My office uses Function Point to track our time and do estimates and billing. This, or a service like this, is really helpful for staying organized and on track.

CHAPTER 11

Search Engine Optimization, Content Marketing, and Digital Marketing

"We think that we are reasonable, rational people and that our decisions are made by careful thinking. But the reality is that the website we pick, what we decide to do while there, and whether we buy or not are decisions and actions that we make in a largely unconscious way."[1]

—Susan Weinschenk

Design and content creation today is not just about how content looks, but how users find it and interact with it. **User experience** (UX) and user interface (UI) design as well as content marketing and search engine optimization (SEO) approaches are critical areas for the success of digital projects. While UX and UI tend to be understood as primarily visual design approaches, there is a significant content organization component as well. This is often referred to as *information architecture*, and agency communicators can and should drive these ordering choices using their expertise in audience understanding and strategic language. These terms have risen in prominence as the importance of excellent web and mobile design has increased, but they are not exclusive to digital realms. Understanding these perspectives adds to a practitioner's ability to work with designers and developers but also informs their broader work, including event planning (the ultimate UX) and structuring writing about complex subjects.

As users, many of our web-based decisions have more to do with SEO and UX design than we realize. SEO website design, **SEO copywriting**, and digital marketing go together like peas and carrots, or as author and search expert, Neil Patel likes to say, peanut butter and jelly.[2]

Objectives

- Understand how public relations correlates to developing the user experience.

- Distinguish between search engine optimization, search engine marketing, and search engine copywriting.

- Summarize the fundamentals of website design and functionality.

- Learn how to develop an integrated public relations strategy based on the importance of internet search, content marketing, and digital marketing.

---

[1] Weinschenk, S. (2009). *Neuro web design: What makes them click?* Berkeley, CA: New Riders, p. 1.

[2] Patel, N. (2014, January 20). 7 smart ways to combine content marketing with SEO for more qualified search traffic. *Quick sprout.* Retrieved November 10, 2017, from https://www.quicksprout.com/2014/01/20/7-smart-ways-to-combine-content-marketing-with-seo-for-more-qualified-search-traffic/

Regardless of the analogy, one thing is certain: SEO and digital strategy are paramount for effective external communication. Think about this:[3,4]

- Ninety-three percent of online experiences begin with a search engine.

- Google accounts for over 94% of all mobile and tablet search traffic globally, followed by Yahoo at 3% and Bing at 1%.

- Over 76% of all global desktop search traffic is completed through Google, followed by Bing at 8%, Baidu at 7.5%, and Yahoo at 7%.

- Google receives over 57,000 searches per second daily, translating into nearly 2 trillion searches annually.

- The first five results in Google receive a 67% click rate.

- Nearly 40% of individuals search only on a smartphone in an average day.

An effective digital presence starts with thoughtful design. Whether consumers buy, read, donate, or browse, companies are interested in driving up the number of visitors to their webpages. There are essential elements and language to web design that every practitioner should familiarize themselves with. Websites must be designed both to attract and capture traffic through SEO as well as to provide a useful experience for the people who find them.

Rawpixel Ltd/Alamy Stock Photo

A great deal of thought goes into creating captivating websites. User experience must be kept in mind when designing a new site.

Principles of Web Design

A basic understanding of web writing, design standards, and coding is valuable for today's public relations professionals, as they must often update digital content and connect to it through social media channels. While practitioners may not be coding websites, they must understand the capabilities, limitations, and best practices in working with agency and client teams on digital projects. However, a slightly deeper understanding of website development, structure, function,

[3] McEvoy, M. (2016, November 29). SEO statistics to know in 2017. *Web presence solutions*. Retrieved December 19, 2016, from http://www.webpresencesolutions.net/seo-statistics-2017-seo-stats/

[4] Patel, N. (n.d.). SEO made simple: A step-by-step guide. *Neil Patel*. Accessed January 16, 2017, from http://neilpatel.com/what-is-seo/

and interaction is necessary to manage web development projects, often with agency, client, designer, and developer involvement. Learning basic web design vocabulary is a significant first step:

- *Backward compatibility*: A important design consideration; the functionality of programs developed for current operating systems, hardware, and web browsers should still be accessible with older technology

- **Content management system (CMS)**: WordPress, Drupal, Wix, and Joomla! are among the leading systems that allow for relatively easy website creation and updating

- *Cascading style sheets (CSS)*: A web design and layout system that allows for flexible sizing based on the display size

- *Flash*: A software technology for creating and managing interactive multimedia web applications such as websites, animations, movies, games, advertisement banners, and more. It gives almost unlimited options in the design of web pages, but is less compatible and accessible than other programming languages.

- *Hand coding*: Writing website code without the use of design programs or templates

- *HTML/XHTML*: The basic web design language, very useful for displaying text and adding images and links

- *Information architecture*: The layout and organization of information and content on a website in a way that makes it simple for users to find what they need through search, navigation, and menus

- *JavaScript*: An object-oriented computer programming language commonly used to create interactive effects within web browsers[5]

- *Parallax*: Web design language that allows for moving images and graphics, often used for highly stylized designs and long-scrolling sites.

- *PHP*: Hypertext Preprocessor is an open source, server-side, HTML-embedded scripting language used to create dynamic web pages

- *Responsive design*: The creation of websites that will adjust to function in desktop and mobile form.

---

[5] JavaScript. (2017). *English Oxford living dictionaries*. Retrieved December 14, 2017, from https://en .oxforddictionaries.com/definition/javascript

- *Re-skin*: Using a content management system, overlaying a new design template (skin) on top of existing content. This provides a relatively easy way to refresh a site's design.

- *Site map*: Also known as a *web tree*, the site map provides an overall structure for the site, listing every page. In today's designs, the traditional *tree* with clear branches has been replaced by a matrix, where multiple pages link to each other at multiple levels of the interface, allowing for more user choices and flexibility.

- *WordPress*: The most popular content management system, WordPress is open source and very robust, with a wide variety of functionality and regularly updated plugins.

Public Relations and the User Experience

UX design may sound wildly outside the bounds of PR oversight, but it is an area where agency practitioners have a lot to contribute. Practitioners should take advantage of their deep understanding of organizational publics and their behaviors and preferences to support the work of designers and developers regarding the organization and structure of digital content. Because our expertise is related to dealing with audiences and information dissemination—the tools public relations uses to build relationships—it makes practitioners uniquely qualified to support the work of usability experts as well as in-house information technology and development staff to improve design. According to usability testing expert Steve Krug, "web teams aren't notoriously successful at making decisions about usability questions," as they are too close to the content and processes at hand.[6] PR teams—and agency teams in particular—have the audience knowledge and external perspective to improve these decisions.

In the same way that PR practitioners are trained to adapt their writing styles for different audiences, these adjustments also allow for informed choices when developing a website. From selecting the text size and color scheme of a website to the need for isolated web pages for differentiated content (a blog-style setup for regularly updated, shareable content as opposed to a scrolling **parallax design**—a site with more static content but more complex visual design elements), the choices that a practitioner makes are directly tied to the final design. What might the target audience respond to? How long are they likely to stay on the site? Are they more likely to interact with the brand through its website directly or through social media channels? The answers to such questions can heavily influence the direction of a specific creative project—and PR professionals often are in the best position to have these answers.

---

[6] Krug, S., Bayle, E., Straiger, A., & Matcho, M. (2014). *Don't make me think, revisited: A common sense approach to web usability* (3rd ed.). San Francisco, CA: New Riders, p. 103.

Principles of Digital Dialogue

In 1998, Michael Kent and Maureen Taylor introduced the notion of online dialogic relationship building by proposing five theory-based dialogic principles of website communication:[7]

1. **Principle One: The Dialogic Loop**— Feedback from an audience should be embedded in the PR tactic. This allows for an organization and its public to communicate interactively. A person should be available to respond to concerns, questions, or requests.

2. **Principle Two: The Usefulness of Information**—Sites should include information that is valuable to organizational stakeholders and publics.

3. **Principle Three: The Generation of Return Visits**—Sites should create and regularly update information that makes visitors want to come back.

4. **Principle Four: An Intuitive Interface**— Visitors should find sites easy to understand and navigate.

5. **Principle Five: The Rule of Conservation of Visitors**—Website visitors should be valued; therefore, it is recommended that sites include only essential links that drive traffic back to an organization's site.

The dialogic principles have become a cornerstone for PR research and are still used by PR and communication scholars and practitioners. Today, researchers are discovering new ways to apply these principles to digital communication beyond website development.

Krug's Seven Traits of Usability

In his book, *Don't Make Me Think*, author Steve Krug lists seven traits of usability for digital design:[8]

- **Useful**: Digital activities and content must be valuable for a user.

- **Learnable**: Users should be able to intuitively complete all major tasks.

- **Memorable**: Structure and tasks should not need to be relearned.

- **Effective**: It accomplishes its intended purpose for the organization and users.

- **Efficient**: It should not require more time or effort than necessary to navigate or complete tasks.

- **Desirable**: Users want to take advantage of content and actions.

- **Delightful**: Users should enjoy the experience of accessing information and completing tasks.

---

[7] Kent, M. L., & Taylor, M. (1998). Building dialogic relationships through the World Wide Web. *Public Relations Review, 24*, 321–334. doi:10.1016/s0363-8111(99)80143-x.

[8] Krug, S., Bayle, E., Straiger, A., & Matcho, M. (2014). *Don't make me think, revisited: A common sense approach to web usability* (3rd ed.). San Francisco, CA: New Riders, p. 9.

Designing for Usability

In *Designing Web Interfaces*, Scott and Neil emphasize a number of key principles for creating interactive digital channels. One is to "keep it lightweight," emphasizing the importance of minimizing the number of choices that a user can have at all points so that the choice can be made more easily and frequently.[9] As Krug states, this is accomplished by efforts to "eliminate distractions," "create effective visual hierarchies," and "take advantage of conventions."[10]

A second important concept or metric for creating interactive digital channels is *flow*, the idea that a user should move naturally through a given task without having to consciously consider the steps needed to complete it.[11] Flow is equally as important in the design of apps—app users often have less patience to complete the task at hand. PR practitioners are in a particularly valuable position to utilize this metric when evaluating interfaces and user experience. Flow is significantly increased with the increased ability to scan: When a user can quickly sort through content or make decisions, they are much more likely to have an easy, enjoyable process and return.

Calls to action (CTAs) are a critical part of a website or web page's functionality. They often determine the success or failure of its ability to sell tickets, gather email addresses, or elicit feedback. Whatever the objective, a CTA funnels a user's attention toward a specific purpose. Scott and Neil recommend CTAs for singular or "simple 1-2-3" tasks.[12] They describe the most effective versions to be visually distinct and compelling, inviting clicks or action by visual separation from the rest of the content or by providing empty boxes, enticing the user to fill them in.

Evaluating Usability

In its simplest form, usability is about creating intuitive interfaces. Krug describes the object as to "get rid of the question marks" for the user.[13] When navigating through a website, and particularly when testing a process the user needs to complete, practitioners should put themselves in the shoes of the user to anticipate potential challenges: Are links clearly clickable? Do menus bring up anticipated destinations? Are terms unambiguous? Ideally, practitioners should observe actual users putting themselves through this process with draft pages and tasks, known as **usability testing**. Particularly for web-based businesses, there is no better feedback than watching customers attempt to accomplish important tasks and seeing where any hiccups occur. For a business, such tasks may include making

---

[9] Scott, B., & Neil, T. (2009). *Designing web interfaces: Principles and patterns for rich interactions.* Sebastopol, CA: O'Reilly Media, Inc., p. 76.

[10] Krug, S., Bayle, E., Straiger, A., & Matcho, M. (2014). *Don't make me think, revisited: A common sense approach to web usability* (3rd ed.). San Francisco, CA: New Riders, p. 29.

[11] Scott, B., & Neil, T. (2009). *Designing web interfaces: Principles and patterns for rich interactions.* Sebastopol, CA: O'Reilly Media, Inc., p. 102.

[12] Ibid., p. 185.

[13] Krug, S., Bayle, E., Straiger, A., & Matcho, M. (2014). *Don't make me think, revisited: A common sense approach to web usability* (3rd ed.). San Francisco, CA: New Riders, p. 13.

a purchase, contacting support, or seeking additional product information. For a nonprofit organization, important actions might include the ability to make a donation, signing up to volunteer for an event, or examining the organization's mission and partners. Traditional testing processes begin with recruiting individuals from outside the organization and asking them to complete these types of basic tasks. While some practitioners may be intimidated with this process, even a simple setup with over-the-shoulder observation can be extremely useful. With larger-scale development, there is always the opportunity to bring in user experience specialists to perform larger, more quantitatively rigorous usability studies.

Krug recommends beginning usability testing as early in the design process as possible and repeating as often as possible, even if it is only one user at a time.[14] Receiving early feedback provides an opportunity to fix potentially major structural flaws beyond the cosmetic. Gathering this feedback sometimes leads to practitioners and clients hearing what they do not want to hear, but it allows informed decisions to be made and challenges to be prioritized. This is not to say that usability testing should not happen later in the development process as well, but the feedback and goals of these sessions can be narrowed and refined as issues are resolved.

The basic principles of usability apply to mobile design as well.[15] As apps grow in popularity, brands should consider their usability features just as intensely. Unlike websites, which often interconnect users with outside information, apps function in a more all-encompassing manner. For this reason, apps should be *learnable*, meaning no instructions are needed.[16] PR practitioners should help clients understand the financial and time investment required to create either a highly usable app or a successful website.

Once an organization has developed the structure of a website, it's time to optimize the content. Social media relies on content, and any content that an organization produces is searchable and should be optimized accordingly. Various activities that are within the realm of SEO include **search engine marketing (SEM)**, social media optimization (SMO), **social media marketing (SMM)**, content marketing, email marketing, and digital display advertising. A generally accepted definition of SEO is as follows: SEO is the process of optimizing a company's online content so that a search engine will show the content as a top result for searches of certain keywords.

Optimizing Content With SEO Strategies

Content that is optimized can increase a business's visibility using search engines such as Google, Bing, and Yahoo by triggering the page to rank higher for the desired search terms. Any content can be created with the goal of attracting search engine traffic. According to the Content Marketing Institute (CMI),

---

[14] Ibid., pp. 114–115.

[15] Ibid., p. 144.

[16] Ibid., p. 157.

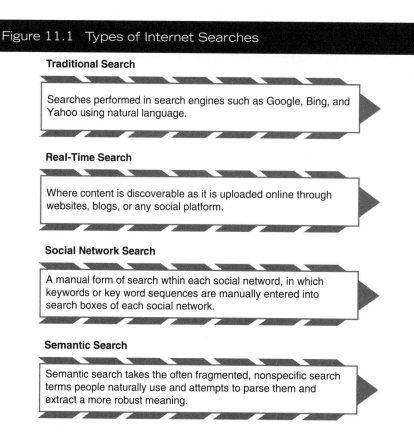

Figure 11.1 Types of Internet Searches

Traditional Search

Searches performed in search engines such as Google, Bing, and Yahoo using natural language.

Real-Time Search

Where content is discoverable as it is uploaded online through websites, blogs, or any social platform.

Social Network Search

A manual form of search wthin each social netword, in which keywords or key word sequences are manually entered into search boxes of each social network.

Semantic Search

Semantic search takes the often fragmented, nonspecific search terms people naturally use and attempts to parse them and extract a more robust meaning.

"content marketing is a marketing technique of creating and distributing relevant and valuable content to attract, acquire and engage a clearly defined and understood target audience—with the objective of driving profitable customer action."[17] Copy is tied directly to relevant keywords, inbound links, and clever promotion.[18]

When optimizing content, the first step that a PR practitioner should complete is to research keywords that are relevant to your target audience. Tools such as Google AdWords calculate the search frequency and competitiveness of specific keyword terms, helping practitioners to choose language with other industry organizations in mind. AdWords may show that certain keywords are highly searched and highly competitive, rarely searched and highly competitive, highly searched and noncompetitive, or rarely searched and noncompetitive. PR practitioners may want to focus, when possible, on keywords that are higher in search volume and

[17] What is content marketing? (n.d.). *Content marketing institute.* Accessed February 8, 2017, from http://contentmarketinginstitute.com/what-is-content-marketing/

[18] Solis, B. (2010). *Engage! The complete guide for brands and businesses to build, cultivate, and measure success in the new web.* Hoboken, NJ: John Wiley.

lower in competition. Keywords should be integrated into the copy—the key term is *integrated* rather than *saturated*—but copy should still be written primarily for human readers rather than for search engine algorithms.[19] Once the content is complete, it can be posted to a blog, website, and social channels so that your audience can share with members in their social sphere.[20]

Google displays search results based on authority and relevance to the users' experience; therefore, selecting the right keywords and then using those keywords in your content is fundamental.[21] While the exact formula is regularly adjusted, these basic foundational principles of search are here to stay. According to Dave Robinson, founder of *Red Evolution*,

©iStockphoto.com/pressureUA

> Google determines the relevance of a company's page by analyzing its content based on where and how often certain keywords are used in a specific piece of content; while authority is measured by the number of links pointing to that page and how trustworthy those links are assumed to be. SEO and content marketing need to have a consistent content output, which means that it is more important than ever for SEO and content marketers to work closely together.[22]

Search engine optimization (SEO) follows a process that should help increase ranking results on search engines such as Google, Yahoo!, and Bing.

Liraz Postan, the SEO manager for Outbrain's digital marketing team, suggests that SEO and content are aligned.[23] Before a company can begin to strategize on how to write quality content, they need to understand what constitutes high-quality content for the major search engine's algorithms. Google provides the following questions as indicators of quality content. These questions emphasize the

[19] Wall, A. M. (n.d.). *SEOBOOK: Search engine optimization.* Oakland, CA: Author. Retrieved December 17, 2017, from https://inlocalmarketing.com/wp-content/uploads/SEO-Training-by-seobook.pdf

[20] Patel, N. (n.d.). SEO copywriting: How to write content for people and optimize for Google. *Neil Patel.* Accessed February 6, 2017, from http://neilpatel.com/blog/seo-copywriting-how-to-write-content-for-people-and-optimize-for-google-2/

[21] Robinson, D. (n.d.). What is SEO? It's simpler than you think! *Red evolution.* Retrieved February 6, 2017, from https://www.redevolution.com/what-is-seo

[22] Robinson, D. (2008, June 18). The red evolution team, creatives, geeks & web geniuses. *Red evolution.* Retrieved December 17, 2018 from https://www.redevolution.com/our-people/itemlist/tag/seo%20basics

[23] Postan, L. (2016, September 19). Content marketing and SEO. *Outbrain.* Retrieved November 10, 2017, from http://www.outbrain.com/blog/content-marketing-and-seo

human aspect as well as attempt to address certain outdated SEO tactics that are now punished in the updated algorithm:[24]

- Would you trust the information presented in this article?

- Is this article written by an expert or enthusiast who knows the topic well, or is it more shallow in nature?

- Does the site have duplicate, overlapping, or redundant articles on the same or similar topics with slightly different keyword variations?

- Would you be comfortable giving your credit card information to this site?

- Does this article have spelling, stylistic, or factual errors?

- Are the topics driven by genuine interests of readers of the site, or does the site generate content by attempting to guess what might rank well in search engines?

- Does the article provide original content or information, original reporting, original research, or original analysis?

- Does the page provide substantial value when compared to other pages in search results?

- How much quality control is done on content?

- Does the article describe both sides of the story?

- Is the site a recognized authority on its topic?

Brian Honigman notes that one question every practitioner should be asking themselves when creating SEO-driven content is this: "Are the topics on your site driven by genuine interests of readers of the site, or does the site generate content by attempting to guess what might rank well in search engines?" The reason being, any metric for judging quality content depends on the readers and audience that a company is attempting to reach. The first stage of content planning and strategy is to consider your audience and their genuine interests. Honigman suggests a simple strategy: Companies should find a niche that is narrow enough to be unique but broad enough to meet business objectives. Then locate the ideal customer within this niche and discover what drives them—what blogs they read, what social sites they use, and even what types of events they attend. Finally, create a persona reflecting this average customer so that the company can gain an understanding of their demographic makeup as well as their psychology, beliefs, and habits. Use this persona as a guideline for focusing your content marketing efforts.

---

[24] Honigam, B. (2015, January 20). How to optimize your content for SEO the right way. *Digital current.* Retrieved November 10, 2017, from http://www.digitalcurrent.com/content-marketing/how-to-optimize-website-content-for-seo/

In his book, *Google Semantic Search*, David Amerland argues that the "four Vs" that govern big data processes can also be used to inform SEO and content marketing decisions. These include the following:[25]

1. Volume: This is the simplest of the four, but the volume of material that you release about your desired topic will be a big indication to Google of your authority on the subject.

2. Velocity: The overall frequency of your content will also give Google a hint as to your expertise. Posting once a week for a year likely looks better than posting once a month over the course of four years.

3. Variety: While you don't want to venture too far with your content's subject, covering a variety of areas within your niche of interest will signal to Google that you have authority on the topic.

4. Veracity: Having content that is received well by readers (that is shared, talked about, etc.) is perhaps the strongest indication to Google that they should serve content from your site to readers interested in the concept you chose to focus on.

Ensuring that your broader content strategy satisfies these conditions provides a focused strategy, which makes it more straightforward to see how individual pieces of content fit. In this way, better strategy leads to quality writing, improved engagement, and search benefits that are greater than the sum of the individual pieces.

Reflect and Discuss

1. When should usability testing come into play for web development efforts?

2. What are the differences between SEO and content marketing?

3. What should professionals keep in mind when developing SEO strategy?

4. How can agency professionals research and select the best keywords for a particular client project?

5. Why is creating high-quality readable/viewable digital content still so crucial in our search-focused environment?

---

[25] Amerland, D. (2013). *Google semantic search: Search engine optimization (SEO) techniques that get your company more traffic, increase brand impact and amplify your online presence.* Indianapolis, IN: Que.

Susan Emerick

Susan Emerick is the coauthor of *The Most Powerful Brand on Earth: How to Transform Teams, Empower Employees, Integrate Partners and Mobilize Customers to Beat the Competition in Digital and Social Media*—a must read for anyone striving to build brand advocacy. Emerick, a passionate data-driven marketing change agent who's navigated the evolution of internet marketing since its inception, advises clients across the globe in developing marketing programs that apply insights from analytics and research to foster long-term, high-value relationships with customers and drive ROI.

Always honing her craft, Emerick stays on top of the evolving emerging technologies landscape by capturing new market opportunities created by the global adoption of digital, social, and mobile. For example, while leading global enterprise social business and digital marketing programs at IBM, Emerick and her team developed an influencer intelligence system by tapping into IBM Watson's machine learning, natural language processing, and artificial intelligence power to establish the technology giant's digital and social media strategy. An early pioneer in digital and social networking for business, Emerick was instrumental in creating IBM's social insights practice to continuously apply social listening insights to marketing planning and engagement strategies.

Why is SEO so important today?

In the past 20+ years, the commercialization of the internet has brought an explosion of growth, resulting in what we know today as the digital economy. As companies have advanced their capabilities to conduct business on the web (and, increasingly, through mobile apps), we have witnessed what is typically referred to as *digital transformation*. During this same period, SEO became a critical way for web developers, content marketers, digital strategists, and the like to optimize their web-based content so it could be easily found, resulting in the most relevant content being presented in search results when a person performs a search query. This process affects the visibility of web-based content in natural and/or organic search results. SEO has become critical, as more than 80% of buyers turn to search as their first step when considering a purchase. This is true for any kind of purchase, consumer or business related.

On a basic level, how does SEO work?

As a digital or internet strategy, SEO considers how search engines work, what people search for (i.e., the actual search terms or keywords typed into search engines), and which search engines are preferred by their targeted audience. Optimizing web-based content involves editing its content and code to increase relevance for specific keywords. The content can then be found and indexed by search engines and ultimately served in the search results. In addition to keyword optimization, increasing the number of links to the source content can also help boost results.

What should someone know about the connection between search engine marketing and PR?

Even looking at traditional public relations tools, such as news releases, you can see they are indexed by search engines the same way that websites are. In fact, this is true for any content type, so it is critical that PR practitioners understand the basics of SEO to ensure that the content they are creating is optimized for search. Practitioners should also understand that the value of earned media is significantly greater because of the SEO impact of content created by media outlets.

What is SEO-driven copywriting and how does one improve it?

One of the most important initial steps in SEO copywriting is to understand the natural language that your audience uses and relates to. Once you have completed this research and have chosen the keyword or keyword phrases relevant for your audience, use the keyword(s) as you write your content. It is important to include the keyword consistently throughout the copy (i.e., headline, body copy, link copy, and web page *meta-data* [the tags or associations related to each search term]). Additionally, be sure to use the same keyword and/or keyword phrase that you have selected in backlinks to your content; this will help boost backlink relevance.

Are there any functional or stylistic guidelines for digital writing?

Writing for the web is fundamentally different than writing for other media, such as print. There are numerous books on the topic, each of which provides guidance on how to create engaging digital content that will help you target and attract web audiences. The following are recommended resources (and are all available on Amazon):

- *Outside-In Marketing: Using Big Data to Guide Your Content Marketing* by James Mathewson and Mike Moran

- *Audience, Relevance and Search* by James Mathewson, Frank Donatone, and Cynthia Fishel

- *Optimize: How to Attract and Engage More Customers by Integrating SEO, Social Media, and Content Marketing* by Lee Odden

What has been the impact of digital video?

Explosive growth in video consumption is driving more digital video media investment. The link to a great report on this trend published by eMarketer called "Mobile Spearheads Digital Video Advertising's Growth" is provided here: https://www.emarketer.com/Article/Mobile-Spearheads-Digital-Video-Advertisings-Growth/1013611

(Continued)

(Continued)

Top 5 Characteristics Every PR Professional Should Have

1. Data-driven marketing basics (i.e., using data to understand customer behaviors, needs, and goals). Translate those insights into a marketing strategy to address business goals.

2. Understanding of measurement techniques and the process of illustrating that the outcomes are actually driving results for the business.

3. Digital, social, and electronic commerce experience—we all expect companies to satisfy our needs via digital and mobile devices. To stay on top, companies must have customer experience, UX design, marketing, and communications/ development teams that make this happen.

4. Be curious and a voracious reader, always learning and observing. The marketing and communications profession is changing at lightning speed, and those who are studying these trends and applying them to their daily work will be leaders of the change.

5. Learn how the global economy is not only becoming increasing digital and mobile but also more collaborative; think Uber and Airbnb. You can see how the sharing economy is giving rise to peer-to-peer commerce.

Top Must-Haves

- **Must-download app:** It may sound silly, but many practitioners are reliant on texting. Make sure that you can message anyone around the globe. Apps such as Facebook Messenger, WhatsApp, and Viber are good choices.

- **Must-read book/blog/ news outlet:** Set up your feeds based on specific interests so you have news/info delivered directly to you. Consider reading *eMarketer*, *Business Insider*, *Forbes* and *Harvard Business Review*. Must-read book? There are so many! Anything written by Malcolm Gladwell—his books just make you think! Also, books by Simon Sinek promote a maturation of leadership skills and help teams collaborate better. Of late, anything that you can get your hands on related to AI and neuromarketing.

- **Must-use tool:** Google apps. In general, any collaboration tool works well, but especially Google Docs and Google Drive, particularly for projects that need simultaneous editing.

The Business of Agency Public Relations

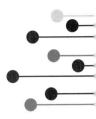

CHAPTER 12

Client Service

The Counselor Role and Seeding Creativity

V eteran agency practitioners have all had the experience of walking into a client meeting with a sense of uncertainty. Will a client understand and appreciate the significant efforts made on their behalf? Despite dozens of valuable media placements, a newly designed piece of marketing collateral to unveil, and positive news on a new partnership, not everything has gone according to plan. The client may love the cover photo of their business in a trade publication, the headline on a new brochure, and the significant increase in social media engagement on LinkedIn. Or they may not have appreciated the way they were portrayed in a prominent news article, found a typo in collateral materials, or received a call from a stockholder urging them against forming a new partnership. Agency practitioners should believe in their work and can make the case for its value, but success is not always judged on the quality of the work alone: It is measured by how effectively that work meets the needs of the clients and how well they understand this connection. The best

Objectives

- Define the elements of excellent client service.

- Learn tools to harness the creativity of agency and client teams.

- Understand the need to customize language, workflow, and reporting for different client organizations.

- Introduce the art of saying "Yes, and . . ."—a structure for agency practitioners to build on client ideas rather than only criticizing them.

© iStockphoto.com/DragonImages

practitioners are able to manage the execution of public relations campaigns as well as the need to explain the results and subsequent impact.

Building Trust: Excellent Work and an Awareness of Client Needs

Given the delicate nature of public relations, clients want to work with partners that they can trust. Agency practitioners must be prepared to (1) deliver great work, (2) promote and advocate for the value of their work, and (3) build relationships and provide strategic counsel that goes beyond it.

These challenges fit under the umbrella of **client service** or account management. Croft defines this as "bringing the agency's management, professional and creative services to bear against a client's problems and opportunities."[1] That said, account management must also consider the importance of personal relationships and making the most of every team members' contributions, including agency and client resources. On one hand, the concept of how to make and keep clients happy might seem straightforward, if difficult: by sharing expertise, by setting and living up to expectations and agreements, and by adding value to the client's organization. At the same time, practitioners must determine what will define excellent work or strengthen the bond with a particular organization or individual. Some client contacts may put more value in personal relationships, while others prefer to keep things strictly professional. Happy clients are those with whom we build fruitful relationships; however, one successful relationship may look very different from another.

Understanding a specific client or individual client contact is more art than science. It begins by answering a number of basic questions: What are their individual goals (in addition to the organization's goals)? What do they see as the highest PR priorities? What are their most important organizational and departmental priorities? Do they have a preferred personal communication style? What are their greatest challenges within their organization? What keeps them up at night? What do they enjoy most about their job? Where do they feel their expertise truly lies? These questions may apply to an individual, the main point of contact overseeing an account, or several individuals, from front-line PR and marketing staff to chief executive officers (CEOs). Taken together, the answers can illuminate a framework for creating successful working relationships. The answers to these questions may point toward emphasizing certain tactics over others as part of a campaign, building reports in a specific order, or ensuring that meetings regularly include leadership to ensure approval. These seemingly subtle adjustments may be able to significantly improve workflow with clients when they reduce stress and improve the agency and client team's ability to focus on the communication challenges at hand.

---

[1] Croft, A. C. (2006). *Managing a public relations firm for growth and profit.* New York, NY: Haworth Press, p. 113.

Strong relationships with clients grow from awareness and appreciation for their needs, both personally and professionally. Client service may never be fully effective without committing significant effort toward improving organizational goals and objectives, but that is only one component. Building a strong professional relationship requires a deep understanding of the clients' day-to-day work, their roadblocks, their frustrations, and their aspirations. Agency practitioners have a unique flexibility to customize programs and processes in order to better reflect the situation at hand. Strong relationships and hard-earned trust can smooth day-to-day work processes and often make interacting with clients more enjoyable, efficient, and productive. Of course, relationships are not the entire answer and never replace effective strategic work, but they can make it easier to achieve the buy-in necessary to accomplish both short-term and long-term goals.

Efficiency is a constant challenge for busy practitioners balancing client and agency projects.

Challenges to Agency–Client Partnerships

Despite our best efforts, relationships between agencies and their clients can become strained. As Zitron shares in *This is How You Pitch*, a frank account of life in a PR agency, "even if you understand what a client requires, it doesn't mean that they do."[2] This potential misalignment can be among several recurring sources of tension that become obstacles to a successful partnership:

- Agencies often move more quickly than their clients. They tend to make decisions rapidly and be optimistic about similar rates of approval from their clients. This can be both intimidating and frustrating for in-house practitioners and organizations not used to moving at the speed of today's journalists or social media users.

- Client communicators may feel threatened by agency practitioners. If a consultant is hired to do work previously handled in-house, it may make them feel superfluous, or they may worry that executive leadership will view them as unnecessary. It is critical for agencies to

[2] Zitron, E. (2013). *This is how you pitch: How to kick ass in your first years of PR*. Muskegon, MI: Sunflower Press, p. 56.

position themselves as part of the same team. Internal communicators are often the main information conduit and advocate for agency efforts.

- Internal communicators also often face significant pressures from executive leadership that are not always apparent from an agency perspective. Understanding some of these pressures, and hopefully helping to alleviate them, can be a significant agency victory.

How do successful agencies overcome these challenges? Most importantly, it comes from a deep awareness of the client's perspective. Understanding differences in planning and the speed of execution allows practitioners to ease clients toward a faster pace but also to plan for realistic project deadlines. An awareness of internal politics and pressures helps agency practitioners to be supportive of clients' communication teams rather than increasing their anxiety. It often means showing our own empathy and humanity to deepen each relationship.

At its root, this approach reflects a consulting mind-set. An effective consultant considers themselves a strategically savvy sage and an action-oriented coach, both excelling at connecting with others on a personal level. A sage believes in the specialized knowledge that he or she has to share and his or her ability to strategize and solve problems. A sage can effectively convey this confidence to others to energize and inspire them. A coach works to empower others, to pull the most from each member of the team. A coach will connect with everyone on an individual level and put both agency and client professionals in positions to succeed. Consultants must understand their subject matter thoroughly and be able to explain it efficiently to someone outside their field. There is no single way to accomplish these tasks, but they often require a balance of confidence, persuasiveness, and flexibility. Consultants must be able to take in significant amounts of information about an organization and quickly synthesize it into solutions and prescriptions. In public relations, this may relate to a specific media situation or crisis, the long-term stability or positioning of a brand, or the internal communication function of an organization.

Howard and Mathews refer to the challenge for practitioners as "earning the right to counsel," which can be defined as the process of proving to clients, and to ourselves, that we have the strategic, organizational, and industry knowledge to provide valuable insights.[3] In-house PR practitioners oftentimes have opportunities to earn this trust, but effective client management requires it of agency professionals. Effective PR work is founded on an individual's personal reputation. It is not enough to understand and speak to such values; practitioners must embody them. As Howard and Mathews emphasize, "Every action you counsel, everything you do and every word you write is a litmus test of your integrity; not

---

[3] Howard, C., & Mathews, W. (2013). *On deadline: Managing media relations* (5th ed.). Long Grove, IL: Waveland Press.

your employer's or your client's integrity, but your own."[4] This does not happen overnight, but over months and years of hard work to best serve an agency and its clients as well as the communities where they work, the media they interact with, and the stakeholders that support them.

Providing Strategic Counsel

Effective consultants establish themselves as strategic counselors, able to support clients on a wide variety of issues and challenges including, but not limited to, communication. Agency practitioners should be able to position their advice and recommendations holistically within the framework of an organization's success. The more that an agency counselor can frame communication strategies and victories by their connections to central goals and values, the more they will resonate with organizational leaders. By utilizing a consistently strategic approach driven by research and presented to solve the needs of an organization's publics, practitioners demonstrate professionalism, business acumen, and a counselor's spirit.

Effective consulting entails a certain attitude and drive: an optimism and commitment to useful, productive change. Clients respond to a can-do mentality. It opens doors and sparks conversations. For those entrenched in organizations, challenges can easily be perceived as insurmountable, particularly for those who may have been fighting the same battles for years. An effective agency practitioner can help clients believe that positive change can be accomplished. Agency practitioners have the power and the responsibility to create opportunities by cultivating environments and attitudes conducive to strategic change.

Thinking in Solutions

One of the most difficult transitions that young practitioners encounter is the shift to framing recommendations as solutions rather than tactics. Tactical responses to problems apply existing or singular tools (a press release, an ad campaign, an event) to unique, complex problems, often with a poor or incomplete fit. Successful counselors approach client-related issues with customized, integrated, and strategic solutions. They begin by setting a clear, measurable objective and then identify supporting strategies. Multiple tactics pointing in the same direction then provide a more cohesive, comprehensive, and effective approach. Holistic solutions, those that come from the focus on an idea/problem/solution, may be more complicated, harder to implement, and more difficult to sell to clients. Yet, the counselors who truly understand their clients' needs and challenges will recognize their value. Successful agency leaders can create effective strategic solutions, convince others of the value of their approaches, and lead the execution of these plans with the confidence of sound direction.

---

[4] Ibid., p. 220.

Generating such novel ideas is not easy. Lencioni reminds consultants that, often, good ideas, particularly genuine breakthroughs, come unexpectedly.[5] They may appear sandwiched between a terrible idea and an implausible one. They may grow organically from a mistake, a joke, or an aside. Good ideas often arrive precisely when an outside perspective and a change to the usual environment connects with the deep knowledge that organizational leaders hold. The consultant's job often entails creating situations, processes, and teams that generate ideas, both broadly and toward organizational goals. At their peak, counselors have the ability to help clients to restructure their goals and missions to better reflect the constant changes in the environment, resources, and expectations for their work. Applying these ideas to organizational problems and opportunities puts the agency facilitator in the position of distilling, or focusing, such abstract ideas into workable solutions.

Adapting to Different Personalities

Client service is never one-size-fits-all. In the early days of working with a new client, it is important to understand what the client is comfortable with and their expectations in terms of communication (frequency, length, detail), hierarchy (working at multiple levels within the organization), and decision making. Some organizations are very insular, and simply signing the contract with an agency to gain additional perspective is a significant and potentially jarring step for them. Others would prefer to quickly hand as many tasks as possible over to an agency. Neither extreme tends to be the most successful approach. A client's natural organizational culture may not be particularly conducive to the type of program they need. For example, a high-profile company with many media opportunities to tackle can only succeed in working with a PR agency if the structure is in place to manage inbound media relations opportunities swiftly and effectively. This could mean pushing a client or specific client contact well outside of their comfort zone, forcing them to quickly make decisions and act on a journalists' tight time line. A change like this rarely, if ever, happens overnight, but it is essential in taking on new opportunities or overcoming existing challenges. Agencies create successful partnerships in large part because they act as forces for change in organizational cultures.

In order to cultivate such relationships over time, practitioners should display flexibility in response to explicit or perceived client needs. This might mean adjusting meeting structure, timing, and attendance to allow a client more time to make decisions. It could entail shortening or lengthening reporting documents to help a client share them with others in their organization more effectively. It might also require adjusting the language choices used in all communication to more closely reflect the client's industry. There will rarely be clients, particularly

---

[5] Lencioni, P. (2010). *Getting naked: A business fable about shedding the three fears that sabotage client loyalty.* San Francisco, CA: Jossey-Bass.

those new to working with an agency, who will clearly define what they need. This responsibility is on practitioners to ask and identify the ways in which they can continuously improve their communication and relationship with a given client.

Gathering Ideas and Insights

One critical skill for improving client understanding is learning to ask questions in order to gather the appropriate information and insights. Following this practice allows the practitioner to make more informed decisions and develop relevant and efficient strategies. Internal communicators may have detailed and valuable knowledge. Yet, as clients, they don't always realize what an agency practitioner does not know. Therefore, consultants must not only use the information that they are immediately provided but understand how to identify what is not being said or explained and then plan to collect it. Additionally, organizations may be aware of some strategic challenges, but not others. They may see some obstacles as inherently insurmountable. Skilled consultants work to change the perspective and mind-set of the organizational leaders that they work with in order to reframe the problem, motivate the client, and (hopefully) provide the tools to overcome these obstacles.

Involving clients at appropriate stages in the process allows them to provide valuable insights and contributions and also to build supportive coalitions for agency initiatives. There is a sweet spot: Too much client inclusion can make already challenging creative processes more unwieldy as well as take up a client's time unnecessarily. Conversely, a lack of input may allow projects to veer off course, away from fulfilling organizational objectives. It can also make client communicators, who often have the responsibility of evaluating agency work, feel disconnected or, even worse, excluded.

Structured approaches for capturing client input minimize the constant back-and-forth within agency–client relationships. Allowing client contacts to provide insights and perspective also makes them feel included in the process. Formalizing the methods for collecting this information allows practitioners to be more efficient and clearly respectful of clients' time. Every client wants to feel that they have contributed to a campaign's success, but no client appreciates being bothered unnecessarily. Striking the right balance of independence and inclusion goes a long way toward building an effective working relationship with client contacts.

Asking Questions

From one perspective, delivering client service can be seen as a process of asking the correct questions, paired with the appropriate external research, to put together the best possible plans and programs. Research (qualitative and quantitative, secondary and primary) contributes to stronger campaigns, better strategic decisions, and, ultimately, better relationships between agencies and their clients. Practitioners must know how to find unbiased data to support

The counselor role does not mean that agency professionals have all of the answers. Success often comes from learning how to ask productive questions, listen, and organize the knowledge clients already bring.

strategic recommendations as well as insightful expert analysis on an industry or trend. The best agency leaders have also developed the skill of interpersonal, qualitative listening to clients— not entering conversations with overly rigid ideas and solutions. From the start, asking questions and letting the interviewee (the client) drive the conversation allows the client's insights to come through. Our tendency is to use the questions and answers that fit our preconceived approaches to situations. Having open-ended conversations, led by the client, can uncover more information than is usually possible through more prescriptive approaches.

In his business fable, *Getting Naked*, author and consultant Patrick Lencioni speaks to the importance of listening for consultants.[6] His narrative compares two consulting firms and approaches, one that strives to research its way to finding all the answers and devising strategies before meeting with a client, and one that grounds its expertise in the process of developing those answers with their clients. From the eyes of a hypercompetitive, traditionally trained, preparation-obsessed consultant, it looks as if his competitor is walking into a meeting wholly unprepared. But, from the perspective of the client, asking questions makes the meeting process one of mutual inquiry, discovery, and creativity, rather than a lecture from an outsider. This is not to deemphasize the critical importance and significant value of research at multiple stages of PR processes. In fact, it should reinforce its value: Agency practitioners should involve clients in the research process itself and never underestimate or undervalue their perspective and knowledge.

To integrate client perspectives into research, practitioners must be vulnerable, admitting that they don't have all of the answers. Lencioni lays out several principles of effective consulting centered on the idea of embracing this vulnerability. He explains that in client acquisition and service, practitioners operate with three central fears: (1) fear of losing the business, (2) fear of being embarrassed, and (3) fear of feeling inferior.[7] By letting go of these fears, being confident in our own knowledge, and allowing the best interests of our clients to drive our actions, consultants can reduce the oppositional nature of the agency–client relationship. Successful counselors listen and tell the truth; they avoid telling their clients

---

[6] Ibid.

[7] Ibid., pp. 153–181.

only what they want to hear. In doing so, they "enter the danger"[8] and embrace the awkward, potentially challenging situations that may arise. These situations are often the ones that lead to genuine insights and go the farthest in deepening agency–client relationships.

How can agency practitioners overcome these fears? It begins by being honest with ourselves and ensuring that others are honest with us about our strengths and weaknesses. It continues by embracing the information that we do not know: by asking questions that we may feel are embarrassing. It acknowledges that the client's well-being is more important than a counselor's pride. Practitioners should own and celebrate their mistakes rather than run from them. Counselors should not be afraid to roll up their sleeves to "do the dirty work" when it's in the client's best interests.[9] Each of these reminders not only strengthens agency–client relationships, but it also produces better PR outreach.

Creativity

Interestingly, and not unsurprisingly, the same qualities that build trust are conducive to creativity within client and agency teams. As organizations rarely hire agencies when they want to follow the same communication path, creativity and new ideas are intrinsic to effective consulting and client service. In Andy Green's *Creativity in Public Relations*, he defines *creativity* as "the ability each of us has to create something new by bringing together two or more different elements in a new context, in order to provide added value to a task."[10] This definition points out that creativity is not only available to inherently creative individuals, but it is also a learned skill. It reminds us that creativity is about adding value. Even the most captivating or unique ideas must directly address the objectives at hand.

Green describes effective creative thinking as utilizing a "red light/green light" approach.[11] Practitioners must be able to tap their creativity and toggle between an uninhibited and open-minded "green light" brainstorming mind-set and an analytical, skeptical, and practical "red light" perspective.

©iStockphoto.com/kzenon

Idea generation techniques help practitioners harness the creative and strategic insights of agency and client teams.

---

[8] Ibid., p. 159.

[9] Ibid., p. 173.

[10] Green, A., & Chartered Institute of Public Relations. (2010). *Creativity in public relations* (4th ed.). London, UK: Kogage, p. 8.

[11] Ibid., p. 24.

Creativity Tips From Andy Green

Five I's of the Creative Process

Generating creative ideas is not about a lightning flash of inspiration; it is a process. New ideas are discovered through research and a deep understanding of the situation. Ideas need time to grow and mature and also should be evaluated and separated from other concepts. Below are Green's five "I's" of the creative process:[12]

1. Information
2. Incubation
3. Illumination
4. Integration
5. Illustration

Creativity Suggestions for Green-Light Thinking

In order to open the discussion for green-light thinking, practitioners must set the ground rules for agency and client team members. Such suggestions reinforce the mind-set for everyone to maximize connectivity and cultivate ideas, rather than questioning and critiquing.[13]

- Narrow the ideas to one specific challenge, opportunity, step, or message
- Suspend judgment
- Aim for quantity over quality of ideas
- Put elements of different ideas together
- Allow time for creativity to happen

In this way, they can both generate a vast number of ideas and effectively narrow them down to the approach that will add the most value.

Idea-generating activities are standard practice within the agency world. Facilitators lead such sessions by setting the structure, process, constraints, and tone. Effective facilitators can but are not required to be active participants in the process. Another key responsibility of the facilitator is determining **prompts**: the questions, concepts, or materials that serve as the spark for the process itself. Stories, videos, and images, among other content, can serve as effective prompts.

According to Green, bold ideas must be presented "within the context of a relationship."[14] The success of bold strategies does not emerge out of thin air but must be earned through increasing trust and delivered with a clear understanding of the perspectives and challenges facing the client. It is this connection and understanding of the client situation that allows the best agency practitioners to craft and generate support for campaigns that are both unique and successful relative to their client's goals.

---

[12] Ibid., p. 30.

[13] Ibid., p. 56.

[14] Ibid., p. 53.

Brainstorming/Ideation

There are many specific techniques and processes that facilitate the interaction of agency and client teams as well as the generation of new ideas to solve problems. In his book, *Idea Stormers*, veteran facilitator Bryan Mattimore outlines an approach for identifying creative solutions to a variety of organizational challenges, from the naming of products to strategies for overcoming business obstacles. Techniques such as ***ideation***, an umbrella term used to describe brainstorming and a wide variety of other idea generation processes, can be extremely valuable in connecting the existing knowledge from client leaders and communicators with the perspective and expertise of agency professionals. Of course, the collection of ideas is only the first step in the process of developing a new concept or developing a different creative or strategic direction.

Ideation techniques "tap into the power of the collective mind."[15] Mattimore outlines several mind-sets helpful to facilitating this process, including curiosity, openness, following intuition, and embracing ambiguity. For many client communicators, these approaches may at first be uncomfortable or at least unusual. The goal is to avoid *linear thinking*: the step-by-step worldview we use every day to drive efficiency and get work done. Creativity comes from seeing beyond our day-to-day approaches. These concepts are valuable to embrace and can create an environment that encourages client participation in the early stages of an agency–client relationship. By removing individuals from their usual environment, presenting them with fun or unexpected activities, and empowering them to participate, you can help trigger these mind-sets.

There are two underlying principles behind successful idea generation: (1) quality leads to quantity and (2) criticism inhibits creativity.[16] Therefore, idea generation should be about unleashing the collective brainpower of a group of individuals capable of generating a wide variety of ideas. Participants should not be concerned about the quality of these ideas and, in fact, should actively suppress limiting their own ideas or judging the ideas of others. At this stage in the process, effective facilitators and counselors remove barriers from the minds of participants. This can be done by removing them from usual patterns of thinking, by asking new questions, or by specifically disregarding limitations such as budget,

©iStockphoto.com/Luka Lajst

Creative thinking can be facilitated through activities. Having fun allows both agency and client team members to relax, which often leads to a more open flow of ideas.

---

[15] Mattimore, B. W. (2012). *Idea stormers: How to lead and inspire creative breakthroughs*. San Francisco, CA: Jossey-Bass, p. 4.

[16] Ibid., pp. 23–24. Mattimore attributes the breakthroughs and initial "rules" of brainstorming to Alex Osborne of advertising agency BBDO.

time, or feasibility. The most successful approaches often encourage or force ideas to be built on each other. Individuals spur each other's ideas, organically prompting new directions as the process progresses.

Ideation and Idea Generation Techniques

The techniques below, based on Mattimore's *Idea Stormers*, all support the development of new and creative ideas and can be applied in a variety of organizational situations. They are not mutually exclusive and should be seen as easily layered for particular situations.

- **Brainstorming/brainwalking:** In a traditional brainstorming activity, individuals deliver ideas one-by-one and they are recorded for discussion. Many ideation techniques attempt to overcome brainstorming's inherent limitations: inefficiency, privileging the loudest or most aggressive participants, and, most importantly, not allowing participants to share ideas simultaneously. By contrast, brainwalking involves setting up a group of boards, walls, or easels and having a group of individuals simultaneously writing their ideas, then rotating to another station. Individual boards can be themed or can simply reflect the ideas of those who started writing on them. Time is then set aside to review the content across the different locations prior to any discussion. Short (several minute) bursts of activity, quick rotation, the creative value of changing physical location, and the ability to have every individual in a group contribute and build off of everyone else's ideas makes this an extremely valuable and useful technique.

  ○ Potential uses: Naming new products or campaigns, generating potential campaign tactics and strategies, connecting different teams' thinking

- **Reframing and questioning:** Facilitators don't always know the best questions to ask. New paths of inquiry can be a powerful tool, allowing clients to envision problems in a new light. Having participants ask their own questions can be an effective tactic toward generating new ideas. Rather than relying solely on the facilitator for prompts, this technique actively incorporates participants as sparks for idea generation. What do clients want to know about their competitors? What would they ask consumers or patrons of their products and services? Why would they buy (or not buy) a product or service? Facilitators can use themes from these questions to drive further inquiry in that meeting or later meetings.

  ○ Potential uses: Overcoming a strategic obstacle, seeking new product categories or organizational approaches

- **Wishing:** One way to remove obstacles in linear thinking is to ask about dream or nightmare scenarios. Mattimore uses the term *wishing* to describe both the generation of ideal but seemingly impossible scenarios as well as highly negative actions or situations.[17]

---

[17] Ibid., p. 59.

He recommends having a group come up with 20 to 30 ideal scenarios or worst ideas and use the most creative, ridiculous, or compelling to drive discussion for more realistic potential concepts and strategies. These scenarios serve to decouple the group members from the challenges of day-to-day routine thinking in order to find new paths and ideas. Again, this approach recognizes the value of participant-generated ideas to seed creativity.

- ○ Potential uses: Developing new big ideas, generating campaign themes, dealing with a singular obstacle or elephant in the room

- **Visualization:** Images can function as highly effective prompts to generate ideas, help groups make connections between disparate ideas, and encourage new concepts to emerge. Working with language alone may be a barrier for individuals who are stuck in a logical rut when trying to generate new ideas. Using images as a stimulus, or allowing clients to choose images that represent an organization, approach, or challenge, can open up new paths and connections that may not otherwise have been made. It can be helpful both in certain stages of a brainstorming process (such as early definitional work) and in representing difficult-to-describe concepts (such as a brand or organizational persona). This can be accomplished through preselected images as well as through exercises that allow participants to find their own visual representations of the concepts at hand.

- ○ Potential uses: Capturing or developing brand insights and directions, overcoming entrenched strategic obstacles

While it may be difficult to bring a particularly nonparticipative client on board with unusual approaches, trying a small variety of ideas and maintaining a quick pace throughout the discussion will sustain interest and, hopefully, move participants from their normal thinking patterns into a more creative place. While such discussion can and should be uncomfortable, it should also be fun. For more detailed information about execution and a wider array of approaches, *Idea Stormers* provides a valuable overview.

After the initial ideas are generated, they should be sorted and evaluated. Green refers to this as the *red-light phase*, which "emphasizes judgment, reason, evaluation, and what may or may not work."[18] Rather than the freedom of the green-light phase, the second half of the process necessitates generating or acknowledging criteria that would define the successful project. These may be

---

[18] Green, A., & Chartered Institute of Public Relations. (2010). *Creativity in public relations* (4th ed.). London, UK: Kogage, p. 92.

based on logistical factors (feasibility, timing, budget, personnel, or expertise), strategic value (potential audience resonance, novelty, impact, newsworthiness), and organizational factors (brand fit, leadership buy-in, enthusiasm). As the criteria are selected, each idea should be subjected to evaluation. Some will easily be eliminated as too costly, too time-intensive, not relevant enough to the strategic goals at hand, or at odds with the larger organizational brand identity.

A well-structured red-light process and the application of smart criteria-based evaluation should still allow for a variety of ideas to be considered. One approach may stipulate that the evaluators choose their favorite idea based on the criteria, the most realistic idea based on the criteria, and the idea with the greatest potential benefit. They should not limit the process to one "best" idea. Including multiple selections can open up practitioners to new approaches and give organizational leaders more opportunities to take full advantage of an agency's creative and strategic abilities. An idea may be extremely difficult or costly to execute but still have significant potential benefits for the organization. Or an idea may be too costly for an organization today, but not with proper planning the following year. In this way, criteria must restrict the imaginations of agency professionals, but they should do so in ways that still allow for the generation of big, bold ideas.

Structured Discussions and Projects

When in the idea-generation process should clients be involved? When should agency practitioners work independently? Counselors must strike a balance to ensure that client input and time is spent efficiently and effectively on projects. The best results often come from leveraging each individual's skill set as part of the larger project team. Agency practitioners should know and communicate why each person's expertise is important for a specific meeting, ideation, or work session. This means bringing the full team together early in a campaign process to lay the initial groundwork, building the plan largely separately, and then sharing drafts with client decision makers for approval. Too much client involvement during the granular details of the planning process can lead to complications and delays. Generally, in-house communication team members can and should be the most involved and available to answer the smaller questions that might arise about past efforts, organizational relationships, and industry quirks. A larger internal team is often useful to provide a broad environmental and competitive perspective of the organization, its goals, and its challenges at the beginning and end of the process. Agency practitioners should attempt to keep meetings with executive team members either higher level (such as the initial meetings to better understand organizational background) or narrow, such as reviewing and providing feedback to a specific communication plan or evaluating a campaign that has already occurred.

The Power of "Yes, and . . ."

When clients ask their agency for something, there are many potential responses, falling along a continuum from a wholehearted *yes* to a flat *no*. The tendency for many practitioners, particularly early in their careers, is to give an unequivocal *yes*, which can often be the easiest answer in the moment but one that can challenge the relationship over the long term. Counselors must build their client relationships on trust. This often comes from moments where there is disagreement rather than agreement. While effectively saying *no* to clients is a critical and difficult-to-master skill, the more frequently used statement is "Yes, and . . ." This response allows agency professionals to easily frame their work within the context of a client's ideas. While clients should be considered the experts in their industries and organizations, most professionals without experience in public relations or marketing have difficulty translating their situational understanding into strategic, communication-centered solutions. Effective counselors build on client ideas and insights by connecting problems and obstacles to specific objectives and strategies. The qualified *yes* allows for the inclusion and valuing of clients' experiences and perspectives. It demonstrates listening and integration of ideas while reinforcing the outside value and perspective of the agency professional. Client–agency relationships should be seen as partnerships. Taking a "yes, and . . ." approach supports the idea that both sides have something to add, reinforcing the counselor role and emphasizing the value that both sides add to creating effective strategic outreach.

Reflect and Discuss

1. Why does client service include more than just delivering excellent PR work to clients?

2. What are the drawbacks of traditional brainstorming? How can they be overcome?

3. When should clients be involved in the campaign-planning process? When should they be less involved?

4. What are examples of useful criteria for deciding whether a brainstormed idea is worth pursuing?

5. Why is flexibility important for agency practitioners focused on client service?

Nicole Moreo is the director of research and insights leading the research team at Peppercomm, a mid-sized New York–based agency with a broad base of clients in the consumer, financial, and industrial spaces. She came to the agency with a background in economics and has used this unique perspective to provide new approaches to metrics and measurement for her clients. In addition to her work with Peppercomm, she also serves as the vice chair of the North American Chapter of the Association for the Measurement and Evaluation of Communication (AMEC). Her writing on measurement has been featured by the Institute for Public Relations, *PR News*, *The Measurement Standard*, and *O'Dwyer's*, among others, and she is a regular presenter for the Public Relations Society of America (PRSA) on metrics and research-related topics.

How do you decide what should be measured for a client?

For me, a pet peeve is that people always seem to jump to measurement first. You really need to understand the business reason to launch a campaign. By asking the business goal, you can decide what needs to be measured. Is the most important factor paid social, brand awareness, email, or sales? There is a lot of data out there, so start by figuring out what is most relevant and critical to your client's goals and objectives. Those are the first steps in creating metrics that matter.

Additionally, measurement folks sometimes focus exclusively on quantitative data, which can be a mistake. A number without context is just a number. People tend to get bored with it. That's why qualitative research and insights are so valuable. Bringing together quantitative and qualitative data allows us to provide context and meaning for our clients, not just charts and graphs.

What is an example a problem you've had in a measurement process and how did you resolve it?

We might not be siloed, but our clients may be. They may be tasked with just one thing. To expand beyond that is, for them, (1) expensive, (2) time consuming, and (3) often not immediately beneficial. That puts us as the agency in the position of having to advocate for more integrated goal setting, leading to more integrated and valuable measurement and reporting.

It's also easy to focus exclusively on digital metrics because they are readily available, but they rarely tell the whole story. A very large percentage of an organization's audience interaction is offline, so we often have to find additional ways to capture data to provide a more complete picture.

Where are research and measurement important in the campaign process?

One of the key things we try to help clients understand is the difference between measurement and analytics. Benchmarks are pre- and post-campaign. Analytics are a constant. We usually perform a benchmark audit at the beginning of a client relationship or campaign. Then, we highly recommend optimized analytics throughout. If you're doing a paid social campaign, for example, there is a lot of work on content optimization, and the measurement team is there to help with that process.

Then, there are several formats where we share this information. Quarterly measurement reports allow us to say, "Here's what happened." We also will run measurement meetings. We begin by including everyone who could be impacted on the client end. We ask about business goals and the relationship with our communication outreach. Through these conversations, you start slowly learning what information needs to be reported, who needs to be involved, and the best way to share it with that specific client.

What are some specific skills necessary for those interested in practicing measurement and research in an agency setting?

Basic statistics is an excellent start. Being able to negotiate Microsoft Excel really helps in creating spreadsheets to plug in your information and calculate results. The next step would be learning some basic Boolean search language to work with media aggregators and monitoring tools (such as Cision or Meltwater). An understanding of Google Analytics allows you to track an individual's every move on an organization's website, providing invaluable data. Primary research is also critical. Practitioners should know how to craft a survey and conduct an interview that avoids leading questions and generates valid results and insights.

Top 5 Characteristics Every PR Professional Should Have

1. *Design thinking*: The future of PR agencies.

2. Asking great questions.

3. And analyzing the answers to find both results and deeper insights.

4. Integrating measurement across media challenges (including media relations, social media, website analytics, paid media, etc.).

Top Must-Haves

- **Must-use tool:** Talkwalker Alerts are an excellent tool. Their back end pulls in lots of useful data, makes segmentation and tracking easy, and allows me to share those results with our account teams.

- **Must-read book/blog/ news outlet:**

  ○ Huge fan of Jake Knapp's *Sprint: How to Solve Big Problems and Test New Ideas in Just Five Days.*

  ○ AMEC features many of the leading names in measurement. They have excellent resources and many opportunities for measurement-specific education and certifications.

  ○ BMA (Business Marketing Association) has excellent case studies that help PR people learn from the work being done on the marketing side.

Entrepreneurship and Business Development

Why do practitioners choose to start their own businesses? Some may be born with an entrepreneurial spirit, but, for many, it's a personal desire to create something and prove to oneself that they can accomplish it. For others, the journey can be less direct: perhaps it hits you after the fourth year of writing the same press release for the same event at the same company. Maybe it happens as your boss explains, yet again, why your brilliant idea for a new social media strategy is "great, but just not something we can implement right now." There are many motivations that drive successful, creative practitioners to take a significant career leap and strike out on their own, either starting their own firm or working as a sole practitioner. This choice is the *why* behind some of the most important and influential practitioners in the history of the field.

Entrepreneurship should never be taken lightly. It can be a difficult but rewarding journey. As in professions such as law, accounting, and architecture, the nature of

Objectives

- Understand what practitioners need to consider before starting their own agency.

- Define core skills for agency leadership.

- Differentiate among agencies with local, national, and global scope.

- Underscore the value of entrepreneurial skills and a business development mind-set for all agency team members.

©iStockphoto.com/Martin Dimitrov

Agency practitioners at multiple levels can be involved in business development processes, helping to research, recruit, pitch, and win new business.

consulting work can be highly specialized and lend itself to successful small businesses. Specific public relations expertise in health care, finance, or manufacturing can become a highly valued skill that forms the heart of a unique niche for a new firm. Even those not pursuing their own entrepreneurial ambitions may find themselves in agency leadership roles dealing primarily with business development, client retention, or organizational management and growth. These positions demand the mind-set of an entrepreneur who understands the business world, speaks the language of the client or industry, and enjoys the challenge of solving client problems. This consultant role combines the perspective of a strategic communication counselor with the ability to make a clear business case for the value of an agency relationship. Practitioners must be able to answer the following question: What can public relations do for your organization? They must be able to do so succinctly and in language that resonates with business leaders who may have little knowledge of effective communication.

Entrepreneurs must also balance the challenges of running their own businesses (such as hiring and managing staff, cultivating new prospects, and overseeing financials) with the day-to-day work of practicing public relations for their clients. Yet, as Zitron explains in *This Is How You Pitch*, smart leaders build teams to tackle complex challenges: "You're not the one that has to shoulder all of the responsibility."[1] This chapter does not cover the full realm of skills needed to start and manage an agency, but it does provide some insights into the perspectives and processes that are (1) valuable for early career practitioners to grasp and (2) are relevant to all professionals within an agency, not just the founders or principles. Agencies thrive when the entire team embraces an entrepreneurial mindset.

Even the world's largest PR agencies began with a single client and a small team's entrepreneurial drive.

[1] Zitron, E. (2013). *This is how you pitch: How to kick ass in your first years of PR*. Lawrence, KS: Sunflower Press, p. 141.

What Do You Want to Be?

Starting an agency means considering the scope of your ambition. For some, it is to act as an individual practitioner with several select clients. For others, it may be building a global firm to compete with Ketchum, Edelman, FleishmanHillard, and other industry leaders. On this continuum, entrepreneurs should consider what type of agency they would like to run, with the understanding that all agencies start small and evolve through the stages described below. Larger firms typically require larger organizations as their clients, putting some boundaries on the size and scope of the organizations they work with. Each of the following firm structures reflects a conscious, informed choice regarding the clients that they are interested in serving:

- *Individual consultant*: Solo practitioners must be able to manage all parts of the business development process as well as the day-to-day client interaction and project execution. These consultants have all the responsibility on their shoulders but also the absolute freedom to serve their clients in the way they feel is most effective. Generally, individuals build a network of specialist partners to provide clients with specific skills outside of their areas of expertise, which may include design, digital, or crisis communication work.

  - What clients could I serve more effectively or efficiently than a larger firm?

  - What relationships do I already have with potential clients (as well

as journalists, civic leaders, and influences) in different communities or industries?

- *Boutique agency*: Developing a geographic or industry niche, hiring and managing staff, and looking to build client portfolios strategically is critical at this stage in development. Many agencies continue successfully with a few key staff members, several core issue or industry specialties, and a strong personal reputation. Clients benefit from the high level of partner/founder interaction and engagement. Generally, boutique agencies still rely on external partners to supply some client services.

  - What PR needs are not being met by firms in my region or industry?

  - Are there specific vertical markets that could use specialized attention from a PR standpoint?

  - What skills or relationships set me (and my team) apart from competitors?

- *Regional or mid-sized agency*: Agency structure and oversight come to the forefront when managing a larger group of practitioners. Increased specialization and segmentation mean that hiring the best divisional leaders becomes a priority and that their individual expertise may eclipse the principles in those areas.[2] Priorities include developing trust and accountability

(Continued)

[2] See Zitron (2013), pp. 139–141.

(Continued)

to hand over many of the day-to-day tasks to others as well as finding the best role for each individual team member's talents.

- ○ What makes the most effective client teams?

- ○ How can efficiency be maintained as staff and projects expand?

- *National/international agency*: Competing with the world's top agencies is a high bar to reach, but there is always room for those willing to take new approaches. Exciting and rewarding opportunities come from working with larger budgets, higher client expectations, and international audiences. Ambitious practitioners should examine the ways in

which the industry is evolving, structure their approach to win specific significant accounts, and know that it will be an uphill battle. It is always easier for a client to choose an established firm than an unproven one, but, even at the highest level, every organization will respond to carefully crafted strategic approaches that will make a positive impact on the organization as a whole.

- ○ Why would a public company leave their current agency of record?

- ○ What types of work can be done better, faster, cheaper or more seamlessly by a new firm rather than today's global giants?

Growing Your Reputation

Client acquisition is an ongoing challenge for every PR agency, but even more so for newly founded, emerging, or student-run agencies. Without an established track record of success as part of the agency's brand, convincing new clients to sign on can be a challenge. That said, every agency starts without a track record. Some succeed and some fail. Often, those that struggle do not approach their own marketing and business development processes with the same strategic mind-set as their client work. Agency leaders succeed when they translate their expertise into engagement to solve these problems for their clients. As Howard and Matthews put it, "Almost all of the critical problems facing your organization are public relations problems in the broadest sense of the term."[3] Winning new business often means making a clear, meaningful case as to the potential impact of an agency's work. This means understanding the clients' challenges, researching and developing solutions, and engaging with the organization to develop buy-in and enthusiasm.

All agency leaders bring certain knowledge, skills, and expertise to the table. An important part of any agency's health is demonstrating this value to potential clients, often based on the success of past clients or prior in-house experience. Clearly identifying and communicating an agency's niche is critical to getting a foothold. That niche may be based on geography, tactical prowess, or industry

---

[3]Howard, C., & Mathews, W. (2013). *On deadline: Managing media relations* (5th ed.). Long Grove, IL: Waveland Press, p. 212.

media relationships. Croft refers to such a niche as an agency's "unique strategic position."[4] A niche may emerge from an entrepreneur's background and experiences in a specific industry prior to striking out on their own. It may come from a set of valuable reporter relationships in a specific media market, or it may come from a realization that a particular geographic area is underserved. For example, Lippe Taylor, a PR and digital marketing agency out of New York City, specializes in developing campaigns that focus on women as decision makers. Whatever its origin, the niche should reflect the firm's existing strengths as well as its aspirations.

Integrated communication programs for business development should be targeted toward organizations that are the right fit: Potential clients should reflect a specific size, industry, geographic location, or other factor where the agency can excel. Hopefully, they also reflect a cultural fit between individuals at both organizations.[5] An agency accustomed to partnering with established small businesses may struggle when paired with a large public company or with a bootstrapping nonprofit. Even the best agency–client matches on paper may fall apart if, for example, a company culture is particularly laid back while its agency is very buttoned-down. While *fit* can be complimentary and not simply similar, personal and cultural compatibility matter. Identifying potential client prospects of the right

Whatever industry expertise an agency practitioner may have, it can serve as the basis for a specific practice or even the founding of a niche firm.

---

[4]Croft, A. C. (2006). *Managing a public relations firm for growth and profit.* New York, NY: Haworth Press, p. 44.
[5]Ibid., p. 60.

size, type, and culture can create a valuable list to begin more individualized outreach. This is not to say that agencies, particularly growing agencies and budding entrepreneurs, should not stretch themselves to work with clients outside of their usual comfort zone but rather that these choices should be strategic, conscious, and bring an awareness of the added challenges that may occur.

Demonstrating Your Skills

There are a variety of tools that agencies use to build their reputation, showcase success, and win new business. The most effective approaches often employ multiple elements of support, each contributing to an agency's credibility with potential clients. These often begin with a professional digital presence, representing the firm well through a coherent website and with social media. Additional tools support the business development process and are particularly valuable in the early stages of an agency's growth. These tools should be reflective of the firm's identity and its niche. For each of the items described below, their presentation and usage can vary greatly, but their purpose remains the same across channels: to provide additional credibility to an organization as part of the business development process.

Several basic techniques are commonly leveraged to share organizational successes and expertise. Collecting, developing, and sharing **case studies**, with clients' permission, of course, is one strategy used by many agencies to showcase their skills. Case studies should emphasize an agency's strengths as well as reinforce key themes and differentiators from other competitor firms. Client **testimonials** serve as another powerful tool to highlight the ways an agency's efforts add value from the perspective of organizational leaders. Such testimonials, collected and shared with client permission, can be valuable humanizing representations of an agency's impact. **Thought leadership** is another tactic that raises both awareness and perceived value. Put simply, agency leaders should share their expertise with others in the world of public relations as well as within the client industries where they have experience. This can take the form of blog posts, bylined articles in trade industry publications, or expert sources in mainstream media coverage of relevant news.

Despite the seemingly straightforward processes available to generate these materials, the old adage regularly applies: The shoemaker's children go barefoot. Agencies are often their own worst enemies when it comes to marketing their business precisely because they are focused on their clients first. Entrepreneurs enjoy public relations because it allows them to directly help others, but running a successful agency means not losing the balance needed for the agency's own well-being. It requires what often feels like an organizational selfishness that can be difficult to prioritize in the midst of client crises, exciting new business opportunities, and the challenges of hiring and motivating staff. The most successful entrepreneurs are able to balance these competing interests to both serve clients and nurture their own businesses.

Positioning Your Agency to Win New Clients

- What is your niche? As with any organization, PR agencies must define what makes them different from competitors.
  - How can you prove it?
  - How can you deepen or expand it?
- What is your ideal client?
  - What are their characteristics?
    - Size?
    - Industry?
    - Geographic reach?
    - Demographic reach?
    - Privately held or public company?
    - Nonprofit or for profit?
    - Business to consumer or business to business?
  - How can you raise your profile among organizations with those characteristics?
- How strategic are your business development efforts?
  - How are clients/potential clients finding you? Referrals and word-of-mouth? Through thought leadership?
  - Are these inbound opportunities the right opportunities?

- How are you proactively seeking clients?
- What business development/ cultivation structures and processes are in place?
- Is proactive outreach leading to long-term relationships?
- Are efforts focused on clients that are more of the same or on the clients that would be better for profitability, workflow, and efficiency?
- How are you learning from pitches your firm is *not* winning?
  - How are you improving targets (finding the right potential clients)?
  - How is the cultivation process being refined (networking, improving agency credibility, targeted outreach)?
  - Are campaign proposals resonating with targets (crafting and communicating strategy)?
  - Are new business presentations polished and professional (practice and coordination among the business development team, sales training for agency leadership)?

Agencies should be aware of how much profit individual clients generate and the types of clients that provide the best match for the firm's services. Profitability can be measured by the amount of staff time spent on an account relative to its retainer or project fee. Clients, organizations, or industries willing to pay more for the same services should be considered as areas for expansion. Within the agency, not everyone's time should be considered equal. Agency leaders have higher billable hourly rates than account executives. Croft explains that a client who "requires a heavy investment of your most senior peoples' time" will always be less profitable than a client who can be managed day-to-day by junior staff.[6] From this perspective, agencies focused on efficiency often seek out clients and design work-flow to make the client-focused time of their senior staff as effective as possible.

Entrepreneurs should examine whether business-to-business (B2B) or consumer clients are more profitable as well as how the geographic location of their clients affects time and cost to successfully manage accounts. Some agencies may specialize in (for example) local consumer clients and build programs that leverage the experience and media market relationships involved. Others focus on a specific industry or industries where geography is in no way a barrier to expansion. In some cases, agencies might find that working with clients on the other side of the country will be more efficient than those around the block.

Case Studies

Many companies share case studies that highlight successful outcomes. Each example should clearly and concisely outline the client's problem/situation, the strategy applied to solve it, and the final result. Additionally, the best case studies demonstrate creative, original, and memorable approaches and tactics. Each must be crafted for a specific audience, including a potential client. The appropriate format, style, and length vary greatly depending on the audience and what messages the case study will convey. Of course, clients must give their approval, preferably in writing, to allow for a case study's publication.

Agencies should share example projects in disciplines or industries where they would like to expand. For example, a new firm with a desire to focus on social media for independent retail outlets should develop case studies demonstrating their prowess in that niche. A company working to move beyond its practice in event-focused public relations should consciously seek out projects and generate case studies in other areas. A firm looking to move away from restaurant public relations altogether may only include case studies of clients in other industries or emphasize the tactics (such as media relations, social media, and web content creation) rather than the industry. In this way, they demonstrate the work they want and allow potential clients to more easily imagine an agency as part of their team.

Case studies can serve as useful content in a variety of mediums, including websites, blogs, social media channels, or as bylined articles for industry publications. The opportunity to share these stories can help build organizational reputation in the best-possible way: through examples of success. In the early stages of a company's growth, it can be difficult to develop case studies without the backing of strong clients and challenging to win new clients without examples of excellent work. Many young agencies take on pro bono projects as opportunities to create case study–worthy programs. Pro bono work, often supporting local nonprofit clients with specific campaigns or events, allows an agency to tackle higher-profile

---

[6]Ibid., p. 42.

projects or gain experience with different industries, strategies, and tactics that can grow reputations and build relationships.

Testimonials and Recommendations

The practice of continuously compiling positive feedback from your clients allows solo practitioners and agencies to record and share their best impressions with the world. As with case studies, potential clients will often read this content with an eye toward helping make the best possible decision on which firm to hire. It is always valuable to have on a hand a list of **client references**: clients who will be able to share their positive experiences with potential clients as part of the proposal process. Additionally, it never hurts to ask whether these same clients would be willing to have their statements shared publicly. With satisfied clients, the answer, more often than not, is an emphatic *yes*. An additional step is asking for digital reviews of your organization or top staff through LinkedIn, Google, or other highly visible platforms, linking to specific review pages as needed.

Agencies should keep in mind that the source of the quote, both name and organization, is often more important than the quote itself. Consider what current clients (industries, locations, size, etc.) are of interest to your ideal potential clients, and who would grab their attention as a quoted endorser. What credibility can the endorser add? Within which communities does their reputation matter? Do they bring specific industry expertise? Has their company overcome critical challenges or crises? Consider which skills and relationships your agency wants to highlight based on the clients you want, not necessarily the ones you have. Even if existing clients do not fit this mold, young agencies may be able to draw on prior job experiences and professional networks to construct a list of credibility-building testimonials to their individual abilities. Agency leaders may be apprehensive in asking for client permission to share such stories and testimony, but these fears are often unfounded. Clients appreciate knowing that they are valued and that their agency believes they are doing great work for them.

©iStockphoto.com/sshepard

A multitude of community- and business-focused organizations provide opportunities for agency practitioners to network and build relationships, allowing them to better serve clients as well as cultivate new ones.

Thought Leadership

From agency blogs to best-practice articles in trade publications and keynote presentations at major conferences, practitioners who are adept at explaining the strategies behind their success build credibility within and beyond the PR community. Such content and outreach should be targeted toward groups and industries that are logical fits for current and potential clients. Croft recommends keeping such writing and speaking "99 percent non-commercial."[7] Essentially, entrepreneurs should be sharing their expertise and insights rather than speaking directly about their agencies. In this way, thought leadership allows PR agencies to practice what they preach for business development: Create and distribute useful content through earned, owned, and shared media channels.

Networking and Community Involvement

Becoming an agency leader involves representing the organization both in the community to demonstrate the company's civic commitment (which could be a physical community or an industry network) and in professional organizations. PR agencies are well represented on nonprofit boards of directors, within volunteer positions at local chambers of commerce, and, of course, as the major supporters of Public Relations Society of America (PRSA) chapters nationwide. These organizations provide opportunities to learn from other business and community leaders as well as to network and demonstrate strategic acumen to potential clients. Contributing time and expertise to a local nonprofit may be rewarding for its own sake, but agency leaders should also participate to make the most of the relationship-building possibilities with other professionals. The attorneys, accountants, physicians, small-business owners, and in-house communication leaders also serving on these boards may someday be potential clients, recommend an agency to their connections, or be able to provide testimonials to an agency professional's skills and talents.

Within a local business community, organizations such as chambers of commerce, Entrepreneurs' Organization (EO) chapters, and business accelerators all focus on peer-to-peer mentoring and business development. Such groups work to share both skills and consulting or vendor relationships among their own members. Zitron describes asking for help within such networks as a "sign of strength" rather than weakness.[8] In this way, a young PR firm can build relationships with potential clients as well as with partners for design, development, bookkeeping, human resources, and a host of other business needs. The opportunities to learn skills, share experiences, and develop potential client relationships have made such memberships a staple for many agencies. Like public relations itself, networking is not necessarily a skill or activity that will provide immediate benefits. It takes time for each of us to find ourselves in situations where we may be able to help others or where they may find themselves in a position to help us.

Of course, networking also can be digital. Ensuring that both your personal and your agency's social media accounts are regularly updated and visible is a start, but smart digital networkers develop content that is constantly interesting their peers and potential clients. They frame posts in ways that start conversations, and they demonstrate their own expertise.

---

[7]Ibid., p. 54.

[8]Zitron, E. (2013). *This is how you pitch: How to kick ass in your first years of PR.* Lawrence, KS: Sunflower Press, p. 125.

Responding to Requests for Proposal[9]

Clients may choose several paths when selecting an agency to work with. Similar to employee hiring processes, different organizations have different degrees of formality and different levels of openness to outside or unfamiliar candidates. When looking for an agency, some organizations build relationships first and sign contracts without opening a public search. Others, including most large, nonprofit, or government-affiliated entities, put in place a formal structure to outline the scope of work, receive proposals, and vet them. This is often referred to as a *RFP* (request for proposals) *process*.

RFPs exist in an attempt to level the playing field and allow a variety of agencies to bid on a project with the same level of background knowledge. This does not mean that the RFP process is inherently fair, but, when done with the right intentions, it can provide each competing agency with fewer resources and experience to compete based on their strategic acumen.

RFP Standards

- RFPs can be posted publicly or sent only to a predetermined list of agencies.

- Many organizations require agencies to sign a nondisclosure agreement (NDA) regarding the proposal content.

They also may inquire about potential conflicts of interest at the application stage.

- After reviewing all of the proposals, several finalists usually perform an in-person pitch for the decision makers.

RFP Response Tips

- **Make sure your agency is the right fit:** RFPs take a significant amount of time and effort to respond to. If you don't see the potential client as a strong fit, it may be best not to participate in the process.[10]

- **Prepare for a quick response:** Your boilerplate agency language, team member bios, images, and strategy descriptions should all be vetted and ready to go so that you can act quickly.

- **Clarify your plan:** What will make your approach distinctively successful? Ensure that this is articulated and rearticulated throughout the process. No one will read every word of your proposal, so the ability to scan is critical.

- **Bundle pricing:** Rather than having a detailed list of pricing for multiple parts of the process, maintaining a bundled pricing model improves an agency's ability to negotiate rather than have the client seek *a la carte* services.

---

[9]Deeb, G. (2016, October 27). The 10 things you need to know when responding to RFPs. Entrepreneur. Retrieved November 12, 2017, from https://www.entrepreneur.com/article/252061

[10]Willets, A. (2012, April 9). Proceed with caution: Responding to RFPs. *Public relations tactics*. Retrieved November 12, 2017, from http://apps.prsa.org/Intelligence/Tactics/Articles/view/9709/1046/Proceed_with_caution_Responding_to_RFPs#.WZuwypPfr-Z

Developing Long-Term Client Relationships

Clients come and go, but most successful agencies secure a core group of stable, long-term partnerships that create financial and workflow stability and often provide for the most rewarding strategic opportunities. Smart agency leaders cultivate these relationships and manage them carefully in order to keep them flourishing year after year. Securing and executing a successful time-bound campaign project is not the same as working with clients on an ongoing retainer basis. Often, short-term projects are narrow in scope, such as launching a new product, helping an organization manage a crisis, or driving publicity and attendance for an upcoming event. In these situations, clients often dictate the goal and even the objective(s). Long-term relationships allow PR practitioners to become more deeply engrained in their clients' work, build trust, and act as strategic business counselors. They provide practitioners with opportunities to be at the management table as such goals and objectives are discussed.

In this way, practitioners who earn the trust of client leadership can have a significant impact on the direction of organizations, their employees, and their communities. Long-term relationships allow the whole value of public relations and the full expertise of agency counselors to shine. They allow practitioners to form deep relationships with relevant media. They reflect organizations' commitment to the best interests of their stakeholders. They make possible the partnerships and deep client and industry knowledge that allow for strategic insights. Most importantly, they make it possible for the credibility, reputation, and actions of organizations to improve, building each year's work on previous accomplishments. These situations provide the greatest impact for clients and the most rewarding relationships for agency practitioners.

Types of Clients Conducive to Long-Term Partnerships

Strong organizations tend to make the best clients. Companies and nonprofits with clear identities, audiences, niches, and objectives make it easier to for communication professionals to add value. That said, these same qualities make them more likely to already be in successful agency partnerships or have particularly strong in-house PR teams. They may be less likely to need an outside agency. The opportunity to work with such organizations does not come along every day, particularly in smaller markets.

The size of potential clients often has a significant influence on their PR needs. Very large organizations, those with a significant footprint in a specific industry or community, often require a significant amount of communication based on the size and accompanying diversity of their stakeholders. While some organizations in this position choose to bring some of the PR function in-house, the scope of potential challenges makes them likely to seek outside support. Large organizations often prefer to partner with other large organizations (such as selecting a national or global PR firm rather than a local one), but they may also work with multiple local firms. There may be specific industry, geography, or relationship needs that would make a niche firm a preferable option. However, this mentality still may be a hurdle to overcome.

Small organizations, such as start-ups, mom-and-pop businesses, and local nonprofits often find the need to establish basic communication services first. Agencies have an opportunity to significantly upgrade fundamental processes and to make an immediate impact whether through media relations, social media, internal communication, or other means. In these cases, challenges often stem from the lack of resources needed to execute desired plans as well as the lack of internal client support and involvement to keep projects moving forward. Effective agencies must be creative and scrappy to make efficient use of the available resources. Ideally, agencies can increase support as small clients grow, requiring increasingly more sophisticated PR strategies and more public opportunities and challenges.

©iStockphoto.com/pixelfit

Small businesses may have very different needs than large corporations, but agencies can offer customized services to support a wide variety of organizational goals.

Organizations that are more active in developing new products or services, expanding, hiring, or diversifying provide many opportunities for agencies to add value. Outside strategic communication counsel can be particularly critical at certain points in an organization's history when they make significant changes. A company launching a product in a new sector may seek out an agency with existing industry experience and relationships, for example. Active organizations require repeated, ongoing counsel in these areas. Growth and activity can provide additional opportunities for agency input regarding fundamental brand choices for organizations, granting public relations and agencies a true seat at the table and the opportunity to make a positive difference in clients' futures.

Public companies often fit the descriptions of organizations with a significant volume of activity and need for public communication. These organizations cater to a variety of media markets, work with a myriad of industry supply chains, and, consequently, communicate with a breadth of different audiences. In addition to being large organizations with significant employee bases and community relevance, they carry significant legal communication responsibilities to their shareholders; this is known as the subdiscipline of investor relations.[11] As

---

[11] Alexander Laskin, professor of public relations at Qunnipiac University, has written extensively on the role of investor relations in public relations: particularly, his 2014 research for the *International Journal of Strategic Communication*, titled "Strategic Financial Communication" and "Investor Relations as a Public Relations Function: A State of the Profession in the United States" for the *Journal of Public Relations Research*.

this corporate communication is governed by the Sarbanes-Oxley Act and other laws, such work requires additional expertise and understanding of the financial and regulatory structures and requirements in play.[12] Practitioners with expertise in such regulations have a significant advantage in winning business for clients interested in agency support for these tasks.

On the other hand, privately held businesses have a wider variety of communication styles and needs. They may be less forthcoming with news and information, as they are legally required to share less. This approach can make the work of PR professionals more difficult: Less news to share can lead to fewer opportunities. Private organizations also have fewer regulatory restrictions on what they *can* share, leading to the potential for greater opportunity. Strategic agency practitioners are often more able to guide the leaders of privately held businesses in a proactive approach to media relations, due to the lack of regulatory oversight and investor considerations. The leaders of privately held organizations may be more likely to share distinct and journalistically valuable/social media shareable

Clients will *not* be successful long-term partners when . . .

- **external relationships are not prioritized:** Working with insular organizations, where community, customer, vendor, and industry partnerships are not valued, means that the efforts of public relations to strengthen these partnerships becomes a lower priority.

- **the organization is stagnant or overly rigid:** Company or leadership cultures resistant to change will not be able to take full advantage of opportunities that arise through the course of an agency–client relationship. Flexibility and openness to change are critical to success.

- **strategic advice is not valued:** Some organizational leaders do not respond well to outside counsel. While clients are ultimately responsible for the decisions they make on behalf of their organizations, consistent rejection of external perspectives does not support a valuable relationship.

- **leadership is only focused on short-term success:** The function of public relations is most effective as an investment in building long-term relationships with an organization's key publics.[13] Organizations who only measure success based on quarterly metrics may struggle in partnering with agencies. Strategic PR efforts provide the greatest benefits over a period of years, not weeks or months.

---

[12]Laskin, A. V. (2014). Investor relations as a public relations function: A state of the profession in the United States. *Journal of Public Relations Research, 26*, 200–214.

[13]Broom, G. M., & Sha, B-L. (2013). *Cutlip and Center's effective public relations* (11th ed.). Boston, MA: Pearson.

opinions and perspectives because they have fewer stakeholders (and stockholders) to whom they are accountable. This freedom has the potential to create lasting and valuable relationships with PR agencies.

While not directly related to private versus public companies, the style of leadership and decision making within an organization also contributes to its ability to take advantage of PR counsel. Organizations with a decentralized or horizontal structure often struggle to implement PR agency work due to a lack of coordination. Effective media relations, in particular, require multiple layers of an organization working together to provide a united public front to journalists and funnel media inquiries back to the PR team.

Successful Entrepreneurs Work With the Tools at Hand

Despite a litany of potential challenges, PR practitioners regularly make the successful transition to agency leadership or ownership. They overcome such client challenges, in no small part, because of an ability to find unique ways to deliver value, whatever the circumstances. Every client has a different set of circumstances, some that contribute to making their story relevant, newsworthy, and sharable; others not. Entrepreneurs win and sustain new business by understanding the situation at hand, setting client expectations in line with the organizational reality, and delivering results despite obstacles. In order to maintain such success, they demonstrate and educate their clients about the compounding positive benefits of improved relationships with key stakeholders, including customers, communities, and media.

While rarely a straight path, entrepreneurship has allowed many top practitioners to accelerate their careers, build rewarding client relationships, and become their own bosses. It requires more responsibility and a deeper commitment but also provides opportunities for greater success and gratification. Even for those not interested in owning their own business, obtaining a foundation in entrepreneurial skills and the entrepreneurial mind-set will allow them to be greater assets to the growth of any firm.

Reflect and Discuss

1. Describe the challenges and opportunities that come with being an entrepreneur and opening your own PR agency.

2. What makes a great client? How could the same organization be an excellent client for one firm, but not for another?

3. How can agencies without an established track record demonstrate their skills for potential clients?

4. Why are long-term client partnerships beneficial for both agencies and clients?

Mark Winter

Identity is a 25-person integrated marketing and PR firm based in Metro Detroit and serves clients across the country. Mark Winter founded the company in 1998 and has watched it grow to more than 60 clients across the country, representing a wide variety of industries including commercial real estate, hospitality, manufacturing, and technology. The company model is centered on its teams of specialists, including its media relations and marketing team, social media team, and creative team.[14]

What got you started as an entrepreneur in public relations?

Ever since I was in third grade, I've had a "business." I've always been a self-starter. I graduated from college and started working in public relations, but considered starting my own firm for many years before I did it. I understood the work. I knew I could do it better, but I wouldn't have been able to make the jump without nine years at two other firms. You learn about the best and worst traits for each one and apply it to what you want to accomplish. When I sat down to start Identity, from the beginning, I wanted to make sure that I created an environment, in terms of culture and growth, without internal competition. The goal was to make it more like a law firm or an accounting firm.

What do you see as your best trait as a business owner?

I know that I am not the best at doing everything. In the beginning, you have to do everything, but as the company matures, those who have the ability to take a look inward have the opportunity to step up. I know my weaknesses are in operational discipline, in holding people accountable. Success in this environment is about finding people who love and excel in the areas where you need help.

What has been your biggest challenge as a business owner?

Different stages of growth hold very different challenges. At Identity, we've experienced people-related challenges; individuals who didn't buy into our vision, who didn't like change. We've also seen client-related challenges, particularly when we moved from a largely B2B base to a more even mix of B2B and business-to-consumer (B2C) clients. Overcoming these challenges is all about staying connected and maintaining your perspective. Running a company can be isolating, and an entrepreneur alone is an entrepreneur at risk. For me, working with organizations like EO has been fundamentally life-changing. It's not so much about people giving advice, but truly understanding that you're not alone.

---

[14]Disclaimer: The author (Capizzo) was an employee of this firm for four years and grew significantly as a PR professional under the tutelage of its partners. This interview is undoubtedly biased—hopefully in a direction useful to readers—in its premise that many independent firms (and Identity in particular) provide exceptional client service as well as offer young professionals the opportunity to build successful careers in the field.

Genuine peer-to-peer conversation with other entrepreneurs, whether they're in public relations or other industries, is extremely important. Leaders in different industries can bring different skills and experiences that may be extremely valuable. You want to know that no one is there just for personal gain.

How have you managed the work/life balance?

It's all about working hard, but *hard* can mean smart and not necessarily working more. At the very beginning, everyone should know that there is a cost to entrepreneurship. That cost comes in the form of time and effort. It's just hard because you're the only one. You have to own that responsibility. You have to have a spouse or significant other who understands what that commitment means. There's a difference between those who are trying to build a *lifestyle business*, a way for them as an individual to earn money and do their work on their terms, as opposed to a *real business*: scaling it up, adding people, adding clients, and really changing people's lives. With Identity, I knew I wanted to build a real business that would provide opportunity for my employees as well. To do that, you

can't tread water; you have to continue to grow. But that growth, and what it can do for others, is what makes it worth the time and effort. You don't have to pick your direction right away, but you always have to put in the time.

What advice would you give to students or early career practitioners who see entrepreneurship in their future?

Are you a risk taker? What does that mean to you? Are you willing to lose everything? Are you willing to admit that you're not great at everything? Can you let go? Are you the smartest person in the room? Are you a leader or a follower? We are who we are. Entrepreneurship is not for everyone. It's important to get an understanding of how things work before putting up your own shingle. Live in the world first. Study agency billing, proposals, contracts, and relationships. Get a job with an existing agency and learn as much as you can. Give 150% there because you'll always have more to do when you're on your own. Sometimes being the owner means you make less, not more. With the opportunity comes exposure. For me, owning a business is not about freedom from work, it's about the freedom to create.

Top 5 Characteristics Every PR Professional Should Have

1. Hospitality minded
2. Communication skills: written and verbal
3. Ability to think strategically
4. Confidence/Trust/Energy
5. Growth and learning focused/embraces change

Top Must-Haves

- **Must-download app:** Slack. We love this as a tool to stay connected as an agency.
- **Must-read book/blog/ news outlet:**
  - I love *HBR* (*Harvard Business Review*). Great

articles with actionable takeaways.

  - *Take the Stairs* by Rory Vaden
  - *The Go Giver* by Bob Burg and John David Mann
  - Fox News

(Continued)

(Continued)

- **Must-use tool:** Slack, hand written notes, Go to Meeting (or any other video conferencing platform), a telephone. The key is to integrate "old school" relational tools with technologies. We cannot take the *public* piece out of PR.

Putting It All Together

CHAPTER 14

Public Relations Tools and Templates

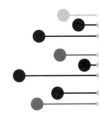

There are several tools and templates that public relations practitioners and agencies use regularly. This final chapter includes the Public Relations Society of America (PRSA) Independent Practitioners Alliance (IPA) proposal template, a ROSTIR (research/diagnosis, objectives, strategies, tactics, implementation, reporting/evaluation) PR planning guide, an executive summary, a strategy brief, a media advisory, a press release, an email pitch, a client report, and a crisis communication plan outline.

PRSA IPA Proposal Template

This PR prospective client proposal template was developed by and reprinted with permission from PRSA's IPA network. The IPA is made up of more than 200 small business owners and freelance PR and communication practitioners. They offer a number of free resources, including this proposal template, on their website (https://www.prsa.org/independent-practitioners-section/):

PR Proposal

Company Name

Date (+ any expiration date)

Name(s): Contact Information

COMPANY NAME HERE

About (YOUR COMPANY)

1. One paragraph about your agency positioning and staff

2. One paragraph about what sets you apart/why you are a good fit for this prospect

   - Promote your key strengths and the experiences that support alignment between you and the prospect/industry.

   - If you are a virtual agency, promote the benefits of doing business with a senior PR professional with low overhead.

3. Link to your website and bio and/or team bios. (Name of Prospect) Situation Analysis

- Start with demonstrating industry knowledge and any trends/opportunities important to your prospect.

- Move on to a brief statement of your understanding of the prospect and their products/services.

- Next, tie these insights to market data and perceived strengths/weaknesses/opportunities/threats to summarize/preview potential communication actions (goals and strategies).

- Make the case for why you/your agency is best prepared to offer assistance.

- Bookend your industry knowledge with a discussion about their messaging and positioning; describe steps for message refinement and the goals of your overall PR program in addressing the current situation.

- Close with a description of what your proposal includes.

For example: This proposal presents a full range of PR strategies and tactics that can be tailored to interact and build upon each other to overcome challenges and best meet the prospect's PR goals. From an initial discussion, the prospect's PR goal, with appropriate supportive objectives, appear include the following:

1. Build on the existing awareness of the Company's products to improve competitive standing in the marketplace.

- Objective: Increase share-of-voice within industry trade publications from XX percent to XX percent over the next XX months.

- Objective: Increase positive word-of-mouth on social media by XX percent in the next XX months.

- Objective: Develop and nurture brand advocates and enthusiasts through social media, increasing the volume of content shared by followers to XX over the next XX months.

To accomplish these goals and objectives, we would prioritize the following PR strategies:

2. Media Relations

- Leverage visibility via a well-balanced media relations program that includes blogs, community offers, and national news articles.

***This template assumes that a verbal discussion with the prospective client has taken place, key questions have been asked, and an understanding of their needs is clear. In this section, summarize what you heard to build PR recommendations on stated needs (i.e., branding, messaging, media relations, search engine optimization, etc.).

- Issue a national press release and customize outreach to community reporters at newspapers in each of the designated market areas (DMA) where the Company has stores.

- Plan and execute a thought leadership program for the chief executive officer (CEO) through writing/publishing editorial pieces and appearing on various traditional news channels, including television and radio.

3. Social Media

- Leverage visual storytelling through a series of posts across Company social media channels, including Facebook, Twitter, Instagram, and Pinterest, triggering strong engagement and emotional responses.

- Sponsor Facebook posts with key demographics (age, gender) and keywords related directly to prospective and competitor customers.

PR Program Elements

This section should include the key program recommendations for this specific prospect. Examples include the following:

1. A consistent and well-executed analyst relations program

- Your explanation on why this program is vital to your prospect.

- Key relationships you already have established in prospect market area listed by analyst firm, name, and practice area.

2. An aggressive media relations effort

- Share what this will consist of, how it will support other areas in the program, and specifics on why it's important.

- Outline your approach and planned focus (business-to-business, business-to-consumer, a combination, etc.) and high-level reasoning behind the recommendations you're making.

- List established relationships with media by media title only, but cite the coverage area of editors to tie in to the industry/product. It is okay to list as many as 50 in a three-column format, but it is not necessary to have that many. You can list a "Top 10" or "CEO List" recommendation.

3. Social media effort (shared and paid/boosted outreach)

- Explain the interplay of different social media channels.

- Underscore the need for a mix of shared, curated, and original content as well as shared and paid/boosted tactics.

4. Key Messages: Distributed (*Sample*)
   - Product reviews and awards
   - Customer testimonials and case studies
   - Developer relations
   - Product launch
   - Tradeshows and user groups
   - CEO thought leadership program
   - Media success measurement

PR Program Pricing

Here, you articulate how much your services will cost and how you will format the invoice. Are you billing by estimating how much time will be spent each month based on known projects (such as an upcoming trade show) or by charging for a monthly fee plus overhead? Will the relationship be a time-bound project or an ongoing retainer?

This is what prospects look for first, so make sure it's clear and straightforward. Potential clients truly value transparency—they are asked to be more transparent, and they appreciate that greatly in their vendors and contractors. Making your costs clear and concise will entice them to read more details before making a decision.

Your Unabashed Pitch on "Why You"

Here's where you restate and add to why you're a great fit, why your business approach is best for them, and how much you look forward to working with them to develop their program.

- Provide them with insight into your management processes (when and how often will you meet; how often will you report and on what, when you will send an invoice, what the terms are, what back up you provide, etc.).

- Tell them why you do business this way and how it benefits them.

- Don't forget to thank them for the opportunity and invite them to contact you with questions and/or for a personal meeting.

We'll be happy to answer any questions you may have about this proposal and would welcome an opportunity to meet in person.
Kind regards,
YOUR CONTACT INFORMATION REPEATED HERE

ROSTIR Strategic Planning Guide

Now that your agency has landed the client, a PR plan will be pulled together. This will serve as an agency's outline for the overall campaign and will demonstrate what the agency has accomplished when researching and, ultimately, when executing the overall campaign for a client. A number of essential components should be included when preparing the ROSTIR strategic planning guide, which will help guide the process of writing and preparation.

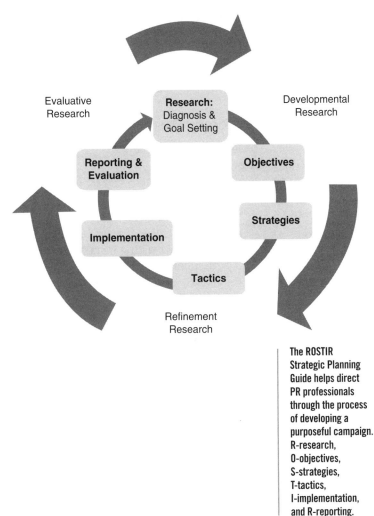

The ROSTIR Strategic Planning Guide helps direct PR professionals through the process of developing a purposeful campaign. R-research, O-objectives, S-strategies, T-tactics, I-implementation, and R-reporting.

Strategic PR Plan

Company Name

Date

Contact Information

Project Lead

Phone Number

Email

TABLE OF CONTENTS

Executive Summary

1. Research—Program Diagnosis and Analysis
   a. Strengths, Weaknesses, Opportunities, and Threats (SWOT) Analysis
2. Objectives and Key Performance Indicators
3. Strategies
4. Tactics
   a. Performance and Monitoring
   b. PESO (paid, earned, shared, and owned media)
5. Implementation and Execution
6. Reporting and Evaluation
7. Conclusion

Executive Summary

The executive summary is a high-level synopsis of the campaign's diagnosis and the solutions offered. This section covers several key points of interest to the client.

Research: Program Diagnosis and Analysis

Research is at the core of all PR activities. Proper research leads to diagnosing the problem and identifying solutions for clients.[1] Depending on the client's needs, various research methods can be used. Research methods can be broadly categorized into two groups:[2]

- *Primary:* This is research conducted firsthand. Research options include analysis of existing content (qualitative or quantitative), surveys and questionnaires, one-to-one interviews, telephone interviews, focus groups, copy and product testing, psychographic studies, and analysis of digital or social media analytics.

- *Secondary:* This method involves gathering information from published or professional sources such as peer reviewed journals, case studies, published reports, white papers, books, professional journals, and archives as well as digital and online sources; internal or proprietary organizational sources; and existing earned media coverage.

Within this section, include a summary of the target audience(s). The research helps to identify key publics and stakeholders. The degree of influence, prestige, power, needs, or level of involvement with the client helps identify potential publics.[3] This section should address the following:

- An explanation of those affected by the PR campaign. This section includes data on the demographics, psychographics, audience personas, and overarching characteristics of key stakeholders.

---

[1] Womeninpr. (2012, January 12). 12 steps to a successful PR campaign. *Women in PR.* Retrieved March 4, 2017, from https://womeninpr.wordpress.com/2012/01/10/12-steps-to-a-successful-pr-campaign/

[2] Wilson, L. J. & Ogden, J. (2016). *Strategic communications planning for public relations and marketing.* Dubuque, IA: Kendall Hunt.

[3] Hayes, D. C., Hendrix, J. A., & Kumar, P. D. (2013). *Public relations cases.* Independence, KY: Cengage.

- Opinion leaders, credible sources, and influencers

- Media to be targeted through PESO

- Benchmarks or metrics that can be used to track progress and success during and after the campaign

SWOT Analysis

A SWOT analysis is a qualitative method that brings together a variety of secondary research about an organization and its competitors/industry peers, combined with primary research to add the input and perspective of organizational leaders. SWOT, which stands for strengths, weaknesses, opportunities, and threats, is an analytical framework that allows organizations to better understand their position in the marketplace.[4] A SWOT analysis enables organizations to pinpoint both internal and external influences that help organizations develop a full picture of all factors necessary for planning.

Objectives and Key Performance Indicators

Once research has been conducted and the problem/opportunity identified, it is time to define the objectives and outline other key performance indicators (KPIs). The objectives should include the end result of the PR activity. Each objective must be SMART:[5]

- **Specific:** Is the objective clearly defined and appropriately focused?

- **Measurable:** Can each objective be measured before, during, and after outreach has occurred to evaluate change?

- **Achievable:** Considering other factors (e.g., budget and time constraints), is each objective achievable?

- **Realistic:** Are you being realistic, given the resources available and constraints?

- **Time bound:** What timing is necessary to achieve the set objectives and by what date do you want to achieve them?

---

[4] Christensen, C. R., Andrews, K. R., & Bower, J. L. (1978). *Ideas for instructors on the use and content of business policy, text and cases.* Homewood, IL: R.D. Irwin.

[5] Beamish, K., & Ashford, R. (2005). *Marketing planning, 2005–2006.* Oxford, UK: Elsevier Butterworth-Heinemann.

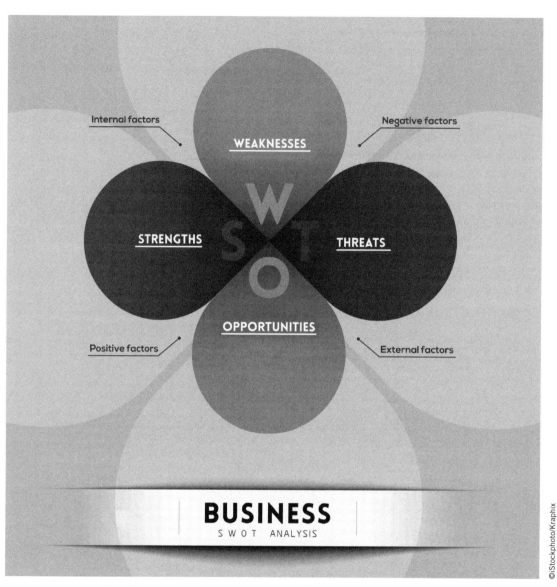

Internal factors

Negative factors

WEAKNESSES

STRENGTHS

THREATS

OPPORTUNITIES

Positive factors

External factors

BUSINESS
S W O T   A N A L Y S I S

©iStockphoto/Kraphix

| An analysis that provides business perspectives, lends objectivity, and helps establish organizational goals.

A KPI is a measurable value that demonstrates how effectively a company is achieving key business objectives.[6] Organizations use KPIs to evaluate their success at reaching targets.

---

[6] KPI Examples. (n.d.). *Klipfolio*. Retrieved March 4, 2017, from https://www.klipfolio.com/resources/kpi-examples

Develop KPIs that are easy to measure, quick to report on, and can be checked regularly. Gijs Nelissen offers the following common KPIs that companies use to measure the success of their PR initiatives:[7]

- New social media followers
- New referral links
- Increased organic website traffic
- New leads or sign-ups

Strategies

Strategies set the foundation for a program that is built on a series of tactics. These tactics are then implemented in order to meet the objectives. Strategies define several channels or other communication opportunities that, when combined, help a campaign achieve its objectives. This section includes a broad statement describing how an objective will be achieved. Strategies provide guidelines and key messages while also offering a rationale for the execution. Strategies and tactics are often interdependent. A *strategy* is the approach, while *tactics* are the tangible aspects of the campaign: A strategy may include using consumer media outreach in a specific geographic market, while accompanying tactics could describe the specific PESO channels, media outlets, or other actions to be taken as part of the implementation of that strategy. There may be multiple strategies in a campaign designed for various targeted audiences.

Tactics

Tactics are the activities implemented to carry out each campaign strategy. Practitioners use a number of integrated communication tools to execute a campaign; however, the challenge is identifying the appropriate tactics for each situation and each audience or public. Depending on the campaign, the right tactic may be proactive media relations, internal communication, lobbying, political advocacy, events, blogger relations, influencer relations, presentations, social media outreach, newsletters (print or digital), case studies, competitions, podcasts, stunts, advertising, and conference presentations in various combinations. Each tactic should help answer the following: What is the next step our organization will need to take to achieve the strategy?[8]

According to Gini Dietrich, an integral component of modern PR planning is thinking holistically by incorporating the PESO model:[9]

---

[7] Nelissen, G. (2014, December 3). Four PR metrics you can start using today. *Spin sucks*. Retrieved March 4, 2017, from http://spinsucks.com/communication/four-pr-metrics-you-can-use-today/

[8] Elson, S. (2016, April 8). PR planning 101: Defining objectives, strategies and tactics. *CommuniquePR*. Retrieved December 18, 2017, from http://www.communiquepr.com/blog/?p=8422

[9] Dietrich, G. (2015, March 23). PR pros must embrace the PESO model. *Spin sucks*. Retrieved February 3, 2016, from http://spinsucks.com/communication/pr-pros-must-embrace-the-peso-model/

- **Paid media**: Paid media for a PR program is social media advertising, sponsored content, traditional advertising, and email marketing.

- **Earned media**: Earned media is commonly referred to as either *publicity* or *media relations*. It's getting a company's name in print. It's having a newspaper or trade publication write about you, your company, or its offerings. Earned media is what the PR industry is typically known for because it's one of the few tangible tactics accomplished.

- **Shared media:** Shared media is also known as *social media*. This area continues to build beyond simply marketing or customer service. Soon, organizations will share it as their main source of communications internally and externally.

- **Owned media:** Owned media is also known as *content*. It is something that you own, and it lives on your website or blog. You control the messaging and tell your story.

Implementation

With the overall strategy in place and the tactics identified, the next step is to create a time line and enter the execution phase of the campaign. It is important to create a calendar to fully coordinate the timing and implementation of each tactic. Timing is vital for a successful campaign. PR professionals look for the exact moment the event should be held, social media should be shared, or an advertising campaign should launch. Clearly articulating the time line for a campaign's implementation is critical to ensure that the client understands how the campaign will be executed while at the same time setting expectations for the process.

A Gantt chart is one of the most popular and useful ways of showing activities such as tasks or events, each displayed against time.[10] Gantt charts are often used by PR professionals to stay on track and communicate deadlines to project teams within the agency and with a client. Typically, the left side of the chart lists the activities to be conducted and the top is a suitable time scale. Each activity is represented by a bar; the position and length of the bar reflects the start date, duration, and end date of the activity. Gantt charts allow you to see

- the various activities;

- when every activity begins and when it ends;

---

[10] What is a Gantt chart? (2017). *Gantt.com*. Retrieved March 4, 2017, from http://www.gantt.com/index2.htm? utm_expid=11664174-46.EjGD5xWgTOia25IJzkiv2w.2&utm_referrer=https%3A%2F%2Fwww.google .com%2F

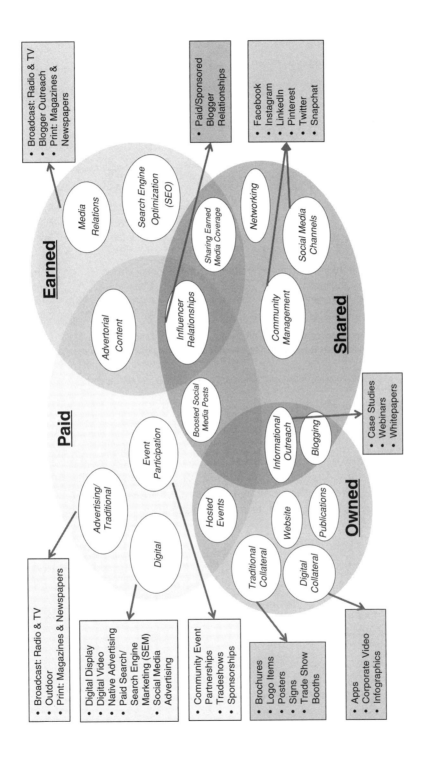

The diagram categorizes public relations tools into four overlapping groups: Paid, Earned, Shared, and Owned.

Paid
- Advertising/Traditional
  - Broadcast: Radio & TV
  - Outdoor
  - Print: Magazines & Newspapers
- Digital
  - Digital Display
  - Digital Video
  - Native Advertising
  - Paid Search/Search Engine Marketing (SEM)
  - Social Media Advertising
- Event Participation
  - Community Event Partnerships
  - Tradeshows
  - Sponsorships

Earned
- Media Relations
  - Broadcast: Radio & TV
  - Blogger Outreach
  - Print: Magazines & Newspapers
- Search Engine Optimization (SEO)
- Advertorial Content

Shared
- Sharing Earned Media Coverage
  - Paid/Sponsored Blogger Relationships
- Influencer Relationships
- Networking
- Social Media Channels
  - Facebook
  - Instagram
  - LinkedIn
  - Pinterest
  - Twitter
  - Snapchat
- Community Management
- Boosted Social Media Posts
- Informational Outreach
- Blogging
  - Case Studies
  - Webinars
  - Whitepapers

Owned
- Hosted Events
- Website
- Publications
- Traditional Collateral
  - Brochures
  - Logo Items
  - Posters
  - Signs
  - Trade Show Booths
- Digital Collateral
  - Apps
  - Corporate Video
  - Infographics

	EXPOSURE	ENGAGEMENT	INFLUENCE	ACTION
Paid	• OTS • Click throughs • Cost per thousand	• Duration • Branded search • Cost per click	• Purchase consideration • Change in opinion or attitude	• Visit website • Attend event • Download coupon
Earned	• Message inclusion • Impressions • Net positive impressions	• Readership • Awareness • URL visits	• Purchase consideration • Change in opinion or attitude	• Visit the store • Vote for/against • Make a donation
Shared	• OTS • Comment sentiment • No. of followers	• Number of links • Number of retweets • Subscribers	• Tell a friend • Ratings • Reviews	• Redeem coupon • Buy the product • Visit the website
Owned	• Unique visitors • Page views • Search rank	• Return visits • Durations • Subscriptions	• Tell a friend • Change in opinion or attitude	• Download white paper • Request more info

The International Association for Measurement and Evaluation of Communication (AMEC) developed standards by which social media is measured. These include exposure, engagement, influence, and action.

- the duration that each activity is scheduled to last;

- where activities overlap with other activities and by how much; and

- the start and end date of the entire PR project.

Including a budget is also an essential part of a campaign. Both fixed and soft costs should be taken into consideration. Companies will want to know all expenses related to the campaign.[11] They do not need to see a complete breakdown, but it's important for agency professionals to include all of the following:

- Professional time

- Campaign-related expenses (travel, creative production, events, paid media)

- Operating costs (administration, office space, materials)

- Communication costs (technology, media monitoring, and distribution services)

There are numerous free budgeting tools available for use and customization. Smartsheet developed a free, downloadable plan that displays the budget allocated for a specific tactic, the actual spending, and the budget variance. The Smartsheet template also breaks down marketing strategies by category, including advertising,

[11] Luttrell, R. (2016). *Social media: How to engage, share, and connect.* Lanham, MD: Rowman & Littlefield.

PR PLAN CALENDAR WITH BUDGET TRACKER				YEAR TO DATE TOTAL		
				BUDGETED	SPENT	VARIANCE
				$ –	$ –	$ –

ADVERTISING						
STRATEGY	TACTIC	DEPLOYMENT MONTH	TARGET AUDIENCE	AMOUNT BUDGETED	AMOUNT SPENT	BUDGETEDVARIANCE
Strategy A						$ –
						$ –
						$ –
Strategy B						$ –
						$ –
Strategy C						$ –
						$ –
			ADVERTISING TOTAL:	$ –	$ –	$ –

WEBSITE						
STRATEGY	TACTIC	DEPLOYMENT MONTH	TARGET AUDIENCE	AMOUNT BUDGETED	AMOUNT SPENT	BUDGETEDVARIANCE
Strategy A						$ –
						$ –
						$ –
Strategy B						$ –
						$ –
Strategy C						$ –
						$ –
			WEBSITE TOTAL:	$ –	$ –	$ –

WEBSITE						
STRATEGY	TACTIC	DEPLOYMENT MONTH	TARGET AUDIENCE	AMOUNT BUDGETED	AMOUNT SPENT	BUDGETEDVARIANCE
Strategy A						$ –
						$ –
						$ –
Strategy B						$ –
						$ –
Strategy C						$ –
						$ –
			CORPORATE BRANDING & GRAPHICS TOTAL:	$ –	$ –	$ –

WEBSITE						
STRATEGY	TACTIC	DEPLOYMENT MONTH	TARGET AUDIENCE	AMOUNT BUDGETED	AMOUNT SPENT	BUDGETEDVARIANCE
Strategy A						$ –
						$ –
						$ –
Strategy B						$ –
						$ –
Strategy C						$ –
						$ –
			SOCIAL MEDIA TOTAL:	$ –	$ –	$ –

WEBSITE						
STRATEGY	TACTIC	DEPLOYMENT MONTH	TARGET AUDIENCE	AMOUNT BUDGETED	AMOUNT SPENT	BUDGETEDVARIANCE
Strategy A						$ –
						$ –
						$ –
Strategy B						$ –
						$ –
Strategy C						$ –
						$ –
			DIRECT MARKETING TOTAL:	$ –	$ –	$ –

WEBSITE						
STRATEGY	TACTIC	DEPLOYMENT MONTH	TARGET AUDIENCE	AMOUNT BUDGETED	AMOUNT SPENT	BUDGETED VARIANCE
Strategy A						$ –
						$ –
Strategy B						$ –
						$ –
Strategy C						$ –
						$ –
PUBLIC RELATIONS TOTAL:				$ –	$ –	$ –

WEBSITE						
STRATEGY	TACTIC	DEPLOYMENT MONTH	TARGET AUDIENCE	AMOUNT BUDGETED	AMOUNT SPENT	BUDGETED VARIANCE
Strategy A						$ –
						$ –
Strategy B						$ –
						$ –
Strategy C						$ –
						$ –
RESEARCH TOTAL:				$ –	$ –	$ –

WEBSITE						
STRATEGY	TACTIC	DEPLOYMENT MONTH	TARGET AUDIENCE	AMOUNT BUDGETED	AMOUNT SPENT	BUDGETED VARIANCE
Strategy A						$ –
						$ –
Strategy B						$ –
						$ –
Strategy C						$ –
						$ –
EVENTS TOTAL:				$ –	$ –	$ –

WEBSITE						
STRATEGY	TACTIC	DEPLOYMENT MONTH	TARGET AUDIENCE	AMOUNT BUDGETED	AMOUNT SPENT	BUDGETED VARIANCE
Strategy A						$ –
						$ –
Strategy B						$ –
						$ –
Strategy C						$ –
						$ –
COLLATERAL TOTAL:				$ –	$ –	$ –

branding, public relations, and social media. You can find this template on the student website that contains ancillary materials.

Reporting and Evaluation

Both reporting and evaluation should be reviewed regularly, particularly in a long-term PR campaign. Evaluation (determining whether, how, and why a campaign is succeeding [or not]) and reporting (communicating campaign progress to clients) should be addressed both during and after the campaign:[12]

[12] Biderbeck, T. (2011, February 8). The creative brief: 10 things it must include. *Felt & Wire*. Retrieved August 11, 2017, from https://www.mohawkconnects.com/feltandwire/2011/02/08/the-creative-brief-10-things-it-must-include/

Ongoing: The ongoing review is what will be carried out throughout the campaign. It is not calculated at the end of all the campaign activity, but constantly throughout. If certain elements of the campaign are not working effectively, this analysis highlights where to refocus. Agency practitioners should have a process for reporting regular updates to clients during a campaign.

End of Campaign: At the completion on all public relations activities, final results can be compared with the campaign objectives, as well as to examine unexpected positive or negative outcomes. To do this, each strategy and tactic should be critically analyzed.

Conclusion

The conclusion ties together the overall PR campaign and discusses future PR plans. Recommendations for future planning and lessons learned are also included.

Creative Briefs and Strategy Briefs

Creative briefs and strategy briefs are documents created for a specific creative project or tactic, usually written as a collaboration between a client and an agency practitioner before any work begins. Their main purpose is to ensure that all parties involved in the project are on the same page as to its purpose, focus, and execution.

As we learned in Chapter 10, effective briefs should answer the following questions:[13]

- Goal: What is the dilemma? What do we want to achieve?

- Tone: What are we trying to say and how should we say it (tone)?

- Design perspective: What action do we want our audience or publics to take? What's nonnegotiable?

Despite their importance in the planning process, briefs should also not be set in stone: The best practitioners adjust briefs to changing circumstances as projects progress. This comes, of course, with the input and approval of all teams involved in the project.

In any given campaign, a variety of creative and strategy briefs may be written. A brochure, a blog post, social media posts, a feature story, an e-marketing email, a direct mail piece, an infographic, advertising pieces, a video, a special event, or a speech are just some of the tactics for which this approach can be helpful. Throughout the project, the brief continues to inform and guide the work. According to the author of *Managing the Design Process—Concept Development and*

---

[13] Oetting, J. (2016, April). 13 questions to help you write a compelling creative brief in 2017. *Hubspot*. Retrieved August 19, 2017, from https://blog.hubspot.com/agency/create-compelling-creative-brief

Implementing Design, Terry Lee Stone, suggests that a good creative or strategy brief will answer these questions:[14]

- What is this project?
- Who is it for?
- Why are we doing it?
- What needs to be done?
  - By whom?
  - By when?
- Where and how will it be used?

The template included in this chapter is meant to give an overarching structure. Each brief should be customized to the client, their needs, and the objectives of the strategic plan.

Strategy or Creative Brief

Project Title

Client Name

Project Overview

This is a short summary of the project to be completed. Include any research conducted for the findings. Here, you should also include a concise analysis of the expectations by the public. For example, if you are developing a social media post, you may include that you want the target audience to comment and share the post with their social connections. This prompts the individuals working on the project to keep that action in mind as they develop time lines, copy, images, and distribution approaches.

Project Lead and Due Date

Indicate who is leading this project other than the account manager and when the project is due to the client. It is also good to indicate other people on the team that will be working on the project.

Include a brief time line that will alert others that are working on the project as to when they must have their pieces completed. For example, if the strategy brief is for a brochure, the copy editor and graphics team will need to work together to ensure that deadlines are met.

---

[14] Biederbeck, T. (2011, February 8). The creative brief: 10 things it MUST include. *Mohawk*. Retrieved December 18, 2017, from https://www.mohawkconnects.com/feltandwire/2011/02/08/the-creative-brief-10-things-it-must-include/

Target Audience

Describe who the target audience is and the demographic (primary, secondary) this tool is directed toward.

Key Messages

Primary message: Primary messages represent the overarching information the company wants to present.[15] In this section, include a list of three to five short statements that articulate the key message the client wants to use in this tool.

Secondary message: Secondary messages support the primary message. Data, facts, images, narratives, and other important information should be included.

Project Requirements

Depending on the project, the requirements may change. Use this area to customize the brief for the specific project.

Image Requirements

List the necessary imagery and resources, such as photography, multimedia, charts, color palette, and so on. Include photo size and resolution needs. For example, do images need to be larger than 300 dpi? If so, include explicit instructions here.

Print Requirements

List the necessary print requirements. Keep in mind the following options:

- Finish: Options include matte, glossy, dull, cockle, finished, textured, or uncoated.

- Finished size: Some common sizes include 11 x 17, 12 x 18, 17 x 22, 23 x 29, 26 x 40, and 28 x 40.

- Fonts: serif, sans serif, decorative, or script. A great resource is 1001 Free Fonts (https://www.1001freefonts.com/).

- Paper weight: Weights include 30 to 115 pounds for items such as magazines, booklets, or posters; 60 to 120 pounds for items such as invitations, postcards, or mailers; or 16, 20, 24, 28, 32, and 36 pounds for traditional print jobs such as stationary, presentations, or fliers.

- Postage: Check with the Post Office for specific rates. Nonprofit organizations may receive reduced rates or bulk rate.

- Quantity: Consider digital printing, offset printing, black and white versus color, or short runs.

---

[15] Mack, S. (2017). Examples of primary & secondary messages in public relations. *Chron.* Retrieved December 18, 2017, from http://smallbusiness.chron.com/examples-primary-secondary-messages-public-relations-69839.html

Social Media Requirements

List the following social media requirements:

- Analytics to measured: metrics to consider include comments, likes, shares, exposure, engagement, influence, impact, and advocacy
- Content calendar: production and distribution time lines
- Hashtags: use tools such as http://hashtagify.me/ to understand popularity, trends, and correlations
- Links: use www.bit.ly to shorten websites as well as track metrics
- Search engine optimization (SEO) terms
- Visual elements: graphics, photos, infographics, charts, or videos

Web Requirements

List the following web requirements:

- Links: Include a list of embedded links to be used, if appropriate.
- SEO terms: If this material is being used on the internet, then include a list of relevant, search-friendly terms and phrases to be used.

Video Requirements

List the following video requirements:

- B-roll
- Copy: titles and on-screen graphics
- Equipment
- Images/Stills
- Location(s)
- Time of year
- Music and sound effects
- Permissions
- SEO terms
- SEM terms
- Storyboards: shot-by-shot overviews of the video to be approved before shooting
- Talent
- Clothing/costumes
- Cost analysis

Distribution Channel

Through which channel will this material be distributed?

- Blog

- Website

- Social media platform

- News media

- Magazine

- Television

- Radio

- Professional journal

- Mainstream media

Comments and Approval

Sign off from a client is crucial, so be sure to include a section for the client to sign off, leave comments, and approve the strategy brief for final execution.

Press Release

Press releases, media advisories, and email pitches are tools used regularly in media relations. The purpose of a press release is to signal to the media that something significant or newsworthy has occurred. Press releases are often used for mergers, new product launches, scientific discoveries, new hires or promotions, fiscal earnings, and other types of stories. Multiple press releases may be distributed over the course of the same project. For example, a product launch may involve a press release announcing that a new product is coming (previewing the launch date), a second press release marking the launch itself, and a third a month later describing the initial product sales and response. Generally, press releases are designed to include most of the information needed for a reporter to write their own story but also to entice them to do additional investigation and sourcing.

If printed, press releases and media advisories should use the following:

- 8 1/2 x 11 paper

- One page; paragraphs are single spaced while spacing between paragraphs is double spaced

- Clearly indicated contact information

- Concise, attention-grabbing headlines

- Answers to who, what, when, where, why, and how

- A standard boilerplate paragraph with background information on the client

- AP style

Printed Press Release

Company logo

Company name

Full mailing address

Phone * Email * Website

FOR MORE INFORMATION, CONTACT:

Name and Title

Phone: xxx-xxx-xxxx (Include the best number to be contacted at during the event, not a desk phone number.)

Email:

Social Media

FOR IMMEDIATE RELEASE

HEADLINE—BOLD, ALL CAPS, CENTERED, 6–12 Words

Subheading—Italics, no punctuation, centered

CITY, STATE, DATE—The lede paragraph should include key information in the event the rest of the release is not read. The most important information should be included using complete sentences; exemplar grammar, punctuation, and spelling; and AP style. Use third-person references: for example, "Pumpkin Waffle Company today announced a new line of organic syrup for the fall season."

The second paragraph expands on the lede and provides further information. Writing should be clear and concise and include only two or three sentences per paragraph.

Include a quote from the appropriate spokesperson.

The concluding paragraph should include additional details such as where to go for more information, to purchase products, to attend the event, and so on.

-30-

Boilerplate: This is the 'about us' section of the press release. Here, include a brief description of your organization. Boilerplates are located at the end of the advisory after the *-30-* or *###*. You can shrink the type size for this paragraph to ensure the release fits on one page.

Online press releases, sometimes called *digital press releases*, do not necessarily need *-30-* or *###*. These symbols once alerted wire services that the release had ended and no further content is forthcoming. In an online environment, such as the company's media center, indications such as these are not necessary.

Media Advisory

A media advisory, or *media alert*, invites the media to a company event, such as a news conference, grand opening, or presentation.[16] Think of it as an invitation. Advisories must clearly and succinctly explain why a reporter would benefit from attending a specific event.

Printed Media Advisory

COMPANY LOGO HERE

MEDIA ADVISORY

HEADLINE—BOLD, ALL CAPS, CENTERED

Subheading—Italics, no punctuation, centered

WHAT:	This section should be brief and to the point. Tell the journalist what is happening.
WHY:	Include why this event is important for the journalist and their audience. Include some relevant content of interest, such as a description of photo/video opportunities, and data or statistics that may be relevant and add to the newsworthiness of the event. This section can include a mix of sentences and bulleted items.
WHEN:	Indicate when the event is happening. Include the time and date (add start and end times, if applicable).
WHO:	Indicate and list the important people that will be at the event that the media would like to interview.
WHERE:	Address
	City
	State

---

[16] Jensen, K. (2017). Differences between a media advisory and a press release. *Chron.* Retrieved December 18, 2017, from http://smallbusiness.chron.com/differences-between-media-advisory-press-release-50929.html

Interested media should call the contact listed below to secure interviews.

CONTACT: PR contact name and title

Name of the organization

Phone number

Email

Social media link

-30-

Boilerplate: Include a brief description of your organization. Boilerplate copy is located at the end of the advisory. If there is little room left for this, you can shrink the type size for this paragraph.

Email Pitch

An email pitch is a PR practitioner's email message to a journalist or blogger about a potential story and why it should matter to their audience. While practitioners write press releases and media advisories for a broad media audience, pitches should be as tailored and personalized as possible, demonstrating research about the reporter's background and interests, their media outlet, and the outlet's audience.

Email Pitch

To: Conduct research to find the appropriate reporter or editor.

Subject: The subject line is akin to a headline, so be creative to catch the journalist's attention.

Dear Mr., Mrs., Ms., or Miss, [Check the AP Stylebook for diversity and inclusive language, particularly regarding the use of *they* as a gender-neutral pronoun.]

As clearly and concisely as possible, explain the story being pitched and the news angle. Any time you write a reporter, think about answering these two questions: So what? Who cares? The reporter must appeal to a large audience, so that is what they are asking themselves when they receive your email. Is what you are offering newsworthy? Will their readers, viewers, or listeners care?

The second paragraph should offer secondary messages that support the news angle. These can be bulleted sentences that include facts, examples, and data. Include a link to the full press release that should be on your company's media center.

The final sentence should let the reporter know when you will follow up.

Sincerely,

Name and title

Organization

Email

Phone

Social media link

Client Reports

Reporting back to the client is paramount. They want to understand how a campaign is going. Weekly or monthly reporting allows the agency and the client to evaluate and communicate progress and challenges. Each reporting document should clearly articulate what has been accomplished (past), what is happening currently (present) and what is in process or coming soon (future). Metrics help to

- track and highlight overall campaign performance monthly,
- evaluate successes, and
- understand what tweaks may be necessary.

Team Gantt, a project management software company, developed a free downloadable template project status report that is easy to customize. Some elements appear within these pages and the template can be found on the student ancillary website.

Agency Logo

Dear Client,

Include an introductory message. Be sure to point out key conversation points, metrics of interest, and even issues that may need addressing.

If you have a call scheduled to review this report, place the date, time, and meeting details here as well.

Thank you,

Your Name

Summary

What happened last week

- Tasks
- Deliverables

- Meetings
- Communications
- Decisions

What's happening this week

- Tasks
- Deliverables
- Meetings
- Communications
- Decisions

In progress

- Upcoming projects and tasks (see list above)
- Content, insights, or approvals needed from the client
- Potential obstacles or challenges to be addressed

Overall project time line completion status: XX% complete (or Stage X of X)

Phase, milestone, or task: XX% complete

Phase, milestone, or task: XX% complete

Total reach grew X% month over month

Overall website visits up X% from [previous month]

**This section could be organized effectively in several different ways, including by campaign objective, by project or initiative, or by previously agreed-upon metrics. Ideally, it should reference larger goals and objectives, contain quantitative and qualitative insights, and demonstrate progress while not ignoring challenges.

Overall budget spent: XX% spent; XX% remaining

**Note: You are tracking hours or dollars here.

Some agencies will report specific time- or dollar-based metrics. Others track specific tasks as well as hours, allowing them to report to a client that, for example, 30% of their efforts for a given month were spent on media relations, 20% on events, 20% on social media, 20% on creative project oversight, and 10% on reporting and account management. Agencies must balance a client's need to know how their dollars are being spent with providing unnecessary or overly granular information.

Upcoming tasks and milestones:

Task/Milestone	Target Date	Detail

Action items:

Action item	Owner	Due Date	Notes

Project issues, risks, and mitigation plans:

Project Issue	Risk	Mitigation	Notes

Crisis Communication Plan

Crisis Communications for a 24/7 News Cycle

Michael Meath (principal; Fallingbrook Associates, LLC; and a visiting assistant professor at Syracuse University's Newhouse School) advises that crises are not a matter of if, but when.

Today, every organization operates in a complicated and interconnected world. The chances of something going wrong and needing a carefully worded and positioned response is inevitable. Meath suggests that to help prepare for this eventuality, organization leaders consider these five key factors to successfully navigate crises and sensitive issues:

Take the "Critical 10"

Answering any inquiry in haste during a crisis may exacerbate the problem. Being on the receiving end of a phone call or urgent message always puts you at a disadvantage as you may not only be unprepared, but you are also operating on someone else's timetable. In these situations, always defer your availability and offer to call back in 10 minutes. ***And then be sure to do it.*** Even these few minutes can make the difference between managing a sensitive issue and a full-blown crisis. Always give yourself time to digest, reflect, and analyze before responding. Then, when you get back to the inquirer, you have a much better chance of being prepared and in control of the conversation and you are better suited to provide valuable information and answers. When negative digital media is employed, don't engage in an online battle. Try to get the person into a conversation offline as soon as possible. Taking the "Critical 10" can keep you from firing back and later regretting it.

Think in 280 Characters

The point here is not to literally think in tweets. It simply means to keep all messaging consistent and concise. When a crisis occurs and all the information is not available, organizations should have prepared *holding statements*, which they can easily modify and use until more information becomes available. These consistent and concise statements are best when they contain three key components: *fact*, *empathy*, and *what's next*. There's no room for speculation. The same process is necessary when crafting key messages later on. Limit yourself to one page of 14-point font, and craft 5 to 7 messages that are useful for *all* audiences. This ensures a consistent and clear voice and enables you to provide valuable and transparent information for all of your information partners (e.g., journalists, regulators, customers, employees, etc.) in disseminating your key messages to larger audiences. And even as you prepare for digital first responses (or even on-camera responses), prepare your key messages in writing first. Too many situations have gone poorly when messages weren't committed to writing for everyone to use and reference.

Who Speaks and Who Is the Designated Backup?

While one person should be designated as the primary spokesperson for your organization (often the CEO or other executive), be sure you train and prepare a backup spokesperson as well as specific subject matter experts to step in as needed. Training can be effectively done by both in-house and outside staff—but be sure you are objective about the training you are getting. Sometimes the CEO wants to be the spokesperson, but this doesn't automatically make him/her the best choice. In this instance, an outside consultant can help with an objective opinion.

And remember this: "You can always go up, but you can't go down," says Meath. If you put your senior leadership person out in front of an incident, be sure she stays there until the situation has been resolved. To do otherwise will undermine your organization's credibility.

Bridge With ATM

During a particularly sensitive interview or inquiry by a reporter, a regulator, or even a customer, think about ATM: acknowledge, transition, message. Acknowledging a question or point may be difficult, but it demonstrates a reflective tone and active listening, an attempt to understand, and show empathy. Phrases such as *No comment, Look, Listen,* or *What you need to know* are dismissive, combative, and demoralizing and can actually hurt your reputation further. Instead, once you've acknowledged the inquiry or concern, begin with the phrase *What I can tell you is* to return to and emphasize your key messages. A gentle approach will better enable you to get back to the important points you need to make during a crisis or sensitive situation.

Always Take Dessert

This seldom used technique is one of the easiest; yet is often forgotten or dismissed. At the conclusion of most interviews or inquiries, an opportunity is almost always offered you to provide additional thoughts. Yet people being interviewed seldom take it. The answer to a concluding question of "Is there anything else you would like to add?" should always be an emphatic "Yes!" Use this gift to reiterate one of your key messages and potentially save the interview. Do not use this opportunity to offer new, additional messages. Keep it simple and prepared.

Meath further suggests that when developing a crisis communication plan, organizations should use the following outline:

Plan Purpose. What is the overarching objective of the plan? Take a few paragraphs to outline what the plan seeks to accomplish (e.g., to communicate effectively to employees, customers, and the public during a crisis situation; to ensure continued operation of the business; or to protect the reputation of the organization). Have the chief executive officer of the company sign the statement to demonstrate the highest level of commitment to the plan.

Risk Scenarios and Issues Management. List the most likely situations that the organization will have to deal with in an emergency or crisis. These may include things such as vehicle accidents, hazardous materials spills, public health risks, improper use of social media, or mishandling of company assets. Be realistic and include the highest priority items.

Incident Assessment. Meath advises use of a high-, medium-, and low-level assessment tool to help determine the possible impact of a crisis. For example, a low-level hazardous materials incident would involve a minor spill with no exposure or injuries; while a high-level incident may involve multiple injuries or fatalities. Create an incident assessment tool that works for your organization.

Roles and Responsibilities. Identify those individuals who make up your Emergency Communications Team (ECT)—those critical people in your organization who will be part of responding to any crisis situation. This list likely includes your CEO, chief communications officer (COO), legal counsel, and key operational staff. Keep the number of people on your ECT as small as possible. Supplement this with an advisory team, which will include key resources both inside and outside the company that you can call on in a crisis situation. Finally, prepare a directory that includes the contact information for both your ECT and your advisory team, and keep that information on your smartphone for easy access. Assign someone to review and update this list no less than twice per year.

Coordination With Key Stakeholders. Identify the key stakeholders that may need careful attention from a communications standpoint during a crisis. For example, in a health care environment, family members of patients and residents are as critical as the patients themselves. Be sure to identify the audiences that are most affected and plan to include them in any communication plan rollout.

Media Response Guidelines. Prepare a generic list of media response guidelines so that your spokespersons and/or subject matter experts can be reminded of best practices for a media interview. Items to be included on the list include the importance of maintaining eye contact and positive body language, avoiding the use of industry jargon, and other useful tips.

Dark/Failover Website Preparation. Work with your web developer to prepare a "dark" or "failover" page that can be quickly mobilized in the event of a crisis. It would allow for key information specific to the crisis situation to be posted and made available to the public. A failover site may also come in handy if your organization website is hijacked or crashes for some reason.

Emergency Communications Action Steps. List out the actual step-by-step actions that need to be taken from a communications standpoint during a crisis situation. This will look different for every organization, but it should include separate step-by-step action items for low-, medium-, and/or high-level situations. It's meant to serve as a checklist when you are quickly building plans during a crisis event.

Incident Review and Evaluation. Build in a specific timetable for reviewing your response to an incident within 15–30 days of the event. What went well? What needs to be changed in the organization's response? Formalize this review process to ensure that the organization learns from the communication strategies and tactics used during the crisis.

Finally, Meath suggests that appendices be added that include time-stamped tracking logs (which can be managed electronically), sample holding statements, an organization phone and email directory (including personal cell phones), and other additional resources that may help you respond during an event.

A good crisis communications plan is as different as the organization preparing it, and it is never something that answers all the questions that come up during an incident. However, it provides a much-needed place to start during a crisis—which is no time to begin preparing one.

Melinda Machado

Melinda Machado is the director of the Office of Communications & Marketing with the Smithsonian's National Museum of American History. She is an award-winning practitioner with diverse experience as a newspaper reporter and political communicator as well as both an agency and in-house PR professional with particular expertise in media relations. Her experiences span a variety of industries (including associations, consumer products, public health, and software/technology) as well as the for-profit and nonprofit sectors. We had the opportunity to talk with her and find out more about what it's like working in public relations.

What has it been like moving among journalism, agency work, and in-house practice?

I started in journalism at a small newspaper, then worked as the press secretary for the first Mexican American woman elected to the Texas State House of Representatives. After a number of jobs in agencies and consulting work, the Smithsonian's National Museum of American History recruited me to bring agency expertise to a four-year project centered on the Star-Spangled Banner. That four-year project ended up taking 10 years, and I'm thrilled to still be here nearly 20 years later.

All of the experience I had, the freelance writing I did in college and throughout my journalism career, and the diverse clients I was exposed to in agency practice prepared me for work at the Smithsonian. My time at Porter Novelli and Edelman also included several intersections with the museum: One of my assignments was to work with Black & Decker and its DustBuster product in a donation to the National Museum of American History, so I had to understand the organization and work with a curator even before I started in my current position.

In my role today, it's not unlike an agency environment. It is definitely not a 9-to-5 job! We're always handling multiple projects at the same time, and we try to staff up as if we were a firm, even though we don't have the same budget. At the time we spoke, our team of three was busy promoting our "Latinos in Baseball" initiative, our "Hurray for Politics!" exhibit opening, and Black History Month; and we were working with a curator who collected six very rare motorcycles from 1902–1916—and that was just one month. We also handle a significant number of documentary film requests, and now we have our own Smithsonian Channel as well.

How do you use the PESO model in your work?

We find PESO very helpful to explain what we do to others inside the organization. Our efforts at the museum are largely focused on earned media, but we do some paid local ads for different exhibitions and events, social media outreach beginning with our blog, and a variety of owned content including our website, our incredible museum space, and the Smithsonian Channel. PESO allows us to consider and communicate how all of these efforts fit together.

(Continued)

(Continued)

Mini Case Study: The Secret Message in Lincoln's Watch

In February of 2009, the chair of the museum's division of political history received a call from the ancestor of a watchmaker who reportedly left a secret message inscribed on the inside of a pocket watch owned by President Abraham Lincoln; now in the care of the museum. The watchmaker's original claim had been made public in a 1906 *New York Times* article, but it had never been investigated. A potentially fascinating and newsworthy historical discovery, the story appeared to be credible, but there was no guarantee that it was more than a family's fable.

Machado and her communication team were initially tasked with developing a strategy that would balance the forthcoming media opportunities while protecting the reputation of a national institution. Handled poorly, a media event featuring the opening of the watch could tarnish the Smithsonian's image if the watch did not yield the expected message. With this in mind, they developed a strategy that would reinforce the values of the institution and create a compelling media story at the same time, preparing for several potential outcomes.

The strategic approach focused on an invite-only media event for the opening of the watch, with select print and radio journalists in attendance. Reporters from the *Associated Press*, National Public Radio, the *New York Times*, the *Washington Post,* and *Smithsonian* magazine were invited to witness the event, along with the museum's curators who could act as expert sources. Machado also contracted

with a video crew to document the event, allowing the organization to both capture and control the footage and images for wider distribution—provided the historical account turned out to be true.

As the day of the event arrived, the selected reporters, as well as Machado and her team, were thrilled to discover that the watchmaker's tale and Smithsonian's hunch had been proven correct. In the end, not one, but two secret messages were discovered on the inside of President Lincoln's watch more than 150 years after they were originally inscribed. Interestingly enough, Lincoln himself was unaware of the existence of these inscriptions.

Each of the invited reporters discussed the discovery with a variety of historical experts, contributing to a detailed account of the event. Then, as a result of the Smithsonian's subsequent media outreach efforts, the story produced vast amounts of publicity locally, nationally, and internationally. Broadcast coverage from the event included features on *The Today Show* and NBC's *Nightly News*, and the story garnered print coverage from *AP*, *Reuters*, and nine of the ten largest newspapers in the country. As the original watchmaker was an Irish immigrant, the story also drew coverage from the *Irish Times* and on radio stations throughout Ireland and England. The *New York Times'* in-depth coverage was particularly poignant, as they had been the paper to publish the original story about the inscription 103 years prior.

Ultimately, the strategy that Machado adopted supported the vision of the Smithsonian in sharing this historical occasion with audiences around the globe. It also ensured that the event would be successful, whatever was found inside the watch: The reputation of the museum was protected, even if everything had not turned out as planned. In the end, the discovery and resulting media coverage reinforced one of the museums central principles: History is made by ordinary people.

Top 5 Characteristics Every PR Professional Should Have

1. The one thing I can't teach you is how to write. I've trained people who have had no intention of being in PR, but if they can write, I can make it work.

2. You have to know what news is. Why should a reporter leave his office or a blogger leave the comfort of her couch to come to your event? Is it really news?

3. You have to be able to see the story: What's the picture?

4. Understand what reporters need to make a great story: A press release? Images? Background information? Interviews? All of the above?

5. Know how to use the PESO model to explain paid, earned, shared, and owned media—it's very helpful for explaining our work to non-PR people in the organization.

Top Must-Haves

- **Must-use software:** Microsoft Word! That's where I write everything. It's still the center of what we do. If it was 1980, I would say the typewriter.

- **Must-use tool:** PR Newswire is an excellent tool. For us, particularly when I'm doing targeted outreach in different languages, it makes my work so much more efficient. We do a lot of work with Spanish language publications, and the translation and distributions functions really help.

Glossary

Acculturation: The process of being integrated into an organization by learning about its processes, norms, and expectations

Additive color: An approach to color creation, used in digital screens and other pixel-based displays, that creates color by adding certain amounts of different colors (usually red, green, and blue). Adding none of these colors creates black, while adding all of them creates white.

Advertising: A form of paid media such as a printed flyer in a traditional newspaper, a sponsored banner on a website, or paid content on a social media channel

Associated Press: A not-for-profit news organization based in New York City that provides global news reporting to local news organizations, acting as an association or cooperative. This approach allows local outlets to pool their resources in order to provide high-quality global news content.

Audience: A group of individuals that receive messages from an organization or brand

Benchmark: In relation to public relations metrics, the term signifies milestones or progress achieved during the life of a project. It can also refer to the comparison of processes, products, or services to those of competitors, particularly to industry leaders.

Binding: Finishing options to make loose pages into books or booklets, including a saddle stich, wire or spiral coil, screw post, or traditional hardcover

Blog: Short for *weblog*; an online journal that is a collection of an individual's or organization's thoughts on a particular topic

Boosted Content: A paid social media strategy that allows organizations to expand the reach of their organically created or curated content, specifically targeting audiences by interest, geography, demographics, and other factors, depending on the platform

Brand: The collection of factors, including name, design, symbol, language, tone, experience, or other features, that identifies an organization's goods or services as distinct from others. Brands are co-constructed by the organization and its publics, who bring their experiences and impressions as part of the definition.

Brand ambassador: An individual who embodies an organizational brand and shares its message with others both internally and with the larger community

Brand equity: The value of a consumer's positive associations with a brand

Brand experience: A consumer's relational experience with a brand

Brand image: The visual impression of a product co-created by an organization's design choices and the image held by its publics

Brand loyalty: Faithfulness of consumers to continue buying a brand over competing brands

Brand persona: Human characteristics given to a brand

Brand strategy: A long-term plan for the development of a successful brand in order to achieve specific goals. The strategy addresses *how*, *what*, *where*, and *when* a company plans on communicating and delivering on brand messages.

Brand voice: Consistent messaging an organization develops to engage consumers and represent or embody its brand

Brainwalking: An ideation technique utilizing the rapid change of both prompts and physical space to maximize creativity

Branding: The process of developing, communicating, and managing brands

Budget: An estimate of income and expenditure for a set project or period of time

Budget (media): Money dedicated to paid media, including advertising, public relations, social media, and marketing costs

Case studies: Carefully crafted descriptions of successful strategic public relations campaigns designed to show off a firm's skills through creative solutions to client problems, innovative tactics, or supremely successful execution and results

C-Suite: A term used to collectively refer to a corporation's executive level employees (for example, *chief executive officer*, *chief operating officer*, or *chief marketing officer*)

Call to action (CTA): A piece of content designed to prompt a specific action from its audience

Channel: The medium through which messages are sent, such as the elements within the PESO model (paid print advertising, earned trade media placements, organizational social media channels, or an organization's website)

Client references: Current or past clients willing to speak—hopefully positively—on behalf of the work an agency has performed for them

Client service: The part of agency public relations work involving the client-facing research, planning, implementing, and evaluating of campaigns and programs. It is particularly critical to understand the industries, individuals, and obstacles that the client faces, building support for agency ideas and initiative as well as building long-term relationships.

Clip (media): A specific piece of media coverage, generally referring to client or organizational content that has been included in a story

Clip (video): A segment of video

CMYK: The abbreviation for cyan, magenta, yellow, and key (black); a subtractive color system

Coding: The process of identifying words, phrases, tones, themes, or other symbols in a variety of materials to look for frequency and patterns during content analysis

Color system: A structure for organizing and differentiating colors in visual design

Communication goal: Also known as a *public relations goal*; informed by organizational goals, communication goals should reflect the most effective use of campaign outreach to support the achievement of organizational goals

Community relations: Building relationships with groups of people that constitute an organization's communities, which could include geographic and physical communities, industry communities, or digital communities

Content creation: Writing original content on behalf of an organization

Content curation: Gathering content relevant to a particular topic or area of interest to share on behalf of an organization

Content management system (CMS): A software application or set of related programs that are used to create and manage digital content

Continuity: Maintaining the logical progression of a video throughout the shooting and editing process

Controlled media: Any channel an organization wholly owns and operates, such as the company website, print materials such as brochures, or hosted events

Conversion: A member of a target group completing a desired action such as donating to a fundraiser, buying a product, or signing up for an e-newsletter

Corporate communication: An organizational department and function that develops messages, cultivates strategic execution of integrated campaigns, and fosters relationships with key publics both internally and externally

Corporate culture: The collective, distinct behavioral and communicative standards and patterns of individuals within organizations

Corporate social responsibility (CSR): A philosophy that emphasizes an organization's obligation to give back to its community and society

Counselling/Counselor: The act of advising management concerning policies, relations, and communications

Creativity: Generating new or innovative strategies, tactics, messages, or processes that add value for clients, often accomplished by bringing together individuals and groups with different perspectives on the same challenge or opportunity

Crisis communication: Using public relations strategies to protect the brand of an organization during a time that challenges its reputation

Crisis management: The process of strategically planning and responding to a crisis or negative incident

Data: The content analyzed through research. Data can take many forms, from interview transcripts and media articles to social media posts and experiment results.

Diagnosis: The process of identifying the core problem or opportunity for communication and public relations efforts. It should be based on information gleaned from internal and external research, balancing the organization's goals, immediate environmental circumstances, and resources to identify where the greatest positive impact can be made.

Digital printing: More flexible and less labor-intensive (with lower overall quality) than offset printing, digital printing is generally faster and has a lower cost per page at low volumes, making it ideal for smaller and quick turn-around projects

Dissolve: A video transition effect that fades from the on-screen image to a black screen

Diversity: Inclusion of different types of people based on ability, age, education, ethnicity, gender, gender identity, religion, sexual orientation, and other factors

Earned media: Published coverage of an organization's press material by a credible third party, such as a journalist, blogger, trade analyst, or industry influencer where the primary factor for inclusion is the quality or value of information

Editorial calendar: An internal tool used to track article ideas, the content creation process, and publication dates

Employee relations: Activities designed to build sound relationships between an organization and its employees.

Evaluation: The analysis of completed or ongoing activities that determine or support a public relations campaign

Facilitators: Meeting leaders who prioritize the inclusion of all voices and generating group consensus. A facilitator's goals involve harnessing the collective ideas and experiences of those involved in a meeting rather than imposing a structure or vision of their own.

Fade: In video production, a gradual dissolve to or from an image and a black screen

Finishing: The steps at or near the end of the printing process, including cropping, folding, or die-cutting materials to meet final specifications

Full script: A script that includes descriptions of background and setting, camera angles, movement, props, and other necessary features in addition to spoken language

Gantt chart: A campaign planning and execution visual that represents a variety of campaign activities and the time line for implementation

GIF: A popular image compression format that is less adept at maintaining high resolution images than JPEG or PNG, but allows for multiple frames (up to short videos)

Government relations: Building relationships among an organization and government entities and decision makers

Gutter: In a bound book, the central blank space between the two pages of text

Hard dollar amount: Fixed expenditures that cannot change during the course of the campaign, such as production of collateral materials, event costs, and broadcast ad purchases

Hashtag: A word or phrase preceded by the symbol # that classifies or categorizes the accompanying text or image. They are often used on Twitter or Instagram.

Head: The white space above the main content on a page

Ideation: The umbrella term for brainstorming techniques aimed at harnessing the creativity of groups to create more creative, insightful, and/or nuanced solutions than individuals would be able to generate on their own

Implementation: The point in the campaign process where the campaign plan is put into action

Influencer: An expert in a specific category that has a loyal and engaged following

Infographic: Data that is graphically represented in the form of a chart, diagram, or illustration

Integrated marketing communication (IMC): The combination of marketing, advertising, and public relations strategies and tactics when planning campaigns

Internal communication: The transmission of information between parts of the organization. It takes place across all levels and organizational units of an organization.

Internal publics: Stakeholders that are a part of the organization itself, including all employees, nonprofit members, boards of directors, and other internal constituencies

Internet: A collection of networks making information stored on disparate computer systems globally accessible

Investor relations (IR): A heavily regulated area of public relations that works closely with investors, financial reporters, and the financial community. It is particularly crucial for large organizations and public companies.

JPEG: A web-friendly image file format designed to optimize high image resolution with small file sizes

Key performance indicator (KPI): A measurable value that demonstrates how effectively a company is achieving key business objectives

Linear thinking: Patterns of thinking that reflect day-to-day work processes, a step-by-step method of solving problems, and a prioritization of efficiency. While these are valuable skills for professional communicators to possess, they can inhibit creativity and solution generation. Many ideation approaches are designed to break such patterns.

Margins: The area outside the printed region of a page

Marketing: The activity related to setting the price, promotion, and distribution of goods and services to customers

Marketing communication (MarCom): A fundamental and complex part of a company's marketing efforts, including the messages and media deployed to communicate with current and potential customers, donors, or members

Media policy: A statement for employees explaining who from the organization is authorized to speak with external media as well as, in many cases, a process for what to do in case media inquiries find their way to an individual outside of the communication team

Media relations: An area of public relations that develops mutually beneficial relationships between an organization and journalists, bloggers, or other gatekeepers to earned media channels

Meeting objectives: The specific desired outcomes of a particular meeting as outlined by the facilitator prior to the gathering

Meme: An amusing or interesting item (such as a captioned picture or video) or genre of items that is spread widely online, especially through social media

Messaging: The process of defining, crafting, integrating, and distributing organizational messages through a variety of communication channels

Mission statement: An actionable description of an organization's unique ability to achieve its goals

Native advertising: Material in an online publication that resembles the publication's editorial content but is paid for by an advertiser and intended to promote the advertiser's product

Newsworthiness: The qualities that make a particular story appealing for journalists to cover, including timeliness, uniqueness, breadth of impact, and relevance to the media outlet's audience

Nonlinear editing: Digital editing processes wherein the editor can continuously rearrange the order of footage, add effects, and adjust audio and graphics

Objectives: A specific, measurable statement of what needs to be achieved as part of reaching a public relations goal

Offset printing: A CMYK- and ink-based printing process used for high-quality and cost-effective large-batch printing

Onboarding: An organization's formal orientation process immediately after hiring, where new employees learn about the organization as well as their specific job duties

Organic social media: Unpaid social media outreach on behalf of an organization, where publics must opt-in (by liking a social media page or subscribing to a blog) to receive updates and content

Organic/participatory organizational structure: Communication structures that facilitate symmetrical organizational communication and employee engagement along with decentralized power and decision making

Organizational goal: Significant, stable, long-term aspirations defined by the management and leadership of organizations

Owned media: The content and experiences produced by an organization and distributed across its numerous communications channels

Paid media: Traditional and nontraditional advertising methods (including print and broadcast ads, social media advertising, digital display, and many others) where the organization maintains nearly complete control of the content shared

Pantone: The industry standard print-focused color system

Parallax design (Parallax scrolling): A web programming approach creating motion and a 3D effect as users scroll

PESO model: An acronym for the integrated, channel-agnostic approach to planning and communicating with publics. PESO stands for paid, earned, shared, and owned media

Pixels/Pixels-per-inch (PPI): A pixel is the smallest element in a digital display. When working with digital images, counting the pixels-per-inch is the standard measurement of resolution.

Podcast: A series of audio and video files that are published periodically for download

Positioning: An effort to influence consumer perception of a brand or product relative to the perception of competing brands or products. Its objective is to occupy a clear, unique, and advantageous position in the consumer's mind.

Post-production: The editing and mixing of video and audio content after shooting

Prepress: Creating print-ready files and generating final printed proofs

Pro bono: Unpaid projects for nonprofit organizations or causes, often taken on by agencies with the dual purpose of (1) giving back to their communities and (2) expanding their professional networks, work experience, and expertise

Production: The process of capturing video and audio content for a video production

Project management: The art and science of ensuring that projects are completed on time, on budget, and within the agreed-upon specification and scope. This is a particularly important skill for public relations practitioners, who often must juggle large project teams at multiple organizations.

Prompt: The spark for idea generation, which could be specific words, images, concepts, and questions

Promotion: The act of generating awareness and driving action for specific objectives, a function that can be part of public relations and marketing efforts

Proofs: A contact proof or prepress proof is an initial run of a print project to test all parts of the process and ensure that setup is correct before a job is fully printed

Public: A group of people connected by shared interests

Public relations: A strategic communication process that builds mutually beneficial relationships between organizations and their publics

Public relations campaign: A public relations campaign is a series of activities utilizing paid media, earned media, shared media, and owned media that are planned in advance and support the achievement of a specific organizational goal

Publicity: Generating public attention for a specific event, issue, person or organization using paid, earned, shared, or owned media tactics, most likely in combination

Reactive public relations: Reacting to media inquiries and only sharing information when asked, rather than proactively reaching out to journalists and other publics

Relationship: A measure of the connection or association between entities. Relationships are a cornerstone of public relations scholarship and practice. They can be measured by satisfaction, trust, mutual control, and commitment, among other variables.

Reporting tools: Documents, charts, and processes designed to assist practitioners in communicating the results of agency work to clients. These can include qualitative and qualitative insights as well as refinement (mid-campaign) and evaluative research (after a project/campaign has been completed).

Reputation management: The act of overseeing an organization's reputation both online and within the community

Research: The methodical collection, analysis, and explanation of information used to increase understanding of needs, gauge progress, and measure success

Research (informal): Useful knowledge-gathering practices engaged in by public relations practitioners through conversations with multiple publics (inside and outside the organization) as well as maintaining a general knowledge of key issues and trends in the media. These processes might include maintaining relationships with leadership, stakeholders, consuming mainstream and trade media, following influencers on social media, and attending relevant community events.

Research (primary): Data collection conducted by practitioners to inform their understanding of the organization, external situation, or a specific campaign

Research (qualitative): Research utilizing primarily language-based approaches, providing a holistic and broad perspective on the data or phenomena being examined

Research (quantitative): Research grounded in numeric approaches to understanding specific phenomena, generally focused on narrowing the scope to one or several key elements to determine their importance and impact

Research (refinement): Research done in the middle stages of the campaign to ensure that strategies and tactics are reaching audiences, having the desired impacts, and balancing channels and resources efficiently

Research (secondary): An early step in the research process, secondary research includes the gathering of insights from research conducted by others, often involving the collection and analysis of a significant amount of existing reports, studies, or other primary research sources

RGB: Abbreviation for red, green, and blue; this additive color scheme is common in digital and web applications

Running Order: The order of clips in the final, edited video

Scope: The boundaries of a particular project or campaign. This can be a particularly difficult to envision, particularly in the early planning stages, but practitioners must be aware of and do their best to define the scope for a campaign to effectively prioritize its efforts.

Search engine marketing (SEM): Paid promotion of websites in search engine results for specific targeted keywords or audiences

Search engine optimization (SEO): Refers to techniques using both language and coding that help an organization's website rank higher in the organic and natural search results

SEO copywriting: The technique of writing website copy using keywords and phrases to optimize website rankings

Shared media: Social media channels that allow for multiple voices (organizations and publics) to share or comment on an organization's posts

Shooting order: The order in which clips will be captured during the shooting process

Shot sheet: A list of all of the necessary shots or clips that must be captured for a particular video project

Social listening: Social media and digital monitoring with the goal of increasing awareness about the opinions and attitudes of publics about an issue, brand, or industry

Social media: Digital communication channels that encourage interactivity among personal networks and facilitate individuals and organizations sharing multiple types of content

Social media analytics (SMA): Analyzing quantitative data regarding the performance of social media activity to assess the quality and value of content, the needs and desires of publics, and the competitive landscape in a particular industry or community

Social media marketing (SMM): A form of internet marketing that utilizes social networking channels as a marketing tool, generally using paid tactics

Social media monitoring: Actively reading and watching the social media channels of an organization as well as key terms, phrases, issues, and competitors for information relevant to a company or organization

Social media policy: Organization-wide guidelines for individual employees' personal social media accounts and behaviors

Social sphere: The interactive digital space created by various social media networks and channels

Storyboard: A technique, often using visual sketches, to describe and plan each stage in production. It serves as a critical link in planning how a script will be brought to life.

Special events: An infrequent event that is put on by an organization

Stakeholder: Individuals with a vested interest in an organization, including internal groups such as employees and board members as well as external groups such as customers/donors, vendors, and community members

Strategic communication: Purposeful use of communication by an organization to fulfill its mission

Strategies: Public-specific communication approaches defining the channel(s) or through which messages are sent to achieve objectives

Subtractive color: Starting with light or white, subtractive color systems such as CMYK mix colors to absorb (or subtract) light in order to create specific colors. Using/

absorbing all colors creates black. Subtractive color systems are often used for printing applications.

Summative evaluation: Evaluation performed after the completion of a campaign or project, designed to explain how and why a campaign met or did not meet its objectives as well as to provide additional insights that could improve understanding of the organization, its publics, or future campaign planning and execution

SWOT analysis: A process to help organizations define their strengths, weaknesses, opportunities, and threats. This is a primarily qualitative research method that brings together a variety of secondary research about an organization and its competitors/industry peers, combined with primary research to add—for example—the perspective of organizational leaders.

Tactics: Specific communication products that carry messages to key publics. Tactics are tangible items such as an event, social media posts, a set of advertisements, or a website.

Tail: The margin at the bottom of a printed page

Target audience: The intended recipients of a specific message, campaign, or program

Testimonials: Quotes from clients and partners attesting to a practitioner's or firm's capabilities, credibility, and skills

Theory: An idea or set of ideas that is intended to explain and predict events and behaviors

Thought leadership: Written articles or speaking engagements that allow practitioners to share their insights and expertise on a specific public relations topic—ideally for an audience of potential clients

TIFF: A high-resolution digital image format often used to store large print-resolution graphics and images

Trade dress: Visual characteristics that make a brand distinctive within a given market or industry. It has legal standing as a form of intellectual property.

Usability testing: A systematic process of understanding how users interact with digital content, generally involving the observation of "testers"—individuals not involved in the creation of the website or app being tested—attempting to complete specific tasks

User experience design: Creating interfaces for digital content (such as websites and apps) with a focus on the interactions between the user and the system, aiming for a final product where completing tasks is seamless and intuitive

Vendors: Subcontractors used by public relations agencies to support certain tools or tasks. This may include traditional and social media monitoring services (such as Cision and Meltwater) or creative production specialists (designers, videographers, printers, etc.) as well as operations and business support services.

Vision statement: A high-level, broad description of an organization's long-term goals

Visualization: Imagining a variety of potential scenarios for dealing with a particular challenge in order to spark creative or unexpected approaches

Web-safe fonts: A small number of fonts generally considered to be universally compatible, often used in web design and other applications where a very wide variety of end users may have vastly different technological capabilities

White paper: A detailed or authoritative report focused on an issue of importance to an organization, often synthesizing primary and secondary research

Index

About the Author

Regina M. Luttrell, PhD, is currently an assistant professor of Public Relations and Social Media at the S.I. Newhouse School of Public Communications at Syracuse University. A contributor to *PR Tactics* and *PR News*, as well as peer reviewed journals, she is a noted speaker where she frequently presents at national and international conferences and business events on topics related to the current social media revolution, the ongoing public relations evolution, and Millennials within the classroom and workplace. She is the (co)author of the following books: *Social Media: How to Engage, Share, and Connect*; *The Millennial Mindset: Unraveling Fact from Fiction*; *Brew Your Business: The Ultimate Craft Beer Playbook*; *The PR Agency Handbook*; and *A Practical Guide to Ethics in Public Relations*. Prior to entering the educational field, she spent the first portion of her career in corporate public relations and marketing. Her extensive background includes strategic development and implementation of public relations and social media, advertising, marketing, and corporate communications. She has led multiple rebranding campaigns, designed numerous websites, managed high-level crisis situations, and garnered media coverage that included hits with the *New York Times*, the CBS Evening News, and the Associated Press.

Luke W. Capizzo is a PhD student and instructor in the Department of Communication at the University of Maryland, specializing in public relations. He is the coauthor (with Regina Luttrell) of *The PR Agency Handbook*. His research interests include global public relations, civil society, financial communication, and public relations education. Before coming to the University of Maryland, he practiced public relations for eight years with a focus on media relations in the financial services, commercial real estate, manufacturing, retail, and technology industries, serving in both agency and in-house roles. Working with a wide variety of clients—from the Fortune 500 to small businesses and nonprofits—he garnered media coverage in top national outlets and trade publications, secured and prepared clients for national cable news interviews, and led projects to improve agency-wide media training, staff on-boarding, and client evaluation and reporting metrics. He has earned the APR (Accreditation in Public Relations) designation through the Public Relations Society of America.